T0247546

Big Dip Energy

88 PARTIES IN A BOWL FOR SNACKING, DINNER, DESSERT, AND BEYOND!

Big Dip Energy

ALYSE WHITNEY

wm
WILLIAM MORROW
An Imprint of HarperCollins*Publishers*

BUTTER
BUTTER

*Dip*dicated to my big dippers:
Grammy, Mom, and Dad.
And to my little dippers, Miso and Ritz,
who always clean up the chip crumbs.
I love you more than ranch.

making dip happen!

Dip Energy

INTRODIPTION: DIP IS ME!

FACE YOUR SCHMEARS (PAGE 131) WITH ME!

Hi, I'm Alyse Whitney and I have Big Dip Energy. And if you're reading this, I bet you do, too.

DIPS ARE A UNIVERSAL LOVE LANGUAGE; the un*dip*feated champion of party foods. I've never met a person who didn't like dip, and I've never met a dip I didn't like. Dip was my first favorite food. It's one of the first appetizers many of us are introduced to as kids, because it's soft, easy to eat, and equally easy to make (or buy). The ones that were imprinted early on my brain were ranch, French onion, and nacho cheese. This trifecta of *dips*coveries brought me from stealing snacks at my mom's Bunco parties to fueling my after-school *O.C.* fan club (and one of the internet's biggest message boards in 2003) with dippable snacks.

Through decades of experimenting with cooking both personally and professionally—working at food magazines and showcasing major PDA (public *dips*plays of affection) on social media with #DipPics and videos—I've become a *dip*ficionado and *dip*termined my MVDs: Most Valuable Dips. In many circles, I'm referred to as the Dip Queen. And that's why we're here together now: to help you become the queen, king—or whichever royal title suits you—of dips, and upgrade every day into a party. This guide to the dip universe will show you whole new worlds of dips and dippers to enjoy on any occasion—or create an occasion just for the dip. Dip is for everyone, dip is for every day, dip is everything.

But this isn't *just* a cookbook about dips and dippers with a cheeky, punny name. (Though, as you can tell, I'm a *dips*graceful human being who is fueled by puns and cannot be stopped.) *Big Dip Energy* is more than just the name of this book—it's a lifestyle and a personality trait. The loose *dip*finition: You're magnetic. People are drawn to you like chips to a bowl of dip. For a good time,

HAVIN' A TIKI KIKI
DIPPIN' (AND SINGIN') CAMPFIRESIDE

people call you because you bring the party and make people come together. You're confident but not cocky. You're the total package.

If you have Big Dip Energy, you don't need to work to draw attention. There's a level of comfort that comes with familiarity, and dips are a food that everyone is well acquainted with. If you have BDE, you exude an energy that makes people around you feel energized and excited. Even strangers may feel like they already know you, because you create a welcoming space for people to be themselves and have a guaranteed good time. Dips are nothing without chips, and chips are greatly enhanced by a dip. You can be a chip, a dip, or a flip (some may call it a switch)! And hey, dip is the best social lubricant. Don't know anyone at a party? Gathering around the bowl and dipping into new conversation—especially if that person you're talking to has BDE—is the party equivalent of the office water cooler, but *cooler* (and tastier).

Having Big Dip Energy means you also possess a certain je ne sais *quality* without being elusive or mysterious. You sparkle like a *dips*co ball, radiating light and reflecting back what you're given. You attract people with your natural shine and magnetism and use that to illuminate new connections, shining light on like-minded people who can be the chip to your dip or the dip to your chip, *dip*ending on what you both need. You always know the friend*chips* you can count on, without needing to feel perfect and polished.

PANIC! AT THE DIPSCO

CHIPS IN MY BAG, SWAG

Dip is not known for being conventionally beautiful. It's a blob of soft food, often off-white or some shade of beige or brown, that you drag other food through as a utensil. Bags of chips often come with half their contents broken, and baby carrots are just ugly big carrots that have been shaved down to little nubs. But in spite of those things, we all love dip and how it makes us feel. Dip makes every party and every day better, and it can turn any moment into a party. Chips and dips have transcended and *dip*fied expectations for many decades of hosting, and in this cookbook, there will be even more surprising innovations, transformations of classic dishes into dips (dippidi-doppidi-doo?), and many non-chip dippers for your dip consideration!

HI, I'M CHIPPY

Hi, I'm Chippy, your friendly neighborhood chip. I'll dip in throughout the book to share dynamic dip tips and dipper flippers. What does that mean? You'll have to flip to find out!

So, let me be your tour guide through the world of dip. First up: Channel your inner BDE, flip through this book, and find the first recipe (or photo) that makes you *feel* something. It may be a name that makes you giggle or a picture that makes you want to rip it out of the book and eat it *right now*. Perhaps the mere idea of enjoying a club sandwich from your favorite diner—but in seven-layer dip form!—for your dad's birthday makes you feel nostalgic and comforted. Or maybe you just want to know how to make dip for one on the couch while watching reruns of *The O.C.*! I hope you feel drawn to certain recipes, make them for friends, and form comforting, *dip*-centric memories. I want you to stain these pages with greasy, cheesy fingers and make these your keepers, the dips you keep coming back for over and over again.

To create the recipes in this book, of course I first mined my own imagination and memories of favorite dishes and ingredients—but I also enrolled all my friends in a monthslong dip focus group to figure out what dips they can't live without and ones they wished existed. Almost every time I *dip*veloped recipes, I hosted dip tastings to get real-time feedback and make the process of trying things over and over again fun. For the biggest football game of the year the month before my manuscript was due, I didn't cook anything. Instead, I had a Super Bowls of Dip party (see page 241 for the *dip*off to my favorite holiday) and had a dozen friends make dips from the book to make sure they were as easy, *dip*licious, and shareable as I intended. It was touchdown after touchdown!

No matter what level of cook you are, you should be able to make every recipe in this book. Some are more *dip*ficult and require more patience, but I promise if you read the recipe all the way through first, you'll find all the answers you need. All the recipes have less than forty-five minutes of active time, and there's even a whole chapter of 5-Minute Dips (page 35) that involve a quick stir-in-a-bowl situation while you wait for everyone to be impressed.

ALL I WANT FOR DIPMAS IS YOUUU!

HIGH (BOBA) TEA TIME

DIP ON DEMAND
(15 minutes or less)

GOLDILOCKS DIP
(in-the-middle timing; 45 minutes or less)

WORTH THE WAIT DIP
(night before prep for chilling purposes or inactive baking time)

And rather than listing the amount of time the recipe "should" take to make—because not all of us work at the same pace or are on the same cooking skill level—I've categorized all recipes into three levels of timing and *dip*ficulty.

There are tested ideas for mo*dip*fications throughout the book and handy tips from Chippy, the *Big Dip Energy* mascot, but I encourage you to use them as guidelines and experiment with different flavors, spice levels, cheeses, or alternative dairies that you enjoy. Get creative and figure out your own motion of the dip ocean! I can't guarantee every swap will work, but I'll give it a try if I see you making a new—and perhaps improved—version of my dips. Just make sure to tag me @alysewhitney on Instagram and TikTok to show off your #BigDipEnergy.

If you're not sure you like an ingredient or flavor profile in one of the recipes but you're trying to expand your horizons, give it a shot in dip form. It's a low-effort way to try something new!

And if you're reading this in the year 3000 after picking up this dusty "vintage" cookbook at an estate sale, I've finally checked off the last item on my bucket list. Dip, dip, hooray!

BABY-CHIPPERS CLUB

THIS DIP IS BANANAS!

dip PRIMER

diptionary:
a love language

DIPSCOSITY (NOUN): The viscosity of a dip, which should be thick enough to not immediately drip or dribble off a spoon when turned upside down. It's similar to the Blizzard test at Dairy Queen, but a dip shouldn't be thick enough to stay upside down for more than a few seconds. Some dips are thinner than others, and some are chunkier. Each one has a purpose and should be appreciated. That's an analogy for life, and human bodies, too.

DIP QUEEN NOTE: The only recipe in the book that doesn't adhere to my *dip*scosity guidelines is Herbalicious Oil Is Bready for Dippin' (page 98), which is a delightful infused oil that I thought *dip*served a space in the dip canon. It's meant just for improving any bread you dip—in this case, more like dunk and swoosh—into it.

The way to *dip*ferentiate between dips and dressings or sauces is whether you'd eat what's in that bowl by the spoonful, even if there was no dipper to be found. A dip should stand on its own and be *dip*licious without needing a vehicle to get it mingling with your taste buds. A dip can be a meal, but a dressing or a sauce cannot. You wouldn't go to a restaurant and order honey mustard for the table, but you *would* (and should) always get the spinnie artie dip.

Still confused? It's like the difference between "your" and "you're." That little apostrophe makes all the *dip*ference between something *you're* excited to eat solo and *your* worst nightmare. I would never eat Thousand Island by itself, but I'd gladly enjoy a spoonful of the similarly flavored Bloom Bloom Room Onion Dip (page 45) before the *Crisp*anthemum Onion Petals are fried up and ready for dippin'. Dip happens!

dip tool kit:
essential supplies

Make someone a dip and you'll feed them for a day. Teach a person how to make dip and they'll dip for a lifetime. That's how the proverb goes, right? Here are all the *dips*sentials you'll need to make dip happen.

BOWLED OVER

What do tiny, small, medium, and large bowls *really* look like? I unfortunately can't peep inside all your cupboards to see what you're workin' with, but I want to give you a point of reference for the sizes I refer to in these recipes. This isn't a dip-measuring contest, so use what you have. It's always best to go a bit bigger rather than smaller, so you have room for *dips*placement when using utensils and dippers.

My most-used serving bowl for dips for four to eight people is the shallow, wide, medium-size Everyday Bowl from East Fork Pottery, which can comfortably hold 3 cups. You'll see a lot of examples from my colorful ceramics collection from the North Carolina–based company throughout the book. My version of a small bowl is their Breakfast Bowl, which is great for dippers and holds 11 ounces. My mixing bowls are a *mix* of vintage Pyrex (my large is 2½ quarts and extra-large is 4 quarts) and reBowls from Material, which are made of repurposed plastic and sugarcane and hold 2¾ quarts.

ALL THE SMALL BOWLS FIT IN QUESO EMERGENCY DIP, PAGE 41

For any dips that need to be baked, I specify the dimensions of the baking dish I used to test the recipe, but if you don't have that exact size or shape, it's okay! It's always better to go a little bigger if you have the option, as the dip will be more spread out, leaving you with more surface area for people to dip in. If you go smaller, you risk overflow and a mess in the oven, or, again, *dips*placement if it's full to the brim.

EXTRA-LARGE
A mixing bowl you'd use to make a batch of brownies, with 4-quart capacity or more

LARGE
A bowl you'd serve salad in at a dinner party, with between 2½- and 3-quart capacity

MEDIUM
A generous serving of soup bowl, between 2 cups (16 ounces) and 1 quart (4 cups or 32 ounces) capacity

SMALL
A cereal bowl, between 1 cup (8 ounces) and 14-ounce (1¾-cup) capacity

PINCH
A pinch bowl (typically used for stove-side salt) or small prep bowl, between 2 and 6 ounces (¼ cup to ¾ cup)

GRATE EXPECTATIONS

My greatest pleasure is also my greatest weakness: cheese. I love cheese in all forms, but I *hate* grating cheese. This is mostly because I always have intricate nail art on and I'm afraid of grating it off, but also because it's a surprisingly intense arm workout, and most cheeses don't want to be grated. Sometimes they schmear onto the grater because the block is too soft, or there's a point toward the end when you are holding a smushed, three-inch piece of cheese that will not go into the holes of the grater without threatening to take part of your finger with it.

You have a few options for achieving *grate*ness without too much *dip*ficulty:

- **Freeze your cheese for 15 minutes and use a grater.** The cheese will grate easier because it starts firmer and won't get soft and gummy midway through grating. I always use the largest holes of a box grater for blocks of cheese like sharp cheddar or mozzarella, but go for the smaller ones or a Microplane for hard cheeses like parmesan.

- **Freeze your cheese for 15 minutes and use the shredding blade of a food processor.** Larger food processors usually come with this accessory that lets you just throw cheese down the chute of the lid for the machine to do all the work. It takes less than a minute to grate an entire pound of cheese.

- **Skip the block of cheese altogether and hit the deli counter!** Really thin cheese slices or sliced cheese cut into small pieces will melt almost as quickly as the shredded stuff, the work is done for you, and you're guaranteed to have the exact amount you need for the recipe. You can still be lazy without compromising the quality of your cheese pulls! You can buy presliced cheese from the refrigerated section of a grocery store, too, but I suggest the deli counter so you can control the exact amount you need and your desired thickness, and you're guaranteed fresher, tastier flavor.

- **For hard cheeses like parmesan, freezing isn't required.** I am not against pre-grated parm, but for flavor and freshness, I suggest buying cheese that is grated in-store and packaged or purchased in the refrigerated section, rather than the shelf-stable shakers.

- **It's what's inside that counts when it comes to dip.** Although I love cheese, you will notice there aren't many cheese-topped recipes in *Big Dip Energy*. It's *dip*ficult to break through the layer of cheese without breaking your dipper, and even with a spoon sometimes things get messy. You can still have a bubbly, crispy top without adding cheese, and if you don't have a dip warmer, cream cheese-based dips still stay dippable and delightful throughout a party in a way that a sharp cheddar-topped dip wouldn't at room temperature. (Congealed cheese is a party foul!) And any one of these topless dips will thicken into a mighty fine bagel schmear the next morning after its slumber in the fridge, or can be mixed into scrambled eggs for richness, creaminess, and flavor.

- **If you're a cottage cheese fan, you can sub*dip*tute 1:1 full-fat cottage cheese for sour cream as long as you blend it until smooth using a food processor, blender, or immersion blender.** It may be slightly thicker in texture, so you can thin out the final dip with a splash of milk or water if you're not happy with the *dip*scosity!

FRESHLY GRATED
Has a fluffy texture in cold dips and melts evenly for grate cheese pulls! Freeze it for 15 minutes first for easier grating.
PRE-SHREDDED BAGGED
Convenient, but added preservatives and anti-caking agents can make it melt weird—or not at all!
SLICED AND CHOPPED
Grab the exact amount you need at the deli counter and use like shredded.

Freshly grated cheese is a transformative eating experience compared to the pre-shredded stuff. It's lighter, airier, and almost fluffy. It piles up like a little cloud and melts on your tongue, almost like snow. That texture allows it to be almost incognito in cold dips (like Freak-a-Leek Beer Cheese Dip, page 82) and melt beautifully without seizing up or over-thickening in hot dips (like Saag Paneer Artichoke Dip, page 60). Why is that? Pre-shredded cheese is coated in cornstarch to prevent caking (sticking together) in the bag. It makes it a harder, sturdier texture when eaten "raw" and melts in globs instead of glorious cheese pulls.

GARLICKITY-SPLIT!

This cookbook uses a lot of garlic. Four cloves minimum for most recipes. There are two things I suggest buying before beginning your BDE journey: pre-peeled garlic (preferably at an Asian market, where it's usually packed fresh onsite without preservatives) and a garlic press. It is the quickest way to "mince" a clove of garlic without it flying all over a cutting board or making your hands smell like garlic forever. I also have a palm-size, push-button-operated teeny-tiny food processor I exclusively use for garlic and that can chop up a whole head's worth of peeled garlic at a time, rather than the one-clove-at-a-time garlic press.

SOFTEN IN A ZAP

You need room temperature cream cheese for a recipe and don't have the time to soften it. You can either microwave a glass bowl (without anything in it) for 2 minutes and then add the cream cheese to the hot bowl so it softens but doesn't melt or get hot, or you can use an electric hand mixer or stand mixer to whip it up before adding the rest of the ingredients.

CRANK THAT PEPPER MILL!

Instead of listing a measured amount of black pepper, I say how many cranks of freshly cracked black pepper you should use in a recipe. Mills vary in size, but I created every recipe using one on a medium-coarse setting. You can add more or less based on how much of a bite you like, but I'd rather you leave the pepper out than try to use pre-ground pepper, which is dusty in texture and flavor.

GUESSTIMATION DESTINATION: HERBS

To guesstimate ¼ cup of fresh tender herbs, grab a fistful of the herb and remove the leaves from the stems. You'll have about the right amount.

IT'S A PROCESS

The most efficient way to make many of the dips in this cookbook is with one small kitchen appliance: a mini food processor, also called a mini prep or mini chopper. For every single dip in this book, I exclusively used a rechargeable

KitchenAid 5-cup food processor when anything needed to be chopped, ground, blitzed, pulverized, pureed, whipped, or otherwise combined into a smooth, delectable dip. Because none of the recipes in this book put aggressive wear and tear on the blade of the food processor—we're not making homemade chicken nuggets by processing our own chicken breasts here, I promise—you can go for an inexpensive, generic brand if you're on a budget. I've had friends test recipes using all sorts of brands, from low- to high-end, and they worked equally well for everyone.

The only thing I cannot guarantee is whether these recipes will work in a blender. Blenders are meant for more liquid-heavy tasks, like soups, dressings, smoothies, and *some* really smooth dips. They have a smaller, often slower blade and whip extra air into mixtures as they blend. There's a smaller margin of error with a blender when it comes to dips, because it can quickly go from zero to sixty and completely puree something you wanted to keep chunkier, with variance in textures, like Trippin' Dip (page 115). Food processors, whether mini prep or standard size, also have wider bowls so you can get more ingredients prepped at a time, and the wider, flat blade can turn a whole roasted butternut squash and a head of garlic into a creamy dip (Curry Squashcotta Sheet Pan Dip, page 119) in seconds. It's my favorite little chef, the closest thing I have to my own Remy (of *Ratatouille* fame)—without the hair-pulling.

BRINGIN' THE HEAT

The second most important kitchen appliance for dips is a slow cooker or warmer. I have an assortment of small Crock-Pots and dip warmers, ranging from ¾-quart to 1½-quart capacities, and a three-section, 2½-quart dip buffet I break out for Dipmas, my all-dips holiday potluck (see the holiday guide on page 241) and other Big Dip occasions. The worst thing you can do to a hot dip is let it get cold. The cheese congeals, the consistency becomes thicker than intended, and it signals the party is over when the dip has been laid to rest in a cold, dark grave. Keep the party going as long as you want—you *can* always unplug it at nine p.m. and ask people to leave—with melty cheesy goodness to *dip*finity and beyond!

If you don't have a dip warmer, you can often find one at a thrift shop for as low as five dollars, but an alternative is to simmer a few inches of water in a saucepan and set the dip in a heatproof glass or metal bowl over it, just as if you're melting chocolate in a double boiler. If you use low heat and warn partygoers to watch out for the hot bowl, you could keep a dip warm all night.

To reheat hot dips that have been made ahead, warm the dip up in a 350°F oven (for about 15 minutes), in the microwave (for 3 to 5 minutes), or in a slow cooker on low (for at least an hour, then switch to the warm setting).

And while we're talking about hot stuff, here's an important *dips*claimer: None of the recipes in this book are very spicy. I have a sadly low spice tolerance, so all my dips hit at a mild-to-medium spice range but can be kicked up heat-wise if you want to add more hot sauce, keep the seeds in your jalapeños, or make other spice ad*dip*tions. I also hate olives and greatly dislike cucumbers and pickles (but love pickled things), capers, and raw tomatoes. They are used sparingly in the book, but if you want to try adding one of them to a recipe, give it a shot. These dips are made to riff on—just please don't come for me if the recipe *detours* de force don't work perfectly.

ICE, ICE, BABY

On the flip side, to keep cold dips chilled throughout the duration of a party, all you need are two bowls. One should be slightly smaller than the other, so they can nest together. Fill the larger bowl with ice about halfway up, then nestle the smaller bowl, filled with dip, inside. You may need to swap out the ice midway through the party, but the water will be so cold that it should be okay if you forget. That said, I've picked up vintage dip chillers at thrift shops and antique malls that have two interlocking bowls designed to fit perfectly and keep the dip securely atop the ice. The only danger in DIYing it is that the dip bowl could tip over when the ice starts to melt if the bigger bowl is much larger.

You can also use this setup with a plate or bowl of dippers you want to keep cold, like shrimp cocktail for Shrimp-less Scampi Dip (page 147).

DIP LIKE BOND

A martini glass is a surprisingly great in*dip*vidual serving vessel, with a wide surface area for dipping at the top and an angled, triangular base to scrape the last of the dip from. Plus it has a built-in stem to hold it securely and a steady-yet-small base that lets you set it down on a table and takes up way less space than a bowl. It's great for things like hanging cocktail shrimp on the edge and piling dips in the middle. Try thrifting some mix-and-match glasses on a budget, or have people bring their own glasses. That way it's easy to tell whose is whose, especially if the glasses have personality or a story behind them.

You can also put out small portions of dips in a shared dip buffet situation in various glassware instead of bowls! Mugs can also work, and ceramic ones will keep hot dip hotter for longer than a plastic plate.

DIPVIDED WE RISE!

If you're fully committed to the *Big Dip Energy* lifestyle, you need to *dip*vide and conquer. Buy kids' divided plates or little sectioned trays, like old-school TV trays. Most of them are dishwasher safe or easy to clean, durable, and colorful. They're great to break out for parties without worrying about actually breaking anything. Check vintage and thrift shops, antique malls, and estate sales for them first, as they'll be cooler looking, proven to be durable, and likely less expensive. But many stores, both for IRL shopping and online—including *dips*count stores like T.J.Maxx and HomeGoods—have them in the kids' section. Bento boxes are also a fun way to plate dips and to take them on the go, whether that's just to the couch, a picnic, or lunch al desko.

THE WAY WE DIP BY: SPOON SIZE MATTERS

The best way to serve dip is with a spoon so people can *dips*pense to their in*dip*vidual plates and avoid double dipping. For serving dips from a small bowl, use a standard teaspoon. For a medium bowl, use a tablespoon. For a larger bowl, a serving spoon is ideal.

MUFFIN CAN STOP US

Some dips take well to being frozen. My favorite way to do so is to fill up a standard 12-cup muffin tin to go in the freezer overnight, then transfer the dip to a container or freezer zip-top bag for microwavable in*dip*vidual portions. When you microwave, do so in a small microwave-safe bowl, covered with a wet paper towel to keep the dip from splattering, and microwave on 50 percent power. It usually takes about 2 to 5 minutes, stirring every 30 seconds or so. You can use the stovetop—a small saucepan over low heat—if you don't have a microwave.

#SendDipPics:

food stylist tips to make your dips picture-perfect

Dip will never be photogenic enough to be named *People*'s Sexiest Food Alive, but you can elevate dip into eye-catching Instagram bait with flame emoji comments galore. *Big Dip Energy*'s masterful food stylist, Nick Torres, helped me make every dip—and dipper—jaw-droppingly gorgeous with a handful of key techniques ranging from swoon-worthy swoops to crisp, lush layers. If you try them out, tag us in your masterpieces @alysewhitney and @nicktorres_alacarte!

SWOOPS, THERE IT IS!

When it comes to swoops, little canals running through a dip, (spoon) size doesn't matter. Choose your tool based on the girth of the swoop that you want—a teaspoon for smaller bowls and subtle swoops and a soup spoon for more dramatic rounded movements. These swooshes are pathways for drizzles, dip confetti, or embedded secondary dips (like the spinach pesto in Trippin' Dip, page 115). Have a dip vision before you start; map out where you want the swoosh to go through the dip so you're not swooshing blind. When you're ready, the key to a perfect swoosh is consistent motion of the dip ocean, keeping your spoon moving in one direction to perfect your style. Don't go backward, even if you mess up, because it will disrupt the flow! It's all in the wrist, pressing the spoon in the dip and dragging through slowly and *dip*liberately. The first pass is your outline, and you can always go back in to make it deeper or wider on the next try. If you mess it up, just smooth it back out and give it another go!

DIPVOT IT LOW

The *dip*vot style features concentric circular moats in your dip. To make them, start with your spoon against the inner edge of the bowl and hold it steady as you move the *bowl* in a circular motion (clockwise or counterclockwise, whichever floats your moat). A lazy Susan or cake stand that spins would be a great tool here, but you can do it without. Go all the way around with the spoon, lift it out of the bowl, wipe it clean, and then repeat an inch or two in from the first circle. Make as many concentric smaller circles as you like, working your way from the outside in. Just remember that the spoon stays in place while the bowl moves, making crop circles to fill in with drizzles, dip confetti, and more.

MUSEUM-WORTHY MARBLING

Swirling or marbling isn't *dip*ficult, but it requires a little patience. Choose your tool: chopstick, spoon handle, or butter knife. Add your base dip (background color) to a bowl, then add spoonfuls of the secondary color or flavor on top. Run the utensil of choice through the dollops, dragged through in a line so the colors gently intertwine. Wipe off your utensil in between each pass. Exercise restraint with your marbling—less is more here—so it doesn't get muddied or turn accidentally monochromatic. As a fail-safe, keep a little bit of the base dip on the side to add dollops and fix over-marbled parts if needed.

DOLLOP PARTON

A dollop is a beautiful finishing topping, mostly used for *dips*serts. Dollops only work with sturdy-yet-airy dips that can stand on their own (like the Simply the Zest *Dips*sert Trio, page 50). For the dollops to not look like blobs in your serving vessel, fill the majority of the bowl, then pile some of the excess on a serving or large spoon and let it fall off the spoon into the bowl. Take a breath and let gravity take over and the dips fall as they may, then flick your wrist up just after the dip drops off the spoon—but not too fast so you don't make a mess in the kitchen—to get that classic point or tip. To fix a limp tip, just scoop up that dollop and redo it. You can also use your skills from the swooshing technique to fix the tip by sculpting it with the back of a spoon or an offset spatula. When layering dollops (like in Whipped Peanut Butter Cup Dip, page 182), cover the bottom of the dish alternating the two colors or bases, then build upward from there.

MORE LAYERS TO LOVE

To get crisp layers that are *dips*tinct, start with a clear dish and choose contrasting colors when *dip*ciding the order of the layers. For the bottom layer, start with your densest dip; it's the most important layer to get straight and perfect so you can build evenly on top. As you build with additional dips, continue to use the densest ones first, so they don't weigh down or crush the lighter layers. Throughout building, you want to keep the edge of the dish clean so the layers are crisp in the cross section. To ensure that, dump the dip in the center of the vessel and spread it out gently from the center to the outside slowly and *dip*liberately. Don't rush this or it will look messy!

If using non-dip solid ingredients (like smoked salmon in the Face Your Schmears Everything Bagel Dip, page 131), shingle beautifully around the outside perimeter (like when you start a puzzle) and then spiral toward the middle. (Since the middle won't be seen in photos, you can scatter more than place these pieces.) If using a spice blend like furikake, sprinkle it evenly across the surface and fill in gaps afterward.

As you're building, don't just look at the top—look at every side of the dish to make sure the layers are coming together properly and aren't crooked or uneven. For in*dip*vidual servings, such as in a coupe glass, you can play around with the thickness of each layer to be *dip*ferent or more intriguing.

DIP CONFETTI (AKA GARNISHES)

The finishing touches on your dips should not be overlooked. They're the first thing people will see before they dip in, so no matter how rushed you are, follow along with these knife skills and garnishing tips.

SHARP SKILLS: Herbs, like our hearts, bruise easily. So use a really sharp knife or you could turn your beautiful green herbs a muddied brown color.

AGGRESSIVE ROUGH CHOP: Sometimes you'll want to be precise and beautiful with your dip confetti—which we'll dive into below—but most of the time, you can just aggressively rough chop it, aka running your knife back and forth across the board over a pile of herbs. (This also applies to what's inside the dip, like onions that will be cooked and don't need to be precisely minced.)

AIM HIGH: Garnishing is more about how you *dips*perse the herbs across the dip than how they're cut. Sprinkle from up high, starting with a small amount and building from there. It's *dip*ficult to fish out excess garnishes without ruining the top of your dip, but you can always add more. You can also find a hero piece of an herb to use whole and showcase what's inside, like baby basil leaves or a whole cilantro sprig. But again, exercise restraint with the greenery. It can easily look like a garden if you overdo it; save that impulse for making Dirt Pudding Dip (page 177).

OTHER SPRINKLES: Aim high to sprinkle all your dip confetti options. For nuts, toast them fresh in a naked pan over medium-low heat until fragrant—stirring frequently without walking away for even a second, because they burn easily!—then set aside to cool. Place in a resealable bag, crush with a rolling pin or a wine bottle, and sprinkle. For spices, whether cinnamon or chili powder, add a pinch at a time from a bowl—not directly from a shaker or other container—for more control. And for *dips*serts, if you're crumbling a cookie or other baked good on top, crumble it into a bowl first, then sprinkle.

DIP RIBBONS: To make beautiful ribbons of herbs like basil, pluck the leaves, stack, roll into a tight log, and slice thinly. The official term for this is "chiffonade."

EXTREMELY BIASED: For sharp, angular scallions that bring the wow factor, slice them thinly on an extreme angle ("on the bias") using a sharp knife or kitchen shears. You can also dunk them in a bowl of ice water and they will curl up to make even more impactful dip confetti!

DO THE HAND CHIVE: Chives are one of the messiest herbs around. Cutting them with a knife usually makes them fly off your cutting board and all over the kitchen. Instead, use kitchen shears and cut them fatter than you think, about ½ an inch, so they aren't so delicate they get lost in the dip. Thicc chives save lives.

VEGGIE TRAILS: When using vegetables as a garnish (like lettuce and tomato atop Drive-Thru Taco 7-Layer Dip, page 128), the key is to use contrasting colors that can really pop and not go overboard. You can always serve more on the side after taking your #DipPic, but you don't want it to look overwhelming or busy. For perfectionists, shred your own lettuce so you can control how thin or thick it is. A quick bath in ice water and thorough drying off will help it stay as crisp as possible. Remove the seeds from tomatoes so they don't make a watery mess. And for raw onion, take the time to uniformly dice or mince instead of doing an aggressive rough chop. As a more substantial and strong-flavored dip confetti, it will stand out in the wrong way if you have weird little irregular shards of onion.

EXTREMELY BIASED
DICED
MINCED
THICC-CUT CHIVES
AGGRESSIVELY ROUGH CHOPPED
EXTREMELY BIASED
EXTREMELY BIASED

DRIZZLE ME THIS

A finishing flourish of olive oil is a chef's kiss, and there are two ways to drizzle. If you make *dip*vots or swooshes, you can just spoon oil into the grooves. If you want to actually drizzle the oil on, decant it into a squeeze bottle so you can control how much comes out at a time, then use a zigzag or swirling motion from high up.

WARM CHIPS > WARM NUTS

A quick lil' zhuzh for chips to make them feel restaurant-quality? Warm 'em up! *Dips*perse the chips—I highly recommend tortilla, but potato, pita, or whatever you like can also work—evenly across a sheet pan and bake in an oven, toaster oven, or air fryer at 300°F for about 5 minutes, until warm to the touch. Bonus: Upgrade with seasonings of your choice—like Tajín for a salty-citrusy moment or cinnamon sugar for a sweet dipper—by sprinkling on while the chips are still hot.

PREDIPTERMINED DIPPERS

If you want to *dips*play some dippers sticking out from your dip artfully, remember that less is more. Spread them out across the circumference of the dip so it isn't too crowded or busy looking. This is your time to be creative and have fun—but just remember that if you stick something in the dip that will get soggy—like softer cookies or chips—remove them before serving so that your guests won't be *dips*appointed by the texture.

PLATTERY GETS YOU EVERYWHERE

If you're making a dip that isn't conventionally beautiful (like Beanie Weenie Hummus, page 108), use a fun platter—like the vintage ones pictured throughout the book—to uplift the dip to wow-worthy level. Think of the vessel as the supportive best friend in a rom-com that helps elevate the otherwise dull dip or dippers. It's the Judy Greer of the dip universe.

CRUDITÉS AND FRUITITÉS

Here are some quick #DipTips for dippers that make the cut.

APPLES: Cut into thick slices and squeeze citrus juice of your choice over them so they don't brown.

BABY BELL OR SWEET PEPPERS: Halve lengthwise with the stem kept intact as a handle and scoop out the seeds.

BANANAS: Using a just-ripe banana (aka yellow with maybe a few brown spots), cut on an extreme bias into long, approximately ¼-inch planks that resemble surfboards.

BROCCOLI AND CAULIFLOWER: Blanch by cooking for 2 minutes in boiling, salted water, then immediately shocking in a bowl of ice water. This keeps them looking vibrant and fresh and takes some of the raw edge off the flavor.

CUCUMBERS, CARROTS, CELERY: Cut crosswise on the diagonal into dippable chunks.

LETTUCES: Any small-leaved, tender-yet-sturdy lettuce can work as a dipper. Just wash and separate leaves of Little Gem, butterhead lettuces such as Boston or Bibb, endive, or the smallest inner parts of a head of romaine and serve with chilled, not-too-heavy (light on the palate and not too chunky in texture) dips like Caesar Salad Dip (page 97).

STRAWBERRIES: Halve the berry and stem together lengthwise so both pieces can have a handle.

SWEET DIPS' POSITION

The arrangement of where your dips and dippers reside on a platter is up to you, but here's a guide to get you started.

BOWL PLACEMENT: If you have a lot of dip—like a party-size portion—it's better to separate the dips and dippers. But if it's a smaller portion that can fit in a bowl on a platter (or part of a *dip*vided platter), surround it with your most beautiful dippers, such as farmers market produce and artisan crackers.

CRACKERS: Shingle them in an arch formation, especially if the platter is rounded!

CHIPS: Always go on the side in a bowl.

CRUDITÉS AND FRUITITÉS: Mix up different textures, colors, or both around the plate. If all your dippers happen to be the same color, lean into the monochrome but accent them with an extra sprinkle of herbs. If you can make a rainbow of colors, it's always impressive, but a few colors are plenty as long as they contrast with each other.

dip etiquette:

only you can prevent double dipping

The first rule of Dip Club is you don't double dip. Full stop. Just don't do it. We all see you! There are many ways to prevent double dipping without compromising your dip-to-dipper ratio . . .

SMOOTH MOVES TO PREVENT DOUBLE DIPPING

Only *you* can prevent double dipping. Set your guests up for success! When filling the serving vessel, leave at least ½ inch of space between the dip and the top of the dish, so it doesn't overflow when people start dipping in. And make sure the dippers are not too small or too big. If they're too short, people could graze their fingers into the dip by accident. If they're too big and the dip and dipper can't be eaten together in one or two bites, there's a higher potential for double dipping.

The following are three of my favorite dipping techniques to ensure no double dipping on your end, and others will catch on once they see them in action. I highly encourage you to do a dipping performance at the start of every party, so everyone knows how to dip the right thing.

DIP FRONT 'N' BACK: Drag your dipper forward in the bowl, then backward. Both sides of the bottom half of the dipper will be coated in dip, which you can spread across the entire dipper or incorporate the dip 'n' flip technique.

DIP 'N' FLIP: After taking a bite of a dipper coated in dip, flip it around so the uneaten side can be dipped separately. Make sure to really emphasize that flip so no one thinks you secretly double dipped!

RIP 'N' DIP: This works best for crusty bread like baguettes, soft pretzels, and bagels. Rip off a small piece of the dipper of your choice to dip into the communal dish. But make sure the ripped dippers aren't too small or you may commit the party foul of touching the dip with your hand.

DIP 'N' SNAP: This works best with crudités. When you have a crunchy vegetable, you can dip then snap in half to have three more potential ends to dip in.

DIP ALONE: If you eat dip by yourself in an in*dip*vidual serving on the couch at home, you can double dip as much as you damn well please. That is always an option!

dip measuring: how to scale up dips for a party

There's nothing worse than going to a party where there's a *dips*proportionate amount of dip to people. So I've done the dip math for you.

- If you're trying to *dip*cide how much dip to make for a party, anticipate that guests will eat about ¼ cup each. So if you're anticipating ten people, make sure you have 2½ cups of dip.
- If you're serving only a dip and no other appetizers, up the quantity to ½ cup per person—so, 5 cups for ten people.
- The serving sizes in the book—Solo (or Duo), A Lil' Get-Together (4 to 6), and A Big Dip Party (8 to 10)—are *dip*termined based on it being the only dip at the party. If you're going to a potluck where your dip will be part of a larger buffet (of all dips or an assortment of food), then you can safely guesstimate that every dip can serve a Big Dip Party.
- And lastly, the math changes if you're dipping solo. When you're the big dipper, you can go for a full cup serving when meal prepping lunches for yourself or you're doing dip for dinner.
- What quantity of dippers should you use for each serving of dip? A good guideline is twice the quantity of dippers to dip, so if you you're serving ¼ cup of Death Breath Dip (page 69) per person, you'll want to serve about ½ cup of crudités and chips alongside it. See the Graze Anatomy guide on page 29 for a visual dip plate guide, which is helpful to reference when assembling dip buffets or spreads where you'll be covering an entire plate in dip. And don't forget that *dip*vided plates and trays are your best friend for dip parties.

CATEGORY IS . . . PREP TIME!

You'll notice there are no prep, active, or inactive times listed. As I noted in the introduction (no sweat if you didn't read it, that's why it bears repeating), rather than listing the amount of time the recipe "should" take to make—because not all of us work at the same pace or are on the same cooking skill level—I've categorized all recipes into three levels of timing and *dip*ficulty: **Dip on Demand** (15 minutes or less), **Goldilocks Dip** (in-the-middle timing of 45 minutes or less), and **Worth the Wait** (night-before prep for chilling purposes or inactive baking time). This way you can read it and *dip*cide if you have time to make it instead of figuring that out an hour before your party when you read the whole recipe through. I highly encourage you to read the recipe in its entirety before even going to the grocery store. This way there are no surprises, except for how exceptional and impressive dip can be!

graze anatomy:
a dipsplainer for the perfect snack plate

Meredith Grey may have departed *Grey's Anatomy*'s Grey Sloan Memorial Hospital, but Mere*dip* Graze is here with big dip energy. Whether you're making a dippy plate for yourself or helping others navigate a dip buffet, here's the official guide to curating the ideal ratios for snacking, *dip*pety-split.

- Create quadrants on your plates so you can fit quadruple the dips and quadruple the fun!
- Separate dips with crudité moats like celery, carrots, cucumber, or lettuce
- You can also use cured meats, like salami
- Keep dippers that can get easily soggy on the outer rim of your plate
- Use vertical space to pile dippers upward on your plate for maximum dip capacity, such as chips
- In case one of your moats collapses, don't mix savory and sweet dips!

astro dips:
your dip horoscope

ARIES (MARCH 21–APRIL 19)

Dip: Miso Eggplant Dip, 113
Why: People will be as passionate about this dip when you casually add it to the party food rotation as you are about . . . everything in your life. Most of the work is hands-off so you won't be hurrying up and waiting for it to be ready.

TAURUS (APRIL 20–MAY 20)

Dip: Garlic Bread Baked Brie in an Edibowl, 85
Why: Bullseye! This cozy, comforting soon-to-be-classic can be a decadent single serving during a solo evening lounging on the couch—or a reliable dip to bring to superb shindigs that will have people singing your praises.

GEMINI (MAY 21–JUNE 20)

Dip: Guava Cheesecake Dip, 49
Why: This dip has a duality of sweet and savory, and you can enhance whichever strikes your fancy—or both. Playful Mini Ham and Cheese Croissants (page 193) are the savory route dipper, cookies or fruit can embrace the guava's tart sweetness.

CANCER (JUNE 21–JULY 22)

Dip: Crab Rangoon Dip, 140
Why: Your connection to crab aside, this is a dip that will be universally beloved for the comforting feeling it brings. You follow your heart and intuition, and they will lead you to crab rangoon.

LEO (JULY 23–AUGUST 22)

Dip: Strawberry Shortcake Dip, 180
Why: There's a big ol' spotlight shining on this dip, just like you. Everyone will be clamoring to take a snapshot of your shining star—especially if you have strawberry inception by dippin' a berry in!

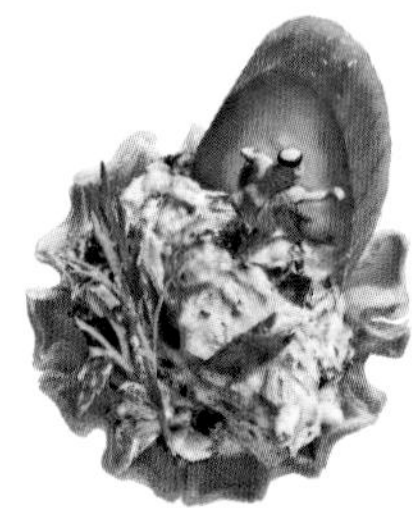

VIRGO (AUGUST 23–SEPTEMBER 22)

Dip: Spanakopidip, 148
Why: This dip is all in the details. How you garnish this twist on the Greek pastry is up to you—go as heavy-handed as you like with a drizzle of luscious olive oil and extra greenery with sprigs of dill—your detail-oriented nature will make it *stunning*.

What's the first dip you should make from this book? It's written in the stars. Alice Hu, my dear friend, founder of Woo Woo Company and career astrologer (learn more at yoursaturn.com), shared her pre*dip*tions for what each sign should make first.

LIBRA (SEPTEMBER 23–OCTOBER 22)

Dip: Black-and-White Sesame Cookie Dip, 164
Why: Stunning inside and out, this combines a black-and-white cookie with roasty-toasty sesame for surprising depth of flavor and major intrigue. It's yin and yang in edible form. And the Dip Queen is a Libra, so . . .

SCORPIO (OCTOBER 23–NOVEMBER 21)

Dip: Curry Squashcotta Sheet Pan Dip, 119
Why: The intense harmony of flavors and textures may make you emotional. Let your tears help season the dish. As a planner, you'll definitely remember to save your squash shell for serving!

SAGITTARIUS (NOVEMBER 22–DECEMBER 21)

Dip: Drive-Thru Taco 7-Layer Dip, 128
Why: This ultimate party food brings everyone together and can light up a room and charm anyone. Sound familiar?

CAPRICORN (DECEMBER 22–JANUARY 19)

Dip: Face Your Schmears Everything Bagel Dip, 131
Why: Like this dip, you have many layers and nuances to your personality. Whether or not you identify as an overachiever, perfecting a layered dip takes a little extra work and patience. Your *dip*termination will pay off.

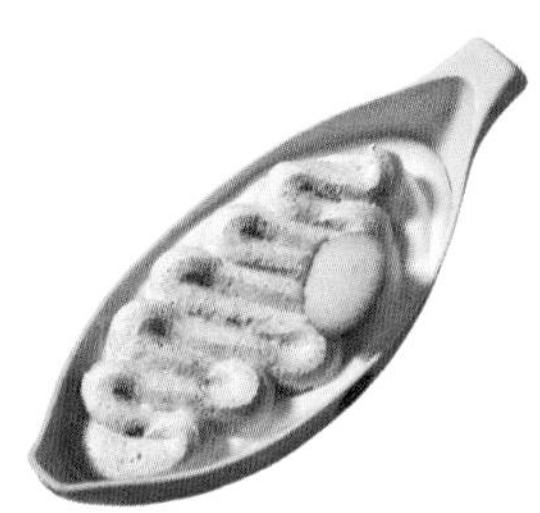

AQUARIUS (JANUARY 20–FEBRUARY 18)

Dip: This Dip Is Bananas!, 167
Why: This innovative dip combines so many favorite banana dishes: banana bread, bananas foster, and banana pudding. It's a triple threat that mirrors your creativity and complexity.

PISCES (FEBRUARY 19–MARCH 20)

Dip: Caesar Salad Dip, 97
Why: Everyone loves this timeless, classic, cheesier-than-average salad, and this is a bold new way to serve it—preferably at a *dip*ner party. It's so dreamy that you'll wonder if you manifested this addictive dip.

THE dips!

5-minute dips

Some people wait a lifetime for a moment like *dips . . .* but you won't have to! All of these dips come together in five minutes (after you gather your ingredients), and they range from sweet to savory and back again. These are for when you need to make *dip* happen for an impromptu hangout or a potluck you forgot about, or just because you want melty cheese for one.

DIPPER MATRIX

HOMEMADE

Double Sesame Mochi Flatbreads, 196

Wonton Lil' Scoopz, 200

Roulette Charred Peppers, 216

Potato Skinny Dippers, 219

STORE-BOUGHT IS FRAN FINE

Fritos Scoops, or another type of corn chip

Tortilla chips, especially Tostitos Scoops

Korean rice crackers

Tempura seaweed chips

Baby corn, corn "ribs," or small pieces of corn on the cob (warning: messy!)

Crudités, such as carrots, cauliflower, broccoli, cucumbers, or sweet peppers

French fries, Tater Tots, or your favorite crispy potatoes

ON DEMAND

corn cheesy like sunday morning dip

SERVES A LIL' GET-TOGETHER (4 TO 6)

I am Korean and love corny puns. And corn as a food and aesthetic. (Just look at all the corn props in the photo on page 39!) So this dip is most in*dip*ative of my personality and Big Dip Energy. I'm also impatient and believe the microwave is an ideal cooking method for warm dips that don't need to have a golden brown, bubbly top. And it's easy (and cheesy) like Sunday morning, but it is also phenomenal after a late night out karaoke-ing.

1 package (8 ounces) cream cheese, cut into chunks for quicker melting

1 cup frozen or drained canned corn

½ cup freshly grated mozzarella cheese

1 tablespoon gochujang

2 teaspoons sugar

1 teaspoon garlic powder

¼ teaspoon kosher salt

¼ teaspoon ground white pepper

1 teaspoon toasted sesame oil

½ cup Kewpie mayonnaise

4 scallions, dark green parts only, thinly sliced on the bias

Toasted sesame seeds, for garnish

1. In a medium microwave-safe bowl, combine the cream cheese, corn, mozzarella, gochujang, sugar, garlic powder, salt, and pepper. Microwave for 1 minute, stir to combine, then microwave for another 30 seconds and stir again. Everything should be smooth and thoroughly combined, but if not, microwave for another 30 seconds.

2. Stir in the sesame oil, mayonnaise (it will break if added earlier), and half the scallions. Top with the remaining scallions and a sprinkle of toasted sesame seeds.

faq

CAN IT BE MADE IN ADVANCE? You can mix the initial ingredients in a bowl and refrigerate, then heat and finish the dip later. But it's so fast that you don't need to!

HOW LONG WILL IT KEEP? A week in the fridge in an airtight container.

elote to love dip

SERVES A LIL' GET-TOGETHER (4 TO 6)

Some of the simplest dips in the book were the most *dip*ficult to get right, including this elote dip. It almost broke me—because the dip kept breaking. When mayonnaise is heated to too high a temperature or for too long, it can separate and become a greasy mess. So after baking, broiling, and cooking this dip on the stovetop, I realized the best way to make it—and Korean-inspired Corn Cheesy Like Sunday Morning Dip on page 37—is in the microwave *without* the mayonnaise, stirring in the mayo after everything else is melty, cheesy goodness. That way it just gets a kiss of residual heat and won't cause a breakdown in the dip, or in your psyche. And although Tajín is prominent in classic elote, I found that more than just a finishing dash of it overpowered the dip with sourness.

1 package (8 ounces) cream cheese, cut into chunks for quicker melting

1 cup frozen or drained canned corn

1 teaspoon garlic powder

1 teaspoon chili powder

½ jalapeño, seeded and minced

¼ cup crumbled cotija cheese, plus more for garnish

½ cup mayonnaise

2 tablespoons freshly squeezed lime juice (about 1 lime)

3 tablespoons aggressively rough chopped fresh cilantro leaves

Tajín or chili powder, for garnish (optional)

1. In a medium microwave-safe bowl, place the cream cheese, corn, garlic powder, chili powder, jalapeño, and cotija cheese. Microwave for 1 minute, stir to combine, then microwave for another 30 seconds and stir again. Everything should be smooth and thoroughly combined, but if not, microwave for another 30 seconds. (If you don't have a microwave, you can do this over medium-low heat in a small saucepan.)

2. Stir in the mayonnaise, lime juice, and 2 tablespoons of the cilantro. Top with the remaining 1 tablespoon cilantro, as much cotija as you want, and a sprinkle of Tajín, if using.

CHIPPY'S TIPPY

This dip can also be served cold. Try omitting the corn and making dippers out of baby corn, corn ribs, or small pieces of corn on the cob (messy but worth it).

faq

CAN IT BE MADE IN ADVANCE? You can mix the initial ingredients in a bowl and refrigerate, then heat and finish the dip later. But it's so fast that you don't need to!

HOW LONG WILL IT KEEP? A week in the fridge in an airtight container.

DIPPER MATRIX
HOMEMADE
Roulette Charred Peppers, 216
Potato Skinny Dippers, 219
STORE-BOUGHT IS FRAN FINE
Fritos Scoops, or another type of corn chip
Tortilla chips, especially Tostitos Scoops
Baby corn, corn "ribs," or small pieces of corn on the cob (warning: messy!)
Crudités, such as carrots, cucumbers, celery, cauliflower, or sweet peppers
French fries, Tater Tots, or your favorite crispy potatoes
CORN CHEESEY LIKE SUNDAY MORNING DIP (PAGE 37)
ELOTE TO LOVE DIP

DIPPER MATRIX

STORE-BOUGHT IS FRAN FINE

Tortilla chips, especially Tostitos Scoops

Potato chips, preferably ridged like Ruffles

Pretzels (hard or soft)

French fries, Tater Tots, or your favorite crispy potatoes

in queso emergency dip

SERVES SOLO (OR DUO)

Sometimes you need emergency cheese. Lucky for you, this insta-queso microwaves into melty goodness in 2 minutes, so you can get to workin' on your night cheese. (Preferably while wearing a Slanket and singing like Liz Lemon.) This was made to serve one, but it is a shareable amount and easy to scale up if you want to dip in with someone else.

2 ounces cream cheese
¼ teaspoon garlic powder
3 ounces white American cheese (about 5 or 6 slices)
2 tablespoons whole milk, plus more as needed

1. Combine all the ingredients in a small microwave-safe bowl. Microwave at 50 percent power (this prevents it from bubbling over and making a mess) for 1 minute, stir, and microwave for 1 minute more and stir. It may need another minute, depending on your microwave's strength. You want the dip to be evenly melted into a cohesive mixture that coats a chip but isn't too runny nor too thicc. Be aware that it will thicken as it cools, but you can add a splash more milk to get the perfect consistency.

2. If you don't have a microwave, the dip can be made on the stovetop over medium-low heat, stirring frequently until everything is combined, about 3 minutes.

faq

CAN IT BE MADE IN ADVANCE? Yes, but it's so fast, just make it fresh when you want it!

HOW LONG WILL IT KEEP? See above.

CHIPPY'S TIPPY

No other cheese will melt as easily and perfectly smoothly as American. Just trust the process(ed).

say kimcheese! dip

SERVES A LIL' GET-TOGETHER (4 TO 6)

Kimchi and cream cheese are two core ingredients to my identity, being Korean and Jewish, so it thrilled me to find they pair together so effortlessly. The spicy funk from the kimchi is toned down by the creamy, slightly tangy cheese and even creamier Kewpie mayonnaise. Toasted sesame oil adds a nice warm note that is complemented by a slight bite of whole scallions (whites, light green, and dark green parts). Garlic powder rather than raw garlic adds its signature touch without overwhelming your palate. Quick-pickled vegetables are a key dipper choice, but you should definitely keep bagels handy, too. It just makes sense. (And it's great as a swap for the herby cream cheese layer in Face Your Schmears Everything Bagel Dip, page 131.)

1 package (8 ounces) cream cheese, softened at room temperature (see page 14)

1 cup kimchi, snipped into small pieces or rough chopped

½ cup Kewpie mayonnaise

3 tablespoons kimchi brine

2 teaspoons toasted sesame oil

½ teaspoon garlic powder

4 scallions, thinly sliced on the bias, a few sliced greens reserved for garnish

Combine all the ingredients in a large bowl and mix well. Transfer to a small serving bowl, top with the reserved scallions, and say "kimcheese!"

MOD*IP*FICATIONS: Have a jar of kimchi that's been sitting around for a while and has soured? Sauté it in a small skillet over medium heat with a tablespoon of neutral oil or butter until lightly caramelized. (If it's really funky, add a teaspoon of sugar or honey.) You can also add this ad*dip*tional layer of flavor with freshly purchased (or made) kimchi.

CHIPPY'S TIPPY

Use kitchen shears to cut the kimchi directly into the dip so you don't stain your hands or cutting board.

faq

CAN IT BE MADE IN ADVANCE? Yes!

HOW LONG WILL IT KEEP? Up to a week in an airtight container at room temperature. After that, the kimchi can age a bit and get a little funkier, so add a sprinkle of sugar to offset that flavor and you can still eat it for a few more days.

DIPPER MATRIX

HOMEMADE

Everything in a Pickle, 218
Veggie Ribbons, 214
Double Sesame Mochi Flatbreads, 196
Wonton Lil' Scoopz, 200
Roulette Charred Peppers, 216
Potato Skinny Dippers, 219
Crispy Rice Dipsticks, 207

STORE-BOUGHT IS FRAN FINE

Korean pickled daikon (bright yellow!)
Korean rice crackers
Tempura seaweed chips
Fritos Scoops, or another type of corn chip
Tortilla chips, especially Tostitos Scoops
Crudités, such as carrots, cauliflower, cucumbers, celery, cauliflower, broccoli, or sweet peppers
French fries, Tater Tots, or your favorite crispy potatoes

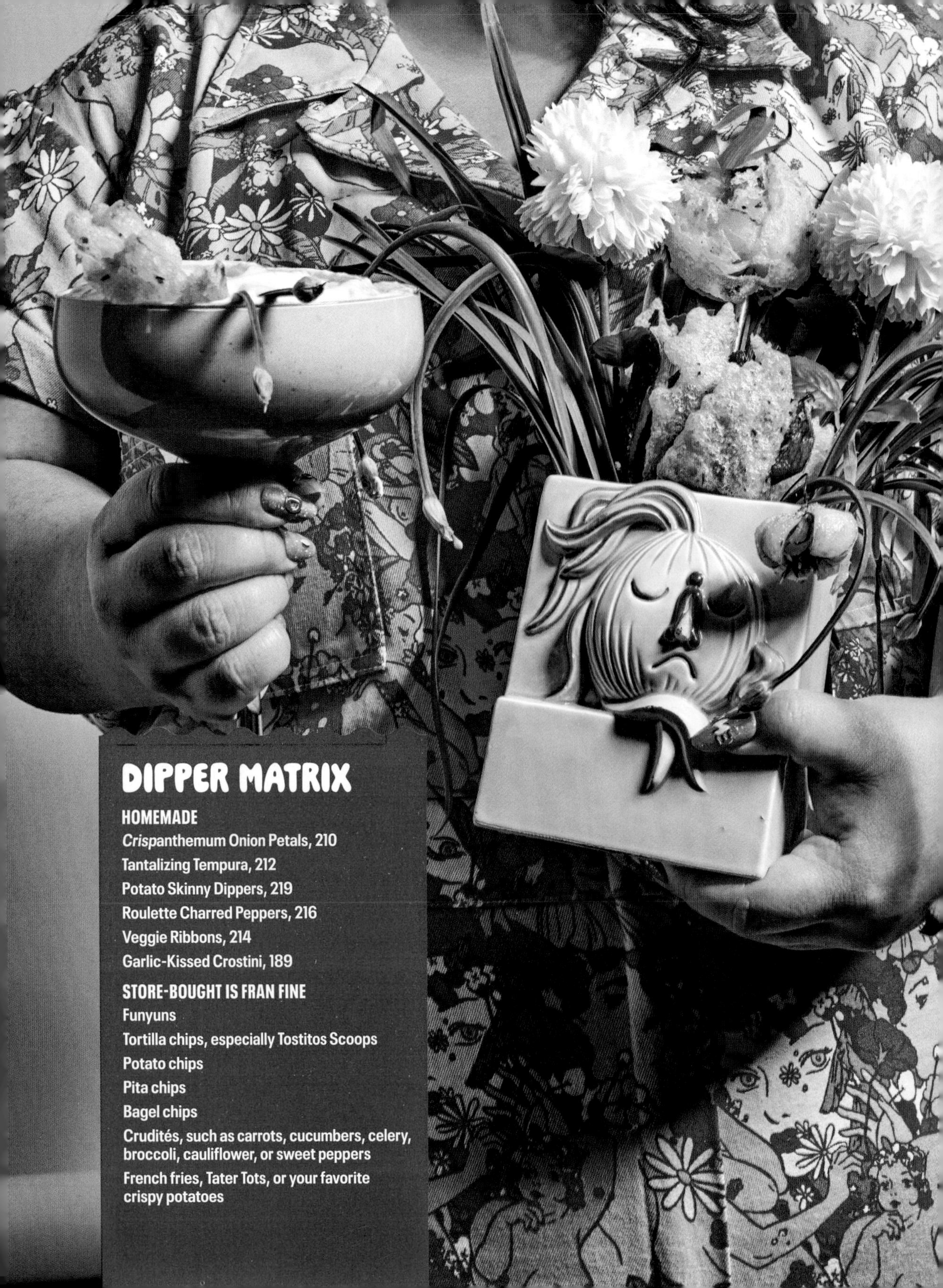

DIPPER MATRIX

HOMEMADE

*Crisp*anthemum Onion Petals, 210
Tantalizing Tempura, 212
Potato Skinny Dippers, 219
Roulette Charred Peppers, 216
Veggie Ribbons, 214
Garlic-Kissed Crostini, 189

STORE-BOUGHT IS FRAN FINE

Funyuns
Tortilla chips, especially Tostitos Scoops
Potato chips
Pita chips
Bagel chips
Crudités, such as carrots, cucumbers, celery, broccoli, cauliflower, or sweet peppers
French fries, Tater Tots, or your favorite crispy potatoes

bloom, bloom, room, onion, dip

SERVES A LIL' GET-TOGETHER (4 TO 6)

Whenever I go to Outback Steakhouse, I ask for extra Bloomin' Onion sauce; the dip-to-dipper ratio they give you is laughable. Maybe 2 ounces dip for an entire edible sculpture of a flower onion? It needs to be quadrupled, at least. This recipe lets you get lost in the sauce, but with a slightly thicker *dips*cosity that's scoopable onto *Crisp*anthemum Onion Petals (page 210) that have the same Bloomin' Onion–inspired spices sprinkled on the outside. But if you don't feel like frying anything, you can just grab a bag of Funyuns or chips, a bag of frozen onion rings, or some veggies. You won't miss the crispy onion bits because there are crushed-up store-bought crispy onions inside the dip, too.

½ cup mayonnaise

½ cup sour cream

¼ cup crushed crispy onions, plus more for garnish

2 tablespoons prepared horseradish

1 tablespoon ketchup

½ teaspoon paprika

½ teaspoon kosher salt

½ teaspoon garlic powder

½ teaspoon onion powder

¼ teaspoon dried oregano

8 cranks black pepper

1 dash cayenne pepper

Combine all the ingredients in a medium bowl, mix well, and garnish with more crispy onions. That's it! That's the dip!

CHIPPY'S TIPPY

The best crispy onions to use in this dip are ones from any Asian market. The texture is superior, and you can buy them as slices or already crushed into small bits. But French's Original Crispy Fried Onions or Funyuns also work, especially if you're planning to use them as dippers as well.

faq

CAN IT BE MADE IN ADVANCE? Yes! As far in advance as you want, within a week or so.

HOW LONG WILL IT KEEP? At least 10 days in a covered container in the fridge, if not longer, as it's just dairy and spices.

piña colada dip

SERVES A BIG DIP PARTY (8 TO 10)

This is as close to Red Lobster's dipping sauce for their coconut shrimp as I could make without storming their test kitchen. It's slightly thicker than its inspiration, so it's more of a dip than a sauce, and it can be eaten with savory and sweet dippers equally. But don't try dipping a Cheddar Bay Biscuit in there unless you're a pineapple-on-pizza person. If you are, the cheesy pineapple combo may speak to you, just like getting caught in the rain and making love at midnight.

- **2 cups sour cream**
- **1 can (15 ounces) cream of coconut, such as Coco López**
- **1 can (8 ounces) crushed pineapple, with juice**
- **Zest and juice of 1 lime**
- **⅛ teaspoon kosher salt**

Combine all the ingredients in a medium bowl and mix well. Taste to see if the dip needs more salt to balance out the sweetness; it should be able to pair equally well with fruit or cookies or crispy coconut shrimp.

faq

CAN IT BE MADE IN ADVANCE? Yes, up to a week in advance.

HOW LONG WILL IT KEEP? Up to 10 days in an airtight container in the fridge.

JEAN DIPS IN TO SAY, "TROPI-CALL ME MAYBE!"

DIPPER MATRIX

HOMEMADE

Crumble Crackers, 229

Wonton Lil' Scoopz or Cinnamon-Sugar Wonton Lil' Scoopz, 200

Phyllo Lil' Scoopz, 202

STORE-BOUGHT IS FRAN FINE

Cooked frozen coconut shrimp

Gluten-free crispy coconut rolls, such as Thai brand or Ava Organic

Fresh fruit, such as apples, strawberries, or bananas

Waffle cones, broken into pieces

Pretzels or pretzel thins

Graham crackers

DIPPER MATRIX

HOMEMADE

Mini Ham and Cheese Croissants, 193

Crumble Crackers, 229

Phyllo Lil' Scoopz, 202

STORE-BOUGHT IS FRAN FINE

Fresh fruit, such as apples, strawberries, or bananas

Pretzels or pretzel thins

Graham crackers

Gluten-free crispy coconut rolls, such as Thai brand or Ava Organic

Shortbread cookies

guava cheesecake dip

SERVES A LIL' GET-TOGETHER (4 TO 6)

The guava cheese strudel from Porto's, a Cuban bakery in Los Angeles, is flawless. The buttery crust encapsulates a sweet-and-savory interior of cream cheese and tangy guava paste that is *so* good I would eat it with a spoon. And now we all can, because I turned that filling into a three-ingredient dip that could be a no-bake cheesecake filling if it firmed up a bit more. Baby ham and cheese croissants made with store-bought crescent dough are a dreamy dipper, bringing an even more savory edge that would make a perfect ad*dip*tion to a brunch spread.

1 package (8 ounces) cream cheese, softened at room temperature (see page 14)

⅓ cup sour cream

8 ounces guava paste, preferably Melissa's

Powdered sugar, to taste (optional)

Combine the cream cheese, sour cream, and guava paste in a medium bowl. You shouldn't need any additional sugar, but the sweetness level of guava paste can vary. If you like, add 1 tablespoon of powdered sugar at a time and incorporate completely.

faq

CAN IT BE MADE IN ADVANCE? Yes, and it stays the perfect consistency even when refrigerated.

HOW LONG WILL IT KEEP? Up to 10 days in an airtight container in the fridge.

CHIPPY'S TIPPY

Melissa's Produce has the best guava paste for this dip, if you can track it down.

GOLDILOCKS

simply the zest dipssert trio:

lemon bar, key lime pie, and creamsicle

SERVES A BIG DIP PARTY (8 TO 10)

Do you remember eating fruit pizza, the pizza-shaped sugar cookies with some sort of sweetened cream cheese spread and assorted fruit on top? They were often at summer barbecues when I was growing up, and my favorite part was always the cream cheese. (Some things never change.) When trying to capture that fruit pizza topping in dip form, I was surprised that vanilla yogurt, sweetened condensed milk, and Cool Whip actually made a better base than cream cheese. This mixture is light and bright and complements citrus flavors to make a trio of dips inspired by lemon bars, Key lime pie, and Creamsicles. They remind me of icebox cakes, so instead of calling them triple threats, I'll refer to them as triple axels. This is *The Cutting Edge* of *dips*serts, after all. Toe pick of the litter!

1 container (5.3 ounces) vanilla yogurt, preferably whole milk

½ cup sweetened condensed milk

1 teaspoon pure vanilla extract

1 container (8 ounces) Cool Whip, preferably Extra Creamy

2 tablespoons lemon curd, such as Trader Joe's or Bonne Maman

2 tablespoons orange juice concentrate

2 tablespoons bottled Key lime juice, such as Nellie & Joe's

Food coloring, preferably gel (optional)

CHIPPY'S TIPPY

The base recipe is designed to be *dip*vided into three bowls so you can mix and match citrusy goodness. If you want to do all one flavor, just triple the amount of the citrus mix-in. Optional dip confetti could be a sprinkle of the zest of a lemon, lime, or orange!

In a medium bowl, combine the yogurt, sweetened condensed milk, vanilla extract, and Cool Whip, taking care not to whisk too much and deflate the Cool Whip. You have two options now: *Dip*vide the mixture among three small bowls and mix in one citrus flavoring per bowl, or triple the amount of one type of citrus and add it to your original medium bowl to go all in on a singular flavor. You can also add food coloring here to make each *dips*tinctly yellow, orange, or green. If you have a multisection serving platter or bowl, it's fun to showcase all three dips at once with dippers, but a small bowl of each flavor with dippers on the side also works great.

MO*DIP*FICATIONS: Love another fruit? Try swapping in that jam or curd and see what happens.

faq

CAN IT BE MADE IN ADVANCE? Yes, it's better if it has more time to set up in the fridge.

HOW LONG WILL IT KEEP? Up to 10 days in an airtight container in the fridge.

DIPPER MATRIX

HOMEMADE

Crumble Crackers, 229

Cinnamon-Sugar Wonton Lil' Scoopz, 200

Ritzy Crispy Treat Chips, 230

STORE-BOUGHT IS FRAN FINE

Fresh fruit, such as apples, strawberries, or bananas

Shortbread cookies

Waffle cones, broken into pieces

Pretzels or pretzel thins

Graham crackers

Gluten-free crispy coconut rolls (such as Thai brands or Ava Organic)

OGs—with a twist!

To those uninformed, OGs means "original gangsters," which is way less gangster to use when you have to explain the meaning. But I *dip*gress. These recipes are dips that you *think* you know, but you have no idea what they could become. Some are elevated, some took a trip abroad and returned with renewed *dip*spiration, and some are expanded past the classics (including seven different types of "cranch," a cream cheese–based ranch that is extra creamy-dreamy).

ranch reinvented:
7 ways to "cranch," from extra-creamy ranch to buffalo chicken dip

SERVES A LIL' GET-TOGETHER (4 TO 6)

Cranch happened by accident. I didn't have any sour cream and wanted to make ranch dip, so I thought, why not cream cheese? Now I won't make it any other way, because cream cheese has this slightly sweet, more decadent, less tangy flavor and a creamier, thicker consistency to make sure you actually are eating a *dip*, not a salad dressing. It's an important *dip*stinction!

You can go with the OG version or level up by adding blue cheese and Buffalo sauce for a vegetarian version of the beloved Buffalo Chicken Dip, or cooked chicken for the best version of the real deal. And there's also Everything Cranch, a French onion-ranch hybrid, and a spicy chili crisp version to play with.

ORIGINAL CRANCH

1 package (8 ounces) cream cheese, softened at room temperature (see page 14)

1 cup mayonnaise

2 packets (1 ounce each) ranch seasoning (about ¼ cup)

2 garlic cloves, grated

2 tablespoons whole milk, for thinning, as needed

1 teaspoon sugar

4 cranks black pepper

BLUE CHEESE CRANCH

Original Cranch plus ½ cup freshly crumbled blue cheese

BUFFALO CRANCH

Original Cranch plus ½ cup Frank's RedHot Buffalo Wings Sauce or Original Cayenne Pepper Sauce

BUFFALO CHICKEN DIP

Buffalo Cranch plus 1 cup cooked and shredded chicken, such as store-bought rotisserie. This can also be done with Chili Crisp Cranch!

FRENCH ONION CRANCH

Original Cranch plus 2 tablespoons dehydrated or fried onions

EVERYTHING CRANCH

Original Cranch plus 2 tablespoons everything bagel seasoning

CHILI CRISP CRANCH

Original Cranch plus 1 or 2 tablespoons chili crisp of your choice (adjust for spice)

FOR ALL THE CRANCHES

1. Combine everything in a large bowl, using an electric hand mixer or your actual hands . . . holding a spatula . . . for an arm workout.

FOR BUFFALO CHICKEN DIP

2. Combine everything in a large microwave-safe bowl, microwave for 1 minute, stir, then microwave for another minute. (You may need to repeat for up to 5 minutes if you have a lower-wattage microwave.)

3. If you don't have a microwave, transfer the mixture to a 9-inch pie plate or square baking dish and bake in a 350°F oven for 15 to 20 minutes, until lightly browned and bubbly. The only benefit to using the oven over the microwave is the browning, but since this doesn't have a cheesy top, it doesn't matter as much, so I opt for the quicker version.

MO*DIP*FICATIONS: You can always sub*dip*tute plant-based dairy, but make sure to taste as you go for salt levels and consistency.

faq

CAN IT BE MADE IN ADVANCE? Yes, even days ahead.

HOW LONG WILL IT KEEP? With no chicken, up to 2 weeks in the fridge in an airtight container. With chicken, 5 days.

VEGGIE RIBBONS + CRANCH 4 EVER!

DIPPER MATRIX

HOMEMADE

Roulette Charred Peppers, 216
Potato Skinny Dippers, 219
Tantalizing Tempura, 212
Veggie Ribbons, 214

STORE-BOUGHT IS FRAN FINE

Fritos Scoops, or another type of corn chip
Tortilla chips, especially Tostitos Scoops
Crudités, such as carrots, cucumbers, celery, broccoli, cauliflower, or sweet peppers
French fries, Tater Tots, or your favorite crispy potatoes

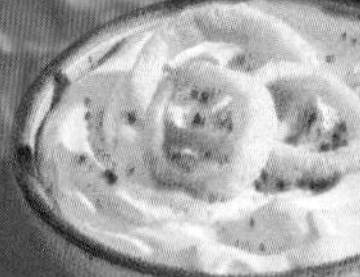
EXTRA CRUNCHY
POTATO
Chips
FRENCH ONION
CRANCH
CHILI
CRISP
CRANCH
BLUE CHEESE
CRANCH
BUFFALO
CHICKEN
DIP
10
20
30
40
50
40

TIME FOR DIPOFF!

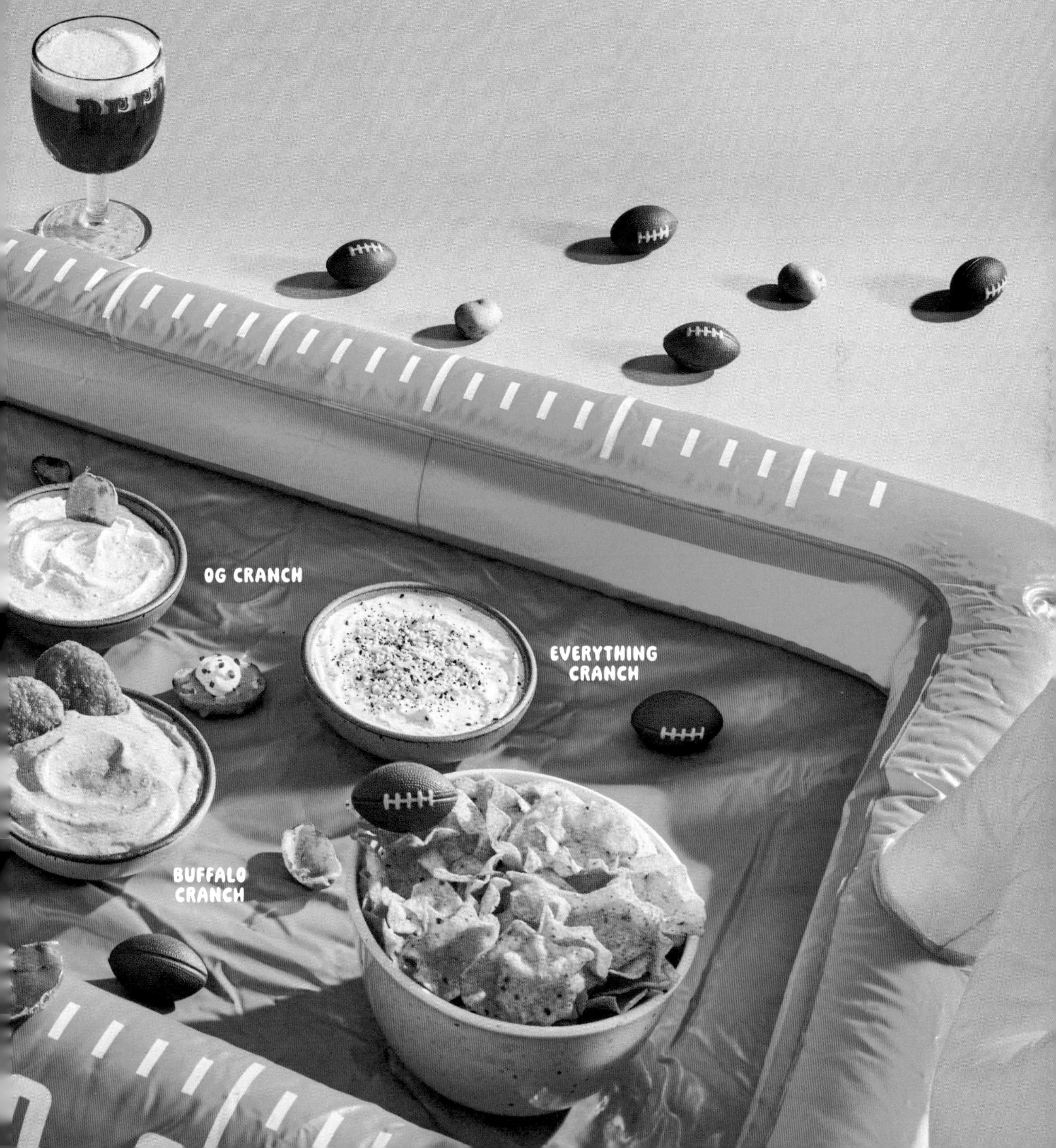

classique spinnie artie dip

SERVES A LIL' GET-TOGETHER (4 TO 6)

It felt wrong not to have the dip I've made probably fifty times in my lifetime in this book, so here's my *classique* spinnie artie dip. I am allowing pre-shredded mozzarella cheese here because it's meant to be ri*dip*ulously easy, but remember that freshly grated mozz will melt better and give you better cheese pulls, so I encourage you to take the extra few minutes and arm workout needed to grate it by hand.

1 can (13.75 ounces) artichoke hearts, drained, wrung out in a towel, and aggressively rough chopped

1 package (10 ounces) frozen chopped spinach, thawed and wrung out in a towel

2 tablespoons olive oil

1 medium yellow onion, finely chopped

4 garlic cloves, aggressively rough chopped

1 teaspoon kosher salt

¾ cup sour cream

1¼ cups shredded whole milk mozzarella cheese (preferably freshly grated, but pre-shredded is okay)

¾ cup freshly grated parmesan cheese

10 cranks black pepper

1. Combine the artichokes and spinach in a medium bowl and set aside. In a large skillet over medium heat, heat the oil. Add the onion and sauté, stirring occasionally, until translucent and just starting to brown, 5 to 7 minutes. Add the garlic and cook for another 1 minute, or until fragrant. Add the artichokes and spinach, ½ teaspoon of the salt, sour cream, mozzarella, and parmesan, and stir until thoroughly combined and the cheeses are completely melted. Add the remaining ½ teaspoon salt and the pepper, then taste to see if the seasoning is good to you; if not, add a little more of one or both.

2. You can serve this *dip*rectly from the skillet or transfer to a slow cooker on low to keep warm.

MO*DIP*FICATIONS: This is an easy skillet dip, but if you want a bubbly, bronzed top, you can also bake it at 375°F for 15 minutes, but I don't recommend putting extra cheese on top, as it will harden quickly and is *dip*ficult to break through with a chip.

DIPPER MATRIX

HOMEMADE

Potato Skinny Dippers, 219
Roulette Charred Peppers, 216
Garlic-Kissed Crostini, 189
Veggie Ribbons, 214

STORE-BOUGHT IS FRAN FINE

Fritos Scoops, or another type of corn chip
Tortilla chips, especially Tostitos Scoops
Crudités, such as carrots or sweet peppers
French fries, Tater Tots, or your favorite crispy potatoes

faq

CAN IT BE MADE IN ADVANCE? Yes, but it may need to be thinned out with a bit of milk if it sits in the fridge overnight. (See page 15 for reheating instructions.)

HOW LONG WILL IT KEEP? About a week in the fridge in an airtight container.

saag paneer artichoke dip

SERVES A LIL' GET-TOGETHER (4 TO 6)

Like Eve 6's iconic song (too niche?), I turned saag paneer inside out to find a new-point-0 version of the classic Spinach Artichoke Dip. (But if you want that one, head to page 58 for my *classique* version.) Instead of the paneer (a firm Indian cheese) being served inside, it's crisped up into Crispy Paneer Dipsticks (page 221) that can scoop the spiced-up dip with a certified cheese-on-cheese situation.

1 can (about 14 ounces) artichoke hearts, drained, wrung out in a towel, and aggressively rough chopped

1 box (10 ounces) frozen chopped spinach, thawed and wrung out in a towel

3 tablespoons ghee or neutral oil, such as vegetable or canola

1 medium yellow onion, aggressively rough chopped

1 large green serrano pepper or jalapeño, seeded (unless you like it spicier) and minced

1 tablespoon peeled and finely minced fresh ginger

4 garlic cloves, minced

2½ teaspoons garam masala

1 teaspoon kosher salt

1 package (8 ounces) cream cheese, softened at room temperature (see page 14)

½ cup whole milk plain yogurt

½ cup mayonnaise

½ cup plus 2 tablespoons freshly grated parmesan cheese

Zest and juice of ½ lemon

¼ cup aggressively rough chopped fresh cilantro, for garnish

1 teaspoon chopped pimiento peppers, for garnish (optional)

1. Preheat the oven to 400°F. Combine the artichokes and spinach in a medium bowl and set aside.

2. In a large skillet over medium heat, melt the ghee. Add the onion and cook, stirring occasionally, until translucent and just starting to brown, 5 to 7 minutes. Add the serrano pepper and sauté for 2 minutes, then add the ginger and garlic and sauté until fragrant, about 1 minute. Add 1½ teaspoons of the garam masala and the salt to the mixture and toast until fragrant, about 1 minute. Set aside to cool.

3. Add the spinach, artichokes, and onion mixture to the bowl of a food processor or a blender. Run the motor until the mixture is as smooth as possible, scraping down the sides if needed. Add cream cheese, yogurt, mayonnaise, ½ cup parmesan, lemon zest and juice, and remaining 1 teaspoon of garam masala, and then run the motor until combined. (This can also be done in a large bowl with an immersion blender.)

4. Transfer the mixture to a 9-inch pie plate, top with the remaining 2 tablespoons of parmesan, and bake for 20 to 25 minutes, until bubbly and lightly browned on top. Top with the cilantro and optional pimientos for a pop of color.

faq

CAN IT BE MADE IN ADVANCE? Yes! See page 15 for reheating instructions.

HOW LONG WILL IT LAST? A week in the fridge in an airtight container.

DIPPER MATRIX

HOMEMADE

Crispy Paneer Dipsticks, 221

Garlic-Kissed Crostini, 189

Potato Skinny Dippers, 219

STORE-BOUGHT IS FRAN FINE

Pita chips

Tortilla chips, especially Tostitos Scoops

Crudités, such as carrots, broccoli, cauliflower, or sweet peppers

tteokbokki sausage dip

SERVES A BIG DIP PARTY (8 TO 10)

The runaway hit of my first Dipmas party, back in 2015, was my friend Katie's sausage dip. It had only three ingredients: a tube of breakfast sausage browned in a skillet, two bricks of cream cheese, and a can of Ro-Tel. It was served with Tostitos Scoops and was the first dip demolished at the party. She got the recipe from her mom, and it was passed to mutual friends for years until it ended up here, in *Big Dip Energy*, with a Korean-ish twist inspired by using leftover sausage dip as a sauce for brunch tteokbokki. I thinned out the leftover dip with a bit of milk and tossed it with cooked rice cakes, along with scallions, toasted sesame oil, and gochujang. It was a damn delight, and that savory-spicy combination was ultimately transformed into this dip, which also includes garlic and onion, extra kick from gochugaru (Korean chili flakes), and a little sugar to balance everything out. Crispy rice cakes and Vienna sausage skewers are the ideal dippers, but this dip is just as good with plain ol' tortilla chips or veggies.

2 tablespoons vegetable oil

1 tube (16 ounces) loose breakfast sausage, such as Jimmy Dean

½ small yellow onion, aggressively rough chopped

4 garlic cloves, aggressively rough chopped

4 scallions, white and dark green parts separated and thinly sliced

2 packages (8 ounces each) cream cheese

1 can (10 ounces) diced tomatoes and green chiles, such as Ro-Tel

2 tablespoons gochujang

2 teaspoons gochugaru

2 teaspoons sugar

¼ cup chopped fresh cilantro leaves, for garnish

CHIPPY'S TIPPY

Add a few dollops of leftover dip into your scrambled eggs the next morning, or use it as a sausage gravy over biscuits.

1. In a large skillet (preferably nonstick) over medium heat, heat the oil for at least 3 minutes. Cut off the end of the breakfast sausage tube and squeeze directly into the skillet for the least messy transfer, then use a spatula to press down into a thin, even layer, as best as you can.

2. Cook the sausage, undisturbed, for 5 minutes, then break into smaller, slider-size pieces and flip. It should be seared golden brown on the bottom. Cook, again without stirring, for another 5 minutes, then break into small pieces that are perfect for sitting on a chip. Add the onion, garlic, and scallion whites, stirring occasionally, for 5 minutes, until the onion is translucent.

(continued)

SAAG PANEER
ARTICHOKE DIP
(PAGE 60)
TTEOKBOKKI
SAUSAGE DIP

DIPPER MATRIX

HOMEMADE

Rice Cake and Sausage Skewers, 224

Crispy Rice Dipsticks, 207

Rainbow Dumpling Chips, page 203

STORE-BOUGHT IS FRAN FINE

Tortilla chips, preferably Tostitos Scoops

Crudités, such as carrots, cucumbers, or sweet peppers

Soft or hard pretzels

French fries, Tater Tots, or your favorite crispy potatoes

3. Add the cream cheese, Ro-tel, gochujang, gochugaru, and sugar and stir until the cheese is melted and the ingredients are combined. Serve warm, topped with the cilantro and thinly sliced scallion greens.

MO*DIP*FICATIONS: Plant-based sausage would work to make this vegetarian, and with vegan cream cheese it could be vegan. Taste as you go—it might need more salt!

faq

CAN IT BE MADE IN ADVANCE? Yes, reheat in a slow cooker on low or in a covered pan over low heat. You may need to add more milk to achieve the desired consistency, where it coats the chip but isn't clumpy or drippy.

HOW LONG WILL IT KEEP? Because there's meat in the dip, I can safely say 5 days in an airtight container in the fridge. But it likely won't last that long anyway . . .

DIP THE RAINBOW WITH RAINBOW DUMPLING CHIPS

cincinnati chili dip

SERVES A BIG DIP PARTY (8 TO 10)

I'm going to get this out of the way right now: I have never been to Ohio. But I have many close friends from all parts of Ohio, including dynamic duo Carolyn and Kevin, who introduced me to Cincinnati chili by way of Carolyn's family recipe. I transformed it into a dip using an Instant Pot for speed, and have had three native Ohioans taste-test it for authenticity.

For the uninformed, Cincinnati-style chili—also referred to as Skyline Chili, aka the most recognizable chili parlor in Ohio—is a bean-less beef chili that leans into Mediterranean flavors with warm spices including cinnamon, cloves, nutmeg, and allspice. Though those spices bring up memories of gingerbread, don't worry—this chili isn't sweet. It does, however, warm you from the inside out with a cozy comforting feeling akin to a hug from a sweet Midwestern friend.

I tried making spaghetti Lil' Scoopz (see pages 200 and 202 for other variations) to go with this, as this style of chili is typically served over spaghetti with a mountain of fluffy, freshly shredded cheddar cheese and raw onions on top. But spaghetti scoopz turned out messy and complicated, so I opted for fried (or air-fried!) pasta chips instead. (Find them on page 209—they've become my favorite dipper for this dip, but there are plenty of other options to mix and match.) And though there are Skyline Chili dips out there with more robust ingredient lists and spice levels, I purposely chose to make a simplified version, using only a softened-yet-unbaked cream cheese cheddar base with the chili on top to help it melt a bit from residual heat, and then more "raw," unmelted cheddar cheese and raw onions on top. On paper, this may weird you out, but I promise it will surprise *and* delight everyone you serve it to, whether they were familiar with the original or not.

*Dips*claimer: The family recipe I based this on calls to brown the beef, which isn't commonly found in Cincinnati chili recipes but adds more flavor from the caramelization. And TBH, I didn't want to make you all whisk raw beef into water, as is traditional!

(continued)

CHILI OUT, WHAT YA YELLIN' FOR?

2 tablespoons olive oil

1 medium yellow onion, aggressively rough chopped

5 garlic cloves, minced

1 pound ground beef, preferably 80/20

1 can (29 ounces) plain tomato sauce (not Italian seasoned)

1 teaspoon ground cinnamon

1 teaspoon ground cumin

1 teaspoon ground allspice

½ teaspoon ground cloves

¼ teaspoon ground nutmeg

1½ teaspoons chili powder

1 tablespoon white vinegar

3 bay leaves

2 teaspoons kosher salt

20 cranks freshly cracked black pepper

ALL ABOUT THAT CHEESY BASE

1 package (8 ounces) cream cheese, softened at room temperature (see page 14)

2 cups freshly grated sharp cheddar cheese

½ cup aggressively rough chopped yellow onion

8 cranks black pepper

CHILI OUT, WHAT YA YELLIN' FOR?

1. Heat a large skillet or dutch oven over medium heat, or if using a pressure cooker, set it to sauté. Pour in the oil, add the onion, and sauté until translucent and just starting to brown, 5 to 7 minutes. Add the garlic and sauté until just aromatic, about 1 minute.

2. Spread the ground beef in an even layer across the bottom of the pot and let brown undisturbed for 5 minutes, then break up into small pieces with a wooden spoon or spatula. Cook, stirring and turning the pieces until they are lightly caramelized and no longer pink, about 5 minutes more. If there's excessive grease, remove it with a spoon or carefully soak it up with a wadded-up paper towel held with tongs, then discard it.

3. Add the tomato sauce, cinnamon, cumin, allspice, cloves, nutmeg, chili powder, vinegar, bay leaves, salt, and pepper to the beef mixture, stir to combine, and bring to a boil over medium-high heat. Cover with a lid, lower the heat, and simmer for 30 minutes. Remove the bay leaves and discard after cooking.

ALL ABOUT THAT CHEESY BASE

4. Preheat the oven to 350°F.

5. While the chili is cooking (or after, whichever floats your boat), in a medium bowl, combine the cream cheese, 1½ cups of the cheddar, and ¼ cup of the onion and mix until thoroughly combined. Crank in the black pepper. Transfer this mixture to a 3-quart baking dish (8-inch round is common) or a wide, shallow, oven-safe ceramic or stoneware bowl and spread it evenly across the bottom.

6. Bake for 15 minutes, or until melty and dippable.

7. Pile the chili in the middle of the cheesy mixture so you can see both layers as you dip in, then top with the remaining ½ cup cheddar and ¼ cup onions.

MOD*IP*FICATIONS: If you don't eat beef, you could try this with ground turkey or a plant-based alternative, but you may need a little more oil to get it nicely browned.

faq

CAN IT BE MADE IN ADVANCE? Yes! The chili tastes even better if you make it at least a day in advance. Store in an airtight container in the fridge or freezer, and assemble and bake together the day you're serving it.

CAN YOU USE A PRESSURE COOKER OR SLOW COOKER? Yes, for the chili! If using a pressure cooker, put on the lid, set to high pressure for 30 minutes, and let the pressure release naturally (about 15 minutes). If using a slow cooker, cook it on high for 3 hours or low for 6 hours.

HOW LONG WILL IT KEEP? Up to 5 days in the fridge in an airtight container. (See page 15 for reheating instructions.) The chili can be frozen for up to 4 months, but the cream cheese's texture gets a little weird after being frozen and thawed. And the chili is *great* on hot dogs.

DIPPER MATRIX

HOMEMADE

Pasta la Vista Chips, 209
Garlic-Kissed Crostini, 189
Roulette Charred Peppers, 216
These Bagel Pretzel Bites Have Everything, 194
Shortcut Garlic Knots, 190

STORE-BOUGHT IS FRAN FINE

Tortilla chips, especially Tostitos Scoops

French fries, Tater Tots, or your favorite crispy potatoes

"'TIL DEATH BREATH DO US PART."
PEPP
SALT

death breath dip

SERVES A BIG DIP PARTY (8 TO 10)

Let's go back, back to the beginning. Back to when French onion dip was the only dip you'd tried. Now it's time to *dip*fy expectations of what onion dip can be and turn up the flavor to the equivalent *dip*cibel of me loudly screaming Hilary Duff's "Come Clean" at karaoke. Death Breath Dip is an allium invasion, with *eight* types of onions and garlic slow-cooked together until meltingly tender, gently caramelized, and sweet in a way that'll fool you into thinking you don't need a mint after. You do, but if you're serving this fragrant dip at a party where everyone is indulging, the collective death breath will cancel itself out.

The most *dip*ficult part of this recipe isn't that you're confiting. (Did I mention you're going to confit? That's just a fancy word for submerging in a nice warm bath of oil and cooking over low heat until the flavors and textures mellow.) Even though this process is mostly hands-off—I prefer using the oven rather than the stovetop, which requires more babysitting—the biggest struggle is remaining patient when the symphony of scents perfuming your kitchen is so intoxicating. But patience is a virtue that will pay off in *dip*idends when you take your first bite of this amped-up, flavor-packed onion dip and *dips*cover that sometimes the reboot can be better than the original.

1 medium yellow onion, quartered

1 medium sweet onion, quartered

1 medium red onion, quartered

1 leek, pale green and white parts only, halved lengthwise and thoroughly rinsed

2 small shallots, halved

1 bunch scallions, white and dark green parts separated

2 garlic heads, lightly crushed to separate the cloves (no peeling or cutting needed!)

4 teaspoons kosher salt

2 cups olive oil, plus more for drizzling, or a budget-friendly neutral oil, such as vegetable or canola (but skip the drizzle)

2 cups sour cream

1 cup mayonnaise

3 tablespoons freshly squeezed lemon juice (about 1 lemon)

¾ teaspoon garlic powder

1 teaspoon Worcestershire sauce or soy sauce, whichever you prefer

20 cranks black pepper, plus more as needed

1 bunch chives, snipped into thicc pieces (see page 22)

1. Preheat the oven to 325°F.

2. To confit the alliums, arrange the onions, leek, shallots, scallion whites, and garlic in a 9 x 13-inch baking dish, sprinkle with 3 teaspoons of the salt, toss to coat, and pour in the oil. Give the veggies a mix and spread into an even layer. Cover with aluminum foil and bake for 1½ hours , stirring twice during baking.

(continued)

3. Meanwhile, watch a couple episodes of your favorite TV show to pass the time. Just before the timer is about to go off, fill a small bowl with ice water. Slice the scallion greens as thinly as you can on the bias (aka diagonally), then drop them into the bowl of water. They will curl up and turn into gorgeous dip confetti! Strain them with a slotted spoon or fine-mesh strainer, then dump onto paper towels and pat until fully dry.

4. In a large bowl, combine the sour cream, mayonnaise, lemon juice, remaining 1 teaspoon of salt, garlic powder, Worcestershire sauce, and pepper and mix well. Mix in half of the scallion greens and the chives and set aside the rest for garnish.

5. When the confit mixture is ready, carefully use a slotted spoon to remove the garlic heads to a small bowl. Transfer the onions, leeks, and scallions to the bowl of a food processor and let cool for at least 15 minutes before blitzing the veggies into a rough paste.

6. Strain the infused oil through a fine-mesh strainer or sieve into a pint container (or medium bowl) and let sit at room temp until cool to the touch, then cover and store in the fridge for another use for up to 2 weeks. (See Chippy's Tippy for a few ways to use it!)

7. Squeeze the confit garlic cloves out of their papery shells—a very soothing activity—and add the garlic to the food processor. Pulse a few more times to combine, then combine all of the confit alliums with the creamy dip base.

8. Transfer the dip to a few small bowls to scatter throughout a party or into one large, wide bowl. (This recipe makes a lot and holds well in the fridge, so I'd recommend serving half to start and replenishing later as needed.) Drizzle the top of the dip with oil then scatter artfully with the remaining scallions and chives.

9. Add a few cranks of black pepper to finish if you like it a little spicier, and serve with the dippers of your choice or a spoon.

CHIPPY'S TIPPY

Don't throw away that allium-infused oil—it's an added allium bonus! Use it in place of regular olive oil in salad dressings, to coat vegetables or proteins for roasting or panfrying, or to cook eggs.

DIPPER MATRIX

HOMEMADE

Potato Skinny Dippers, 219

Veggie Ribbons, 214

Crispy Paneer Dipsticks, 221

*Crisp*anthemum Onion Petals, 210

These Bagel Pretzel Bites Have Everything, 194

STORE-BOUGHT IS FRAN FINE

Potato chips, preferably Ruffles Cheddar & Sour Cream, which adds a cheesy surprise, a little extra tang, and the same ridged surface as OG Ruffles that holds dip in its nooks and crannies

Crudités, such as carrots, cucumbers, celery, or sweet peppers

Pretzel thins

Chicken nuggets

MOD*IP*FICATIONS: Use Greek yogurt instead of sour cream for extra tang and to slightly lighten it up. Plant-based sour cream and mayonnaise can be substituted but will affect the texture and might need a bit of tinkering.

faq

CAN IT BE MADE IN ADVANCE? Yes! The flavors meld better as it sits.

HOW LONG WILL IT KEEP? Up to a week in the fridge, stored in an airtight container.

cheesy af

It's dippin' time, and the living is cheesy. A bowl—or in the case of Cheesesteak Me Out Fon*dip* (page 74), a volcano—full of hot cheese—is the best way to get a party started. Turn to these recipes for easy, cheesy, beautiful guaranteed crowd-*cheesers*. (And for tips on keepin' the cheese hot, refer to the Dip Tool Kit on page 10.)

cheesesteak me out fon*dip* with deli roast beef skewers

SERVES A BIG DIP PARTY (8 TO 10)

How to build the perfect cheesesteak is a hotly debated topic that I'm not about to get in the middle of, so I used all three popular cheese choices—Cheez Whiz, American cheese, and provolone—in this fon*dip*, my lovingly bastardized version of fondue. (Sorry to my Swiss readers—I promise it's done with love and adoration for the fondue format!) I also wanted to give this recipe, which has a bunch of steps, as many shortcuts as possible to make it more doable. This includes using a bag of sliced frozen peppers and onions instead of slicing them yourself and making skewers of rare roast beef from the deli and mini sweet peppers that are seared to emulate the thin, juicy beef in cheesesteak.

FON*DIP* IT LOW

2 tablespoons olive oil

1 bag (12 to 14 ounces) frozen peppers and onions

1 jar (15 ounces) Cheez Whiz

1 can (12 ounces) evaporated milk (or regular whole milk, if you prefer)

¼ pound thinly sliced deli provolone cheese

¼ pound thinly sliced white deli American cheese

1 teaspoon garlic powder

1 teaspoon kosher salt

ZOOT SKEWER RIOT

1 pound rare roast beef, thinly sliced from the deli

1 tablespoon neutral oil, such as vegetable or canola

CHIPPY'S TIPPY

Have the provolone and American cheese thinly sliced at the deli counter while you're grabbing the roast beef. It will melt faster than block cheese and save you from shredding it yourself.

FON*DIP* IT LOW

1. In a large skillet over medium-high heat, combine the oil and the peppers and onions. Cook, stirring occasionally, until all the water has evaporated and the vegetables have developed some nice browning and even blistering, 8 to 10 minutes.

2. Add the Cheez Whiz and evaporated milk and stir to melt together, then reduce the heat to medium-low and add the provolone and American cheese, garlic powder, and salt. Transfer to a slow cooker on low to keep warm or reduce the heat to the lowest it can go and cover with a lid until ready to serve.

DIPPER MATRIX

HOMEMADE

Roulette Charred Peppers, 216

Tantalizing Tempura, 212

Potato Skinny Dippers, 219

These Bagel Pretzel Bites Have Everything, 194

Veggie Ribbons, 214

STORE-BOUGHT IS FRAN FINE

Tortilla chips, especially Tostitos Scoops

Potato chips

Crudités, such as carrots, sweet peppers, cauliflower, or broccoli

ZOOT SKEWER RIOT

3. For the skewers, fold each piece of roast beef in thirds lengthwise and then accordion it into folds onto a 4-inch skewer. Set a grill pan or large skillet over medium-high heat, add the oil and then the skewers, and cook for 1 minute per side, until charred but still a little rare inside.

4. Serve the skewers with the dip, either in a plastic volcano surrounded by dino-shaped chicken nuggets (if you're as extra as me), in a slow cooker on warm, or in a fondue pot.

faq

CAN IT BE MADE IN ADVANCE? Yes, but it may need to be thinned with milk, as it will firm and thicken in the fridge. (See page 15 for reheating instructions.)

HOW LONG WILL IT KEEP? Up to a week in the fridge in an airtight container.

broccoli cheddar soup fon*dip*

SERVES A BIG DIP PARTY (8 TO 10)

Are you ready to brocc 'n' roll? Because this is a *soup*ercalifragilisticexpiali-*dip*ious version of one of the best soups of all time. The base is made of actual soup—condensed cream of broccoli, or if you can't find that, cream of mushroom—and Velveeta. There's cheddar in there, too, but to get the right consistency and nostalgic flavor, there's no sub*dip*tution for Velveeta. Swiss people would probably have a fit over me calling this fondue (and it also has a thicker *dips*cosity than classic fondue) so I'm calling it fon*dip*, which kinda sounds like "Fun Dip." I understand that's confusing because the textures don't match the candy of the same name, but you're dipping fried broccoli inside a broccoli-cheddar soup dip—what's more fun than that?

8 ounces broccoli florets (or 12 ounces frozen chopped broccoli)

2 tablespoons olive oil

½ medium yellow onion, aggressively rough chopped

4 garlic cloves, aggressively rough chopped

4 ounces Velveeta, cubed

1 can (10.5 ounces) cream of broccoli or mushroom soup

1 cup whole milk

2 cups freshly grated sharp cheddar cheese

10 to 15 cranks black pepper

CHIPPY'S TIPPY

Mix leftovers with approximately a 2:1 ratio of leftover dip to cooked rice or pasta and bake it like a casserole at 350°F for 30 minutes. You can add extra vegetables and/or cooked chicken, or just enjoy the cheesy carbs.

1. Aggressively rough chop the broccoli on a cutting board or pulse in a food processor a few times to break them into medium pieces (roughly the size of your thumbnail, unless you have acrylics on).

2. In a large saucepan or high-sided skillet over medium heat, heat the oil. Add the onion and sauté, stirring occasionally, until translucent and just starting to brown, 5 to 7 minutes. Add the garlic and cook until fragrant, about 1 minute, then add the chopped broccoli and cook until tender but a little toothsome, 3 to 5 minutes. FYI: Frozen broccoli may not need this extra time and can get mushier faster, so taste for your desired tenderness.

3. Lower the heat to medium-low and add the Velveeta, soup, and milk. Stir until melted and smooth. Add the cheddar and stir again until fully melted in. You shouldn't need any salt here, but you can go heavier on the black pepper if you like. Start with 10 cranks, then go up from there.

(continued)

faq

CAN IT BE MADE IN ADVANCE? Yes, but thin it out with more milk to reach the desired consistency. (See page 15 for reheating instructions.)

HOW LONG WILL IT KEEP? Up to 10 days in the fridge in an airtight container.

DIPPER MATRIX

HOMEMADE

Tantalizing Tempura Broccoli, 212, or other fried veggies of your choice

*Crisp*anthemum Onion Petals, 210

Garlic-Kissed Crostini, 189

Potato Skinny Dippers, 219

These Bagel Pretzel Bites Have Everything, 194

Roulette Charred Peppers, 216

Veggie Ribbons, 214

STORE-BOUGHT IS FRAN FINE

Tortilla chips, especially Tostitos Scoops

Potato chips or mixed root vegetable chips, such as Terra

Crudités, such as carrots, sweet peppers, or blanched broccoli

French fries, Tater Tots, or your favorite crispy potatoes

pizza your way dip

SERVES A BIG DIP PARTY (8 TO 10)

Pizza is universally beloved but hotly debated. The best styles of crust, sauce, cheese (and whether it goes under or over the sauce), and toppings are all subjective. I'm not trying to please everyone at once, so I'm giving you a choose-your-own-adventure situation where you can go down different pizza pathways. Want a white pizza? Whip up just the garlicky, cheesy base. Want a classic pizza? Sauce up the base! The toppings are entirely up to you, from the meat lovers to the pineapple fanatics.

But the nonnegotiable element is the garlic knots. I engineered this dip to be surrounded by a garlic knot wreath that will make your Dipmas celebrations extra festive, but if you just want to make a big pile of 'em—maybe stack them like a croquembouche?—that's okay, too. Eventually it'll all be ripped and dipped into saucy, cheesy goodness. Feeling overwhelmed by the idea of making your own garlic knots? Do *knot* fret—you can buy a few dozen at your local pizza shop and call it a day!

FOR WHITE PIZZA DIP

2 tablespoons olive oil

6 garlic cloves, aggressively rough chopped

½ teaspoon dried oregano

¼ teaspoon crushed red pepper

1 container (15 ounces) ricotta cheese

1 package (8 ounces) cream cheese, softened at room temperature (see page 14)

3 tablespoons Knorr Garlic & Herb Sauce Mix (half a 1.6-ounce packet)

½ cup plus 2 tablespoons freshly grated parmesan cheese

2 cups freshly grated mozzarella cheese

¼ cup basil leaves, for garnish

FOR RED SAUCE PIZZA DIP

Everything above, plus 1 cup marinara sauce of your choice (mine is Rao's)

FOR BOTH

An assortment of toppings, like pepperoni, thinly sliced onions, cooked crumbled sausage, broccoli, anchovies, or . . . pineapple

1. Preheat the oven to 425°F.

2. In a small skillet over medium-low heat, heat the oil. Add the garlic and sauté until it's just starting to brown, 1 to 2 minutes. Add the oregano and crushed red pepper and cook until fragrant, about 30 seconds more. Transfer to a small heatproof bowl to cool.

3. In a large bowl, combine the ricotta, cream cheese, infused oil, garlic and herb seasoning, ½ cup of the parmesan,

(continued)

DIPPER MATRIX

HOMEMADE

Garlic Knot Wreath, 190

Garlic-Kissed Crostini, 189

Roulette Charred Peppers, 216

Rice Cake and Sausage Skewers, 224

STORE-BOUGHT IS FRAN FINE

Frozen Texas Toast, cooked and cut into dipsticks

Frozen breadsticks, cooked

Tortilla chips, especially Tostitos Scoops

Pita chips

Bagel chips

and 1 cup of the mozzarella. Spread the mixture into a 9-inch pie plate and top with the marinara sauce (if using), remaining 1 cup of mozzarella, remaining 2 tablespoons parmesan cheese, and the toppings of your choice.

4. Slice the basil into thin ribbons (see page 22). Set aside for garnish.

5. Bake for 20 to 25 minutes, until the top is golden brown and bubbly. Top with the basil dip confetti and serve immediately for guaranteed cheese pulls. Transfer to a slow cooker on low heat if you want to keep it warm for the length of a party.

MO*DIP*FICATIONS: A hefty drizzle of pesto can adorn your white pizza dip if you don't wanna go full-blown red sauce.

faq

CAN IT BE MADE IN ADVANCE? Yes, see page 15 for reheating instructions.

HOW LONG WILL IT KEEP? Up to a week in the fridge in an airtight container.

CHIPPY'S TIPPY

If you are a saucy person, you can alternate layers of cheesy ricotta and marinara instead of just pouring one on top of the other. It would be especially beautiful in a clear dish.

MERRY
DIPMAS!

freak-a-leek beer cheese dip

SERVES A BIG DIP PARTY (8 TO 10)

This dip started as a challenge: turn my friend Erin McDowell's cheddar ale soup into a dip. I was leading a conversation with her at the cozy cookbook store Now Serving in Los Angeles in support of her phenomenal book *Savory Baking*. She made everything-crusted pretzel bites—which I also pay homage to with my These Bagel Pretzel Bites Have Everything (page 194) using short-cut store-bought pizza dough—and we got to watch a crowd of carb enthusiasts enjoy our beer cheese bébé.

My favorite part of the original soup was its use of leeks, a highly underrated allium. It's intimidating looking at them in the grocery store, but know that this freaky stalk is only half enjoyable—I discard the tough dark green parts (though some use them for stocks) and cook the rest into submission in butter until they practically melt into a gentle oniony base.

At first I thought there are two options for this dip: leave it chunky or give it a whiz in the food processor. But I realized there's a third, too. Since this is a derivative of soup, in theory you could add some chicken stock and milk and eat it that way. If you borrow the edi*bowl* concept from the Garlic Bread Baked Brie (page 85), you're all set for the most cozy, cheesy party of your life. Report back after you wake up from your food coma.

2 tablespoons unsalted butter

2 leeks, white and pale green parts only, halved lengthwise, rinsed well, and thinly sliced

4 garlic cloves, minced

1 package (8 ounces) cream cheese, softened at room temperature (see page 14)

1 cup sour cream

1 tablespoon dijon mustard

¼ cup plus 2 tablespoons lager beer

2 cups freshly grated sharp cheddar cheese

½ bunch chives, snipped into thicc pieces (see page 22)

15 cranks black pepper, plus more to taste

Kosher salt (optional)

CHIPPY'S TIPPY

This dip can be eaten hot or cold! It also doubles as a great sandwich spread after it's firmed up in the fridge.

1. In a large skillet over medium heat, melt the butter, stirring and letting it brown slightly, for about 2 minutes, then add the leeks. Stir occasionally while cooking until tender and caramelized in spots, about 8 minutes. Add the garlic and cook until fragrant, another 1 to 2 minutes.

2. You can leave the leeks as they are if you want nice texture in your dip, but if you want them smoother, let them cool for

DIPPER MATRIX

HOMEMADE

These Bagel Pretzel Bites Have Everything, 194

Garlic-Kissed Crostini, 189

Roulette Charred Peppers, 216

STORE-BOUGHT IS FRAN FINE

Saltines or your favorite buttery crackers

Pretzels or pretzel thins

Potato chips

Pita chips

Bagel chips

Crudités, such as carrots, cucumbers, celery, or sweet peppers

10 minutes, then blitz them in a food processor or blender (or use an immersion blender in a bowl).

3. In a large bowl, combine the cream cheese, sour cream, mustard, and beer. Whisk until smooth, then fold in the cheddar. Fold in most of the chives, reserving a few for garnish. Crank in 15 (or more!) cracks of black pepper and mix into the dip. I didn't find the dip needed salt, but you can add it if your cheese isn't salty enough.

MODIPFICATIONS: You could use sweet onions or shallots instead of leeks, but it won't be freak-a-leeky!

faq

CAN IT BE MADE IN ADVANCE? Yes, but it may need to be thinned out with milk as it firms up in the fridge. (See page 15 for reheating instructions, if serving hot.)

HOW LONG WILL IT KEEP? Up to a week in the fridge in an airtight container.

CHILLED BEER CHEESE

PIPIN' HOT BEER CHEESE

garlic bread baked brie in an edibowl

SERVES A LIL' GET-TOGETHER (4 TO 6)

Bread bowls are not just for soup anymore. Introducing the *edibowl*, a hollowed-out sourdough boule (or round loaf of your choice) filled with an entire wheel of garlic bread–flavored brie. If you really want to gild the lily, you could toss the leftovers with pasta and transform the dip into a sauce for an innovation in macaroni and cheese that no one saw coming.

2 tablespoons olive oil
½ teaspoon garlic powder
⅛ teaspoon kosher salt
1 large bread boule (about 1 pound), preferably sourdough
1 small wheel of brie (about 8 ounces)
4 ounces cream cheese
6 garlic cloves, grated
1 teaspoon chopped fresh rosemary leaves
1 teaspoon chopped fresh thyme leaves

CHIPPY'S TIPPY

To easily scoop out your loaf, cut into the top at a 45-degree angle—like you're taking the top off a pumpkin before carving—using a serrated knife to get out most of the bread at the center, then scoop more out using your hands. The larger chunk can be cut up and used to make Garlic-Kissed Crostini (page 189), and the smaller bits can be toasted into breadcrumbs!

1. Preheat the oven to 375°F.
2. In a small bowl, mix together the oil, garlic powder, and salt.
3. Hollow out the bread boule, leaving about a ½-inch-thick wall for safety, and then cut 1-inch-deep slits (using a paring knife or kitchen shears) around the entire circumference of the rim—they'll be rip-off toast tabs for dipping later. Drizzle the garlic oil on the edibowl, inside and out. Massage the oil into the edibowl and set it on a sheet pan. Bake for 10 minutes, until lightly golden brown and toasted.
4. Meanwhile, use a serrated knife to saw off the very top rind of the brie. Do not discard it! Hollow out the brie by cutting around the circumference and scooping out the soft inside with a spoon to a small microwave-safe bowl, leaving at least ¼ inch of cheese to protect the bottom rind from ripping. Add the cream cheese, garlic, rosemary, and thyme to the bowl. Microwave for 1 minute, stir, and microwave for another minute, or until completely melted—it may take another 30-second burst or two, depending on your microwave's power settings.

(continued)

DIPPER MATRIX

HOMEMADE

Garlic-Kissed Crostini, 189

Roulette Charred Peppers, 216

Veggie Ribbons, 214

These Bagel Pretzel Bites Have Everything, 194

STORE-BOUGHT IS FRAN FINE

Frozen Texas Toast, cooked and cut into dipsticks

Frozen breadsticks, cooked

Tortilla chips, especially Tostitos Scoops

Pita chips

Bagel chips

Pretzels or pretzel thins

Crudités, such as carrots, celery, sweet peppers, broccoli, or cauliflower

5. Place the top of the brie rind inside the edibowl, cheese side up. Carefully lower the hollowed-out brie rind into the bread bowl on top of that (this residual cheese will melt and form a protective layer between the dip and the edibowl). Pour the dip mixture inside.

6. Bake for 15 minutes, until the dip is bubbling and slightly browned on the top. Enjoy by breaking off pieces of the edibowl to dunk, or use other dippers!

MO*DIP*FICATIONS: Omit the grated garlic and top the brie with a few spoonfuls of your favorite jam for a sweet-and-savory take.

CAN IT BE MADE IN ADVANCE? You can prep ahead, but wait to bake until it's just about time to serve.

HOW LONG WILL IT KEEP? Up to a week in the fridge, but it will never be as good as it was when it was fresh.

chopped cheese (burger) queso with garlic butter hoagie toasts

SERVES A BIG DIP PARTY (8 TO 10)

There's nothing better than melted cheese. The chopped cheese sandwich is legendary in New York City, where I spent the end of my twenties mere blocks from its alleged originator, Blue Sky Deli (formerly Hajji's) at 110th and First Avenue. A cross between a burger and a cheesesteak, the sandwich is ground beef chopped up on the grill and blanketed with American cheese. It is then slid into a hoagie roll—or sub roll, depending where you're from—with ketchup, mustard, shredded iceberg lettuce, tomato slices, mayonnaise, pickles, and onion by request. This sandwich has fueled a lot of my post-karaoke shenanigans in my past, but this queso version can either be a hangover cure *or* hangover fuel, when paired with too many margaritas.

The dip base here was inspired by my Texan friend Allison, who uses a combination of cream cheese and American cheese for ultra-melty creaminess in her original queso. The beef, enhanced by garlic and (red) onion, gets coated in a sweet-and-tangy sauce of ketchup and mustard (similar to a Sloppy Joe), which caramelizes on the meat. If you wanted to get wild, you could dip or smother fries in this mixture, or even thin it out with some milk, add cooked potatoes, and make a truly decadent soup. Jussayin'.

GARLIC BUTTER HOAGIE TOASTS WITH THE MOST

¼ cup (½ stick) salted butter

½ teaspoon garlic powder

3 hoagie rolls, cut crosswise into ¼-inch-thick slices (about 30)

CHOPPED CHEESE, PLEASE

1 cup whole milk

1 pound American cheese, cubed or sliced

1 package (8 ounces) cream cheese

3 tablespoons neutral oil, such as vegetable or canola

1 small red onion, minced

3 garlic cloves, minced

1½ teaspoons kosher salt

1 pound ground beef

15 cranks of black pepper, or more if you like it a little spicier

¼ cup ketchup

1 tablespoon yellow mustard

1 cup shredded iceberg lettuce (go ahead, buy the pre-shredded bag!)

2 Roma tomatoes, seeded and diced

Pickles, if you're into that (I'm not)

(continued)

DIPPER MATRIX

HOMEMADE

Garlic Butter Hoagie Toasts, 90

Potato Skinny Dippers, 219

Roulette Charred Peppers, 216

STORE-BOUGHT IS FRAN FINE

Tortilla chips, especially Tostitos Scoops

Fritos Scoops, or another corn chip

Funyuns

Potato chips, preferably ridged like Ruffles

French fries, Tater Tots, or your favorite crispy potatoes

GARLIC BUTTER HOAGIE TOASTS WITH THE MOST

1. Preheat the oven to 350°F.

2. In a small microwave-safe bowl melt the butter in the microwave. Whisk in the garlic powder. Arrange the hoagie slices on a sheet pan and brush the garlic butter on just the tops. (It will taste the same, and this saves time and annoyance.) Bake for 12 to 14 minutes, flipping halfway through, until lightly golden brown. Let the toasts cool slightly, then transfer to a platter while you make the queso.

CHOPPED CHEESE, PLEASE

3. In a medium saucepan over medium heat, bring the milk to a simmer. Lower the heat to medium-low and add the cheeses. Stir continuously until the mixture is melted and smooth, 5 to 7 minutes. Don't walk away or it can scorch on the bottom! Transfer to a slow cooker on low or reduce the heat to the lowest setting possible and cover with a lid to keep warm.

4. In a large skillet over medium heat, heat 2 tablespoons of the oil. Add the onion and sauté until translucent and just starting to brown, 5 to 7 minutes. Add the garlic and sauté until just aromatic, about 1 minute. Season with ¼ teaspoon of the salt. Transfer the onions and garlic to a bowl and set aside.

5. Wipe out the skillet and heat it over medium-high heat for 3 minutes. (This will help quickly develop a golden-brown crust on the ground beef!) Add the ground beef to the pan—without any additional oil!—and press it into an even layer with a spatula. Let cook un*dip*sturbed for 5 minutes, then season with the remaining 1¼ teaspoons of the salt and the pepper (crank on more pepper if you like). Break the ground beef into large pieces, flip them over in the pan, and let sear on the other side for about 3 more minutes, until a bottom crust has developed. Break up the pieces even further, to large crumbles, and cook for 2 to 4 minutes until golden brown all around. If there's excessive grease, remove it with a spoon or carefully soak it up with a wadded-up paper towel held with tongs, then discard it.

6. Add the reserved cooked onion and garlic, the ketchup, and mustard to the ground beef mixture and stir until well combined. Taste and add more salt and pepper if you like.

7. To serve, pile the ground beef mixture on top of the finished queso. (If you are feeding any vegetarians, serve the meat on the side in a bowl!) Serve with the lettuce, tomatoes, optional pickles, Garlic Butter Hoagie Toasts, and/or tortilla chips. You can make little crostini with everything piled together, or dip chips and add toppings as you go. Dipper's choice!

MO*DIP*FICATIONS: If you don't eat beef, you can try ground turkey or a plant-based ground meat, but add extra oil when cooking.

faq

CAN IT BE MADE IN ADVANCE? Yes (see page 15 for reheating instructions).

HOW LONG WILL IT LAST? Up to 5 days in the fridge in a covered container.

DIPPER MATRIX

HOMEMADE

Garlic-Kissed Crostini, 189

Veggie Ribbons, 214

STORE-BOUGHT IS FRAN FINE

Crackers, such as saltines or your favorite buttery kind

Tortilla chips, especially Tostitos Scoops

Pita chips

Pretzels or pretzel thins

Bagel chips

Crudités, such as carrots, celery, or cucumber

devils on horseback dip

SERVES A LIL' GET-TOGETHER (4 TO 6)

This is the most head-scratching dip of the book. You're probably like, what in the world is a devil on horseback? I hate to tell you, but I don't know either. I just know that I saw a Martha Stewart recipe for bacon-wrapped, cheese-stuffed prunes or dates in a vintage cookbook once and the name stuck with me. I made them exactly once for a brunch party in 2012. They were excellent, but I forgot about them until I thought Devils on Horseback had a nice ring to it. Even if you think you don't like prunes or goat cheese, try this dip. I didn't think I'd like it either, but I keep turning to it for feelin' fancy on a random Tuesday and have watched it disappear first at many parties. It is sweet, salty, and creamy, and leftovers can transform into a schmear for your bagel the morning after the party or a fun tea sandwich spread.

½ cup sour cream

¼ cup mayonnaise

1 package (5.2 ounces) garlic and herb Gournay cheese, such as Boursin

½ tablespoon date syrup

10 pitted prunes, roughly chopped

4 bacon strips, preferably thick-cut, cooked extra crispy and chopped

2 tablespoons goat cheese, crumbled

8 cranks black pepper, plus more for garnish

Olive oil, for drizzling

1 tablespoon thicc-cut chives (see page 22), for garnish

In a medium bowl, combine the sour cream, mayo, Boursin, date syrup, prunes, bacon, goat cheese, and black pepper and stir until thoroughly combined. Just before serving, drizzle with oil and top with chives and extra black pepper, if you're feeling extra devilish.

MODIPFICATIONS: You can use an equal amount of blue cheese instead of goat cheese and/or pitted dates instead of prunes, if you'd prefer.

faq

CAN IT BE MADE IN ADVANCE? Yes, but thin it out with a little milk because it will firm up in the fridge.

HOW LONG WILL IT LAST? Up to a week in the fridge in an airtight container.

CHIPPY'S TIPPY

Prunes are quite sticky, so to cut them without making as much of a mess, heat your knife by running it under hot water before starting, and a few times throughout the prep process if needed.

brighter (and a lil' lighter)

These dips are designed to be eaten in large quantities without making you feel weighed down. They are some of the most innovative and interesting dips in the entire book because I had to calculate how to make something satisfying and bright-and-light (in texture, flavor, and how it makes you feel) at the same time. For Caesar Salad Dip (page 97), that means using romaine lettuce as the base of the dip for a refreshing bite, and I'll go on record here saying that's my favorite dip in the book.

DIPPER MATRIX

HOMEMADE

Garlic-Kissed Crostini, 189—try making with 2-inch cubes from a sourdough boule or loaf to get giant garlic bread croutons!

Potato Skinny Dippers, 219

Roulette Charred Peppers, 216

Veggie Ribbons, 214

Shortcut Garlic Knots, 190

STORE-BOUGHT IS FRAN FINE

Romaine or Little Gem lettuce, cut into little dippin' boats

Rotisserie chicken

Cooked shrimp or shrimp cocktail

Tortilla chips, especially Tostitos Scoops

Potato chips

Pita chips

Bagel chips

Crudités, such as carrots, cucumbers, celery, broccoli, cauliflower, or sweet peppers

faq

CAN IT BE MADE IN ADVANCE? Yes—it can and should! It needs a couple hours in the fridge to get to the right dipping texture.

HOW LONG WILL IT KEEP? Up to 10 days in an airtight container in the fridge.

caesar salad dip

SERVES A LIL' GET-TOGETHER (4 TO 6)

I love all my children equally, but Caesar Salad Dip is my favorite. (I don't care for G.O.B. This is *Arrested* Dip*velopment.*)This *dip*fied all expectations of how dishes can be transformed into dips. This isn't just a Caesar dressing that's slightly thicker and more dippable—it's salad blended into a dip. The base of the dip was inspired by aji verde, a Peruvian green sauce made with a base of pureed romaine lettuce, which adds a subtle vegetal flavor and some of its signature color. I ate it frequently when I lived on New York's Upper West Side (shout-out to Pio Pio!) and was reminded of it by my friend and food stylist Nick Torres during the *dip*velopment process. Watching lettuce get pulverized in a food processor is a little gnarly, but trust the *process* and romaine calm. The water in the lettuce keeps things light and bright even after you add in all of the dairy and garlic, making it refreshingly decadent—and the best way to get yourself to eat a lot of vegetables in one sitting.

1 head romaine, roughly chopped, or 1 bag (7 ounces) chopped romaine (for lazy ease)

4 garlic cloves

3 tablespoons freshly squeezed lemon juice (about 1 lemon)

2 teaspoons anchovy paste or fish sauce

2 teaspoons dijon mustard

2 teaspoons Worcestershire or soy sauce

1 cup grated parmesan cheese (freshly grated or the pre-grated kind from the refrigerated section)

¾ cup mayonnaise

¾ cup sour cream

10 to 15 cranks black pepper, plus more to taste

Kosher salt, to taste

CHIPPY'S TIPPY

Wrap a piece of Garlic-Kissed Crostini (page 189) in a piece of lettuce with optional rotisserie chicken for a dippin' salad bite.

1. Don't let fear stop you—put that lettuce right into your food processor. Blitz it with the garlic until broken down into little bits, then add the lemon juice, anchovy paste, dijon, Worcestershire, and cheese. Run the motor again until the mixture is smooth and evenly combined. Add the mayonnaise and sour cream, then run it again until you have a creamy, green-speckled dip. Crack in as much black pepper as speaks to you and taste to see if it needs any salt (it shouldn't, but you be the judge).

2. Pour the dip into an airtight container and let it sit in the fridge for at least 2 hours to firm up slightly to the right *dips*cosity. You can dip in right away but it will be looser, more like a dressing or dipping sauce.

herbalicious oil is bready for dippin'

SERVES A LIL' GET-TOGETHER (4 TO 6)

Like Oprah, I. LOVE. BREAD! I also love its best friend, butter. (Always salty, sometimes cultured, just like me.) But sometimes when I have a piping-hot, crusty loaf of bread, I want to dip it into a flavorful infused olive oil instead. And this one is herbalicious, *dip*finition: make the bread go loco.

This is the only recipe in the book that doesn't pass the *dips*cosity test of being able to turn over a spoonful and not have it dribble off immediately. But when I was thinking about memorable dips through the years, the bread-dipping oil from Italian American chain Bertucci's stuck out to me. The ample amount of pecorino romano cheese in it adds both a hint of funk and slightly thickens the texture, and even though I hadn't had it in more than a decade, tasting this brought me right back to dining there in Boston.

½ cup olive oil

2 garlic cloves, aggressively rough chopped

1 teaspoon aggressively rough chopped fresh rosemary leaves

¼ cup freshly grated pecorino romano cheese or parmesan, if you prefer it less funkalicious

¼ teaspoon kosher salt

¼ cup aggressively rough chopped fresh parsley leaves

¼ teaspoon red pepper flakes

CHIPPY'S TIPPY

This oil will be excellent tossed with your favorite cooked pasta, especially with toasted breadcrumbs on top. It could also work nicely as the base of a salad dressing, with some vinegar added. Here's a challenge: host a *dip*ner party using it in every course.

In a small skillet over medium-low heat, heat the oil for 2 minutes. Add the garlic and rosemary and cook, stirring constantly, for 1 to 2 minutes, until the mixture is fragrant and the garlic is the slightest bit golden. Remove from the heat and let cool slightly, 5 to 10 minutes. Pour the oil mixture into a small bowl, and *then* stir in the cheese (if it's too hot it can get weirdly gloopy), salt, parsley, and red pepper flakes. Bready or not, here you dip!

MO*DIP*FICATIONS: Not a fan of rosemary? Try thyme. More garlic? Always an option. Customize it as you like, using this recipe as a base ratio and guide.

faq

CAN IT BE MADE IN ADVANCE? Yes, but you will need to leave at room temp for about 30 minutes (the oil solidifies in the fridge) and whisk until recombined. For a speedier serving, gently reheat over low heat in a saucepan.

HOW LONG WILL IT LAST? Up to 2 weeks in an airtight container in the fridge.

DIPPER MATRIX

HOMEMADE	STORE-BOUGHT IS FRAN FINE
B	B
R	R
E	E
A	A
D	D

Bread! Any kind! But preferably a baguette or sourdough loaf, heated in the oven at 300°F for 5 to 10 minutes until it's nice and crusty. Everyone loves warm bread, and as you tear it into chunks, it maintains a lightly toasty and toothsome texture that sops up that *dip*licious oil well.

toum raider
(aka korean-ish whipped garlic dip)

SERVES A LIL' GET-TOGETHER (4 TO 6)

Toum, a Lebanese condiment pronounced "toom," is a cousin to Death Breath Dip (page 69) due to its killer garlickiness. (Lara Croft could probably battle it with enough mints.) I added a twist with ssamjang, a spicy-sweet (in that order) Korean fermented bean and chili paste that you've probably dolloped onto grilled meats at Korean barbecue restaurants. It adds an umami-rich *dip*th of flavor, as well as even more garlic to an already alarming amount of garlic. But somehow this doesn't totally overwhelm your palate, because the texture of the dip is light, fluffy, and airy, and it takes to any dipper that raids the toum.

½ cup garlic cloves (about 15 cloves)

1 teaspoon kosher salt

5 tablespoons freshly squeezed lemon juice (about 2 lemons)

1¾ cups neutral oil, such as vegetable or canola

⅓ cup ice water

2 tablespoons ssamjang

2 teaspoons toasted sesame oil

1. In a small food processor (with a chute or some way to pour ingredients into the top while it runs!) combine the garlic and kosher salt. Pulse until minced, then add the lemon juice.

2. Process until completely smooth, about 2 minutes. Using the chute at the top while running the motor, *very slowly* drizzle in ½ cup of the neutral oil in a tiny stream—it should take about 2 minutes total to drip the whole amount in.

3. Next, keep the processor running and stream in 2 tablespoons of the ice water, also very slowly (about 1 minute) then repeat with another ½ cup neutral oil, 2 tablespoons ice water, then the remaining ¾ cup of neutral oil and 1 tablespoon of ice water. The dip should be thickened, fluffy, and airy as a cloud. Add the ssamjang and sesame oil and blend one more time.

MO*DIP*FICATIONS: You can omit the ssamjang and toasted sesame oil for a plain 'n' simple version.

CHIPPY'S TIPPY

This is the time to buy pre-peeled garlic, preferably from an Asian market, where it is often freshly packed in-house. Avoid the vacuum-sealed bags at other stores, which are often suspended in a bit of water and have a weird preservative aftertaste.

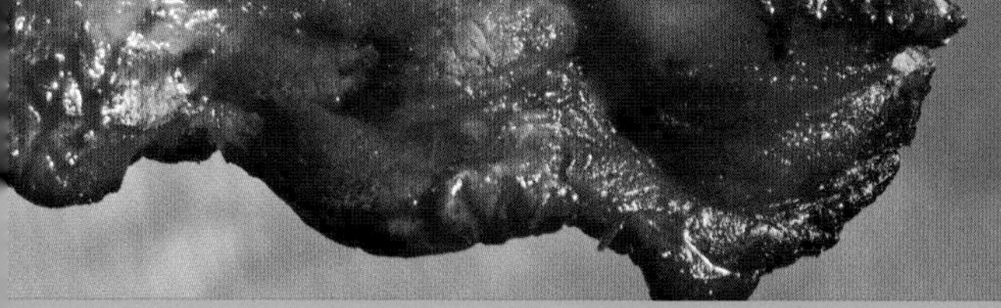

DIPPER MATRIX

HOMEMADE

Potato Skinny Dippers, 219

Rainbow Dumpling Chips, 203

Roulette Charred Peppers, 216

Universally Dippable Marinated Meat Skewers, 226

Veggie Ribbons, 214

STORE-BOUGHT IS FRAN FINE

Tempura seaweed chips

Funyuns

Chips of your choice

Crudités, such as carrots, cucumbers, celery, broccoli, cauliflower, or sweet peppers

French fries, Tater Tots, or your favorite crispy potatoes

faq

CAN IT BE MADE IN ADVANCE? Yes, but the flavors get stronger as it sits.

HOW LONG WILL IT KEEP? Up to 1 month in an airtight container in the fridge.

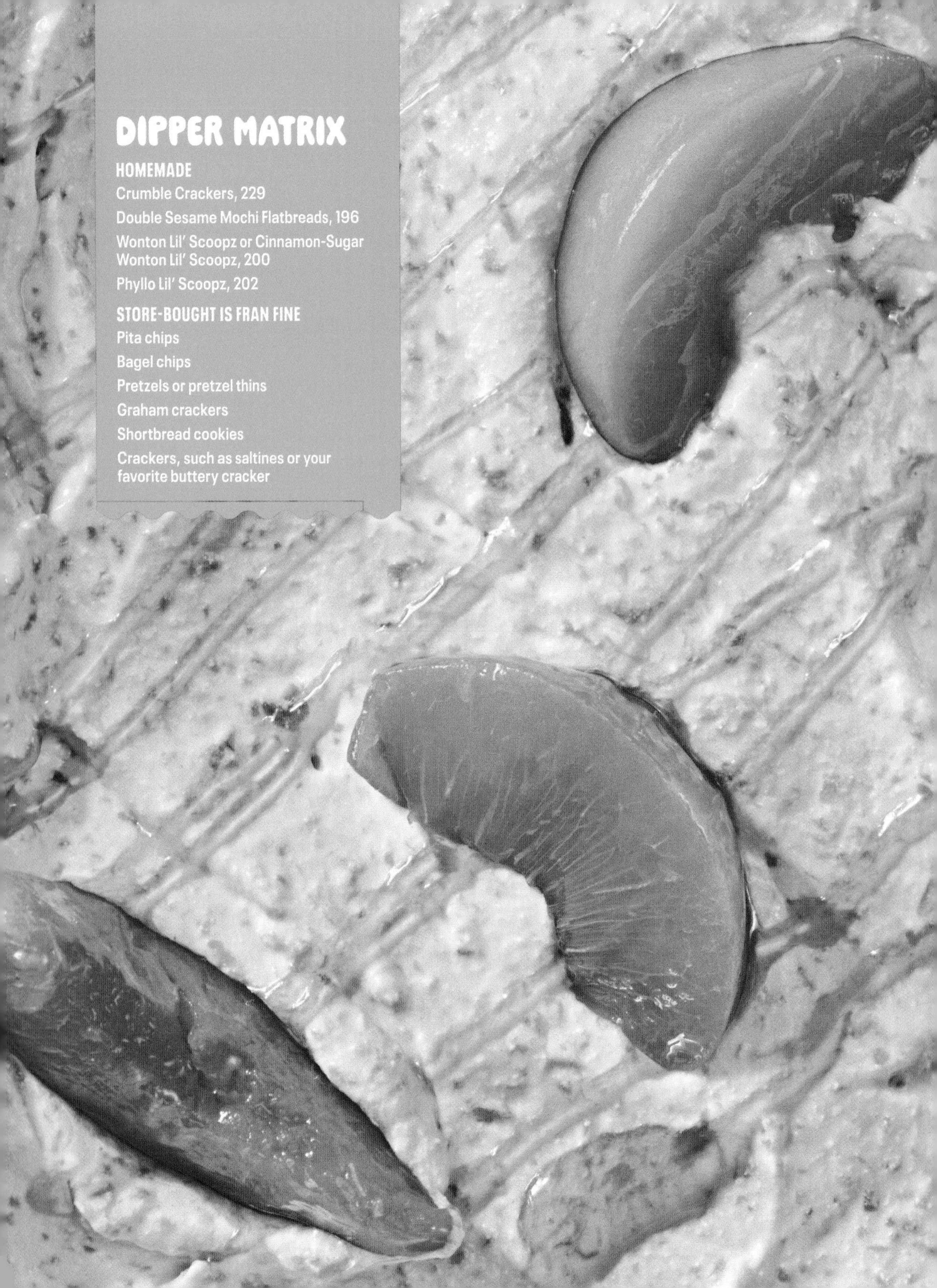

DIPPER MATRIX

HOMEMADE

Crumble Crackers, 229

Double Sesame Mochi Flatbreads, 196

Wonton Lil' Scoopz or Cinnamon-Sugar Wonton Lil' Scoopz, 200

Phyllo Lil' Scoopz, 202

STORE-BOUGHT IS FRAN FINE

Pita chips

Bagel chips

Pretzels or pretzel thins

Graham crackers

Shortbread cookies

Crackers, such as saltines or your favorite buttery cracker

peaches 'n' cream protein dip

SERVES A LIL' GET-TOGETHER (4 TO 6)

Please sing the following to the tune of the opening line of Kelly Clarkson's "A Moment Like This": What if I told you this is made of cottage cheese? Would you believe me, would you eat it? That's right—this *dip*ceptively protein-packed dip (14 grams per ½ cup of the cottage cheese base alone) is certified fresh for breakfast. Sweetened with a quick peach situation (simmering frozen peaches with sugar and lemon juice until jammy), this is a peaches 'n' dream come true. You could eat this before or after a workout, substitute it for protein bites as a snackternoon treat, or bring it to a party—it's dealer's choice whether you divulge the *dip*visive dairy at this dip's core.

- **1 bag (16 ounces) frozen peaches**
- **⅓ cup granulated sugar**
- **1½ tablespoons freshly squeezed lemon juice**
- **½ cup water**
- **1 container (16 ounces) whole milk cottage cheese, preferably Good Culture**
- **¼ cup powdered sugar (optional)**
- **Drizzle of olive oil (optional)**
- **Pinch of kosher salt (optional)**

1. In a small saucepan, combine the peaches, sugar, lemon juice, and water. Bring to a boil over medium-high heat, then reduce to a low simmer and cook for 20 to 30 minutes, stirring occasionally, until the peaches have softened and almost melted into a jammy consistency. Transfer to a medium bowl and let cool at room temperature for at least 20 minutes.

2. Place the cottage cheese in the bowl of a small food processor or blender and run the motor until the cheese is completely smooth, whipped, and ultra creamy. Pour in the jammy peach situation and blend again until smooth.

3. Now you have two options: Add the powdered sugar if you're going for a sweet dip, or add a pinch of kosher salt and drizzle of olive oil if you want it more savory-sweet. Or split the *dip*ference and try it with a little sugar and a little salt!

MO*DIP*FICATIONS: Substitute your favorite frozen fruit instead of peaches 1:1. This also works with canned peaches, and no extra sugar is needed.

faq

CAN IT BE MADE IN ADVANCE? Yes!

HOW LONG WILL IT KEEP? Up to 10 days in an airtight container in the fridge.

green goddess hummus

SERVES A LIL' GET-TOGETHER (4 TO 6)

When a salad and a dip love each other very much . . . Green Goddess Hummus is born. It's herby, garlicky, easy, and vegan. It is, however, not "cheezy." A lot of GG recipes (not *Gilmore Girls*, but should this be called Gilmore Goddess Hummus?) use nutritional yeast, but instead, I opted for the flavor enhancer MSG, which has been unfairly demonized for decades. Just a tiny bit of MSG packs a punch that brings out the umami in this hummus, giving it *dip*th of flavor and shining a spotlight on all the in*dip*vidual ingredients at once so they meld into a downright ad*dip*tive dip. And apparently MSG enhances pun-ability, too.

1 can (15 ounces) chickpeas, rinsed and drained

4 garlic cloves

¼ cup fresh cilantro leaves

¼ cup fresh basil leaves

¼ cup chives

¼ cup fresh parsley leaves

2 scallions, cut into approximately 2-inch pieces

¼ cup olive oil

3 tablespoons freshly squeezed lemon (about 1 lemon)

2 tablespoons red wine vinegar, plus more as needed

2 tablespoons tahini

1½ teaspoons honey, plus more as needed

1¼ teaspoons kosher salt, plus more as needed

⅛ teaspoon MSG

I would never call something a "dump dip," but . . . this kind of is. Dump everything into a food processor, let it whirl until smooth, and taste it. Your palate may want another splash of vinegar, a smidge of honey, or another pinch of salt. Follow your palate.

MOD*IP*FICATIONS: Try canned white beans as a nice neutral base instead of chickpeas.

faq

CAN IT BE MADE IN ADVANCE? Yes, and it gets even better as it sits.

HOW LONG WILL IT KEEP? Up to 10 days in an airtight container in the fridge.

HOW A DIP QUEEN DIPS HANDS-FREE!

DIPPER MATRIX

HOMEMADE

Potato Skinny Dippers, 219

Roulette Charred Peppers, 216

Garlic-Kissed Crostini, 189

Double Sesame Mochi Flatbreads, 196

Veggie Ribbons, 214

STORE-BOUGHT IS FRAN FINE

Pita chips

Bagel chips

Crudités, such as carrots, cucumbers, celery, broccoli, cauliflower, or sweet peppers

sneaky veggies

Dip is known to be a decadent food, but the indulgent nature of multiple types of dairy can be balanced out *slightly* with what I dubbed "sneaky veggies." These are vegetable-forward—or in a few cases, bean-forward—dips that don't taste like you're eating a salad. I'm not calling them healthy, but they are healthier than eating *just* a bowl of cheese and make for a more balanced party food. And if you dip vegetables in them, then that's a double dip of vitamins . . . and the only double dipping you should ever do!

beanie weenie hummus

SERVES A LIL' GET-TOGETHER (4 TO 6)

I bought six different types of beans to try to make into hummus, and somehow, the weirdest one that hasn't *bean* done before was the best one. You are reading the ingredient list right: you're gonna puree a can of baked beans, and you're gonna like it. And you're gonna sauté coins of Lit'l Smokies and like that, too!

This dip has a Sloppy Joe flavor that verges on barbecue sauce but stops just shy of it; it doesn't have any smokiness and has a sweeter edge more than a full-on tang. A dynamic dipper option is Piggies in Snuggies (page 228). (I wanted to repeat the ends in "ie" theme, please don't sue me, Snuggies. I love you.) The possibilities are endlessly weird.

1 can (16 ounces) baked beans, preferably Bush's Original

1 teaspoon garlic powder

1 teaspoon onion powder

¼ teaspoon kosher salt

1 tablespoon olive oil

½ package (7 ounces) Lit'l Smokies, sliced into thin coins

2 tablespoons white vinegar

½ cup firmly packed brown sugar

2 teaspoons ketchup

1 teaspoon yellow mustard

½ teaspoon Worcestershire sauce or soy sauce, whichever you prefer

1. In a sieve or colander over a medium bowl, drain the baked beans over a bowl. *Do not discard the sauce.* Transfer the beans to a food processor and add 1 tablespoon of the reserved bean sauce, ½ teaspoon of the garlic powder, ½ teaspoon of the onion powder, and the salt. Pulse until smooth.

2. In a medium skillet over medium heat, heat the oil. Add the Lit'l Smokies and cook until slightly crispy, about 4 minutes. Reduce the heat to low and add the vinegar, brown sugar, ketchup, mustard, remaining ½ teaspoon garlic powder, remaining ½ teaspoon of onion powder, and the Worcestershire sauce. Let simmer and bubble, stirring occasionally, for about a minute until the sauce looks glazy and slightly thickened.

3. To serve, pour the hummus into a medium serving bowl (preferably a shallow one), carve a wide *dip*vot in the middle using a spoon (for *dip*corating tips, see page 19) so the middle of the dip is lower than the sides. Fill that *dip*vot with the glazed weenies and sauce and *dip*corate using Piggies in Snuggies.

CHIPPY'S TIPPY

Lay a few Piggies in Snuggies and/or octopus-shaped sausages atop the dip as garnishes!

DIPPER MATRIX

HOMEMADE

Piggies in Snuggies, 228
Rice Cake and Sausage Skewers, 224
Potato Skinny Dippers, 219
Roulette Charred Peppers, 216
Garlic-Kissed Crostini, 189
Crispy Paneer Dipsticks, 221
Veggie Ribbons, 214

STORE-BOUGHT IS FRAN FINE

Tortilla chips, preferably Tostitos Scoops
Potato chips
Pita chips
Bagel chips
Crudités, such as carrots, cucumbers, celery, broccoli, cauliflower, or sweet peppers
French fries, tater tots, or your favorite crispy potatoes

MODIPFICATIONS: You can easily swap in regular hot dogs or plant-based hot dogs.

faq

CAN IT BE MADE IN ADVANCE? Yes, but let it sit at room temperature for at least 30 minutes to take the chill off before serving.

HOW LONG WILL IT KEEP? Up to a week in the fridge in an airtight container.

roasted red pepp in your step whipped feta dip

SERVES A LIL' GET-TOGETHER (4 TO 6)

Feta is the most transformative cheese I can think of. What is at first crumbly, dry, and aggressively salty becomes a lighter-than-air, creamy-dreamy dip in seconds when whipped up in a food processor. To help it along, there's also cream cheese in this dip, and a lot of roasted red peppers to give it a vibrant orange color and a flame-kissed flavor. Pair it with Green Goddess Hummus (page 104) and Toum Raider (page 100) for a Mediterranean-leaning trio served with a pile of toasted pita to rip, dip, and delight.

1 package (8 ounces) cream cheese, softened at room temperature (see page 14)

1 cup jarred roasted sliced red peppers, drained

2 ounces feta cheese, drained with brine reserved in a bowl

2 garlic cloves, grated

2 tablespoons olive oil, plus more for garnish

2 tablespoons freshly squeezed lemon juice

½ teaspoon dried oregano

½ cup fresh basil leaves

Calabrian chile paste or oil, to dollop or drizzle on top (optional)

1. In a food processor, combine the cream cheese, roasted peppers, feta, garlic, oil, lemon juice, oregano, and half the basil. Pulse or run the motor until completely smooth.

2. To serve, pour into a medium serving bowl (preferably a shallow one), make some *dip*vots or a moat using a spoon (for *dip*corating tips, see page 19), drizzle with either more oil or, if you want things spicier, Calabrian chili paste, and garnish with small whole basil leaves, or tear larger ones for rustic dip confetti.

CHIPPY'S TIPPY

If you like things spicy, add some Calabrian chile paste inside *and* on top of the dip, but be forewarned—it gets spicier as it sits in the fridge!

faq

CAN IT BE MADE IN ADVANCE? Yes, but you may need to thin with feta brine or milk as it firms up in the fridge.

HOW LONG WILL IT KEEP? Up to a week in the fridge in an airtight container.

DIPPER MATRIX

HOMEMADE

Roulette Charred Peppers, 216

Potato Skinny Dippers, 219

Garlic-Kissed Crostini, 189

These Bagel Pretzel Bites Have Everything, 194

Veggie Ribbons, 214

STORE-BOUGHT IS FRAN FINE

Crackers

Pretzels or pretzel thins

Crudités, such as carrots, cucumbers, celery, broccoli, cauliflower, or sweet peppers

DIPPER MATRIX

HOMEMADE

Tantalizing Tempura, 212

*Crisp*anthemum Onion Petals, 210

Rainbow Dumpling Chips, 203

Wonton Lil' Scoopz, 200

Roulette Charred Peppers, 216

Veggie Ribbons, 214

Universally Dippable Marinated Meat Skewers, 226

STORE-BOUGHT IS FRAN FINE

Tempura seaweed chips

Pita or bagel chips

Funyuns

Crudités, such as carrots, cucumbers, broccoli, cauliflower, or sweet peppers

GOLDILOCKS

miso eggplant dip

SERVES A LIL' GET-TOGETHER (4 TO 6)

VEGAN!

I could give up cheesy dips if every vegan one tasted this good. I'm lactose intolerant-*ish*, meaning I can usually eat cheese but sometimes dairy betrays me. (I take the gamble and carry Lactaid with me at all times.) I didn't work with vegan "cheese" in this book because silken tofu is the greatest plant-based base—and I know, I tried every firmness of tofu to test this theory. It takes on any flavors you want it to . . . like a sponge, but an exceptional sponge, like a Scrub Daddy. In this case, those flavors are miso-roasted eggplant and roasted garlic combining into a super dip that just happens to be vegan.

6 garlic cloves

3½ tablespoons olive oil

1 teaspoon plus a pinch kosher salt

3 medium Japanese eggplants (about 1 pound)

1 bunch scallions, white and light green parts cut into large chunks and dark green parts sliced thinly on the bias

¼ cup white miso

1 tablespoon hot water

1 tablespoon soy sauce

1 tablespoon mirin

3 teaspoons toasted sesame oil, plus more for finishing

1 tablespoon sugar

½ teaspoon ground white pepper

8 ounces silken tofu

1. Preheat the oven to 400°F. Line a sheet pan with aluminum foil (for easy cleanup) and set aside.

2. Lay the garlic cloves on a separate piece of foil, drizzle with ½ tablespoon of the olive oil, and add the pinch of salt. Wrap it up like a little bundle and set aside.

3. Cut off the tops of the eggplants and halve them lengthwise. Using a paring knife, carefully slice through the flesh of the eggplant (not cutting all the way through) in a crosshatch pattern, making little diamonds for the glaze to nestle into later.

4. Transfer the eggplant halves to the prepared sheet pan, skin side down. Drizzle 2 tablespoons of the olive oil and the remaining 1 teaspoon salt over the crosshatched sides of the eggplants. Flip them over so they cook flesh-side down, drizzle with the remaining 1 tablespoon olive oil, and arrange the garlic packet and white and pale green parts of scallions on the tray. Roast for 25 minutes, until the eggplant is tender and offers no resistance when gently prodded with a knife.

(continued)

CHIPPY'S TIPPY

No silken tofu? Any kind of tofu will work; firmer tofu will just take longer to get smooth and will have a heartier texture and thicker *dip*scosity.

faq

CAN IT BE MADE IN ADVANCE? Yes, a few days is totally okay. You can also roast the eggplant in advance and blend the dip when you're ready to serve it.

HOW LONG WILL IT KEEP? Up to a week in the fridge in an airtight container.

5. Meanwhile, to make the glaze, in a small bowl, whisk the miso and hot water until smooth. Add the soy sauce, mirin, sesame oil, sugar, and white pepper and whisk to combine.

6. Flip the eggplants, pour the glaze over the eggplants and scallions, then return to the oven for another 10 to 15 minutes, until the vegetables are nicely caramelized (set the pan under the broiler for 1 to 3 minutes if the veggies need a little help; you want them bronzed and bubbly).

7. Open the garlic packet carefully; the cloves should be soft and lightly golden. Let cool slightly. Scoop out the eggplant from the skin. In a food processor, combine the tofu, roasted garlic, scallions, and eggplant and puree until smooth.

8. Scoop the whole shebang into a medium serving bowl—preferably a wide, shallow one. Make optional swooshes in the surface for flair (see *dip*corating tips on page 19), drizzle with more sesame oil, and top with thinly sliced scallion greens.

MO*DIP*FICATIONS: White miso is mild and slightly sweet. For more salty umami oomph, try red miso!

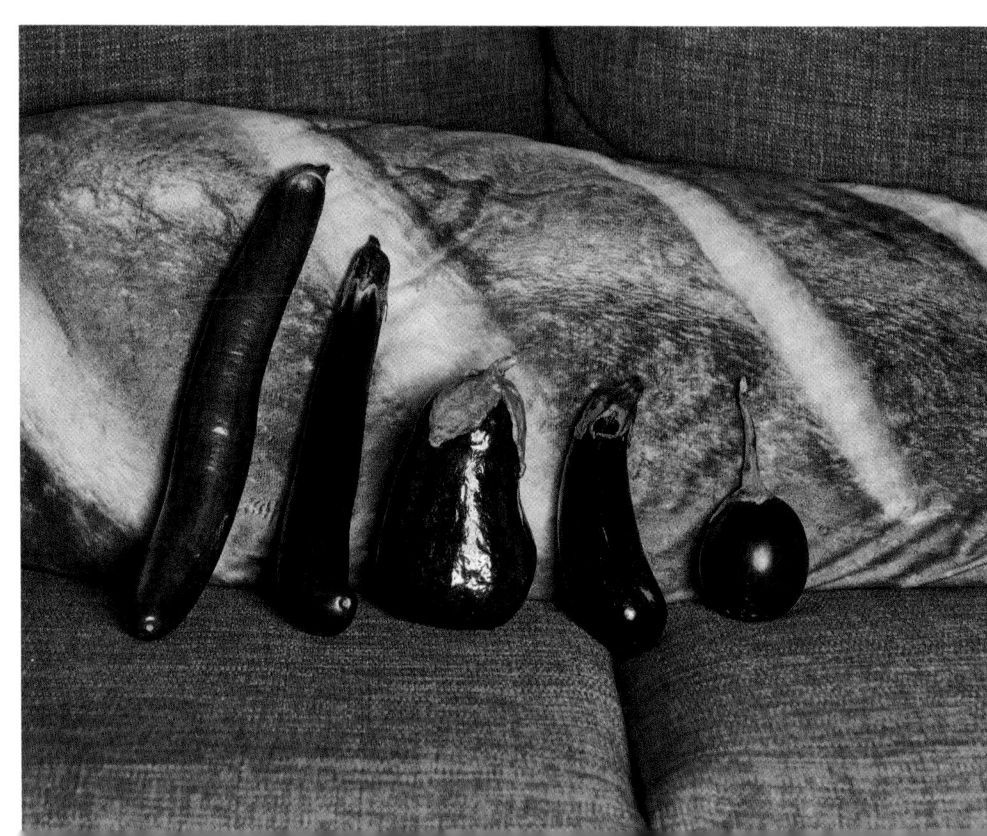

trippin' dip: mushroom dip with pesto swirl

SERVES A BIG DIP PARTY (8 TO 10)

This dip started as a fun name and ended up exceeding all my expectations. There's been a 'shroom boom (or as Feist put it, "Mushaboom") in recent years, and I have more mushroom accessories and home decor than the average forest. In spite of its name, the only trippy thing about this dip is the funky swirl of spinach-cilantro pesto running through the otherwise kind of murky brown-gray dip.

The secret ingredient here is a packet of French onion soup mix. There is no sub*dip*tution for it—it is the backbone of the dip. It balances out the pile of earthy mushrooms, and kind of makes this a mashup of French onion soup, French onion dip, and cream of mushroom soup. Make 'shroom for it in your party appetizer lineup—ideally with tempura mushrooms (page 212) for double the fun(gi).

PESTO, CHANGE-O!

- 1 cup baby spinach
- ½ cup fresh cilantro leaves (about two fistfuls)
- 3 garlic cloves
- ¼ cup neutral oil, such as vegetable or canola
- 1 teaspoon freshly grated lemon zest
- 1 teaspoon freshly squeezed lemon juice
- ¼ teaspoon kosher salt

'SHROOM FOR MORE DIP

- 1½ cups sour cream
- 1 cup mayonnaise
- 1 packet (1 ounce) French onion soup mix, preferably Lipton
- 10 cranks black pepper
- 6 tablespoons olive oil
- 2 shallots, aggressively rough chopped
- 6 garlic cloves, aggressively rough chopped
- 6 ounces oyster mushrooms, aggressively rough chopped
- 6 ounces shiitake mushroom caps, aggressively rough chopped
- 6 ounces large portobello mushroom caps, aggressively rough chopped
- 1 teaspoon kosher salt
- 1 tablespoon thicc-cut chives (see page 22)

CHIPPY'S TIPPY

Store-bought pesto is absolutely fine here. Just thin out with a splash of hot water to make it a more swirlable *dips*cosity!

PESTO, CHANGE-O!

1. Combine all the ingredients in a food processor or blender and blend until smooth. Set aside.

'SHROOM FOR MORE DIP

2. In a large bowl, combine the sour cream, mayonnaise, French onion soup mix, and pepper. Set aside.

(continued)

3. Heat two tablespoons of oil in a large skillet over medium heat. Add the shallots and sauté, stirring occasionally, until translucent and just starting to brown, 4 to 6 minutes. Add the garlic and cook until fragrant, about 1 minute. Add the remaining 4 tablespoons oil to the pan—mushrooms soak up a lot, like sponges—then all the 'shrooms. Sauté for 5 minutes, until the water released from the mushrooms is evaporated. Add the salt and sauté until the mushrooms are tender and golden brown, 5 to 7 minutes.

4. Transfer the mushrooms to the bowl of a food processor and let cool for a few minutes, then pulse into small pieces, about the size of your pinkie nail (unless you're wearing acrylics). Mix the mushrooms into the sour cream and mayonnaise base, then transfer to a serving bowl. Dollop the pesto on top and use a chopstick or butter knife to swirl it in artistically, or use a spoon to carve swooshes in a squiggly pattern across the surface of the dip and add pesto to those moats. Garnish with the chives. (For more *dip*corating tips, see page 19.)

MO*DIP*FICATIONS: Use a store-bought pesto.

faq

CAN IT BE MADE IN ADVANCE? Yes, but you may need to thin with milk as it firms up in the fridge.

HOW LONG WILL IT KEEP? Up to a week in the fridge in an airtight container.

DIPPER MATRIX

HOMEMADE

Tantalizing Tempura, 212
*Crisp*anthemum Onion Petals, 210
Potato Skinny Dippers, 219
Roulette Charred Peppers, 216
Garlic-Kissed Crostini, 189
Shortcut Garlic Knots, 190
Veggie Ribbons, 214

STORE-BOUGHT IS FRAN FINE

- Tortilla chips, especially Tostitos Scoops
- Potato chips
- Pita chips
- Bagel chips
- Crudités, such as carrots, cucumbers, celery, broccoli, cauliflower, or sweet peppers
- French fries, Tater Tots, or your favorite crispy potatoes

curry squashcotta sheet pan dip

SERVES A LIL' GET-TOGETHER (4 TO 6)

The unsung dairy hero of dips is ricotta cheese. It's typically reserved for dessert dips—or as I call them, *dips*serts—like Espressomartinimisu Dip (page 172) and Holy Cannoli Dip (page 171). But ricotta adds a creamy, dreamy, milky flavor base that is somehow rich without being heavy and decadent, yet light at the same time. This dip was inspired by my friend and James Beard–nominated pastry chef extraordinaire Caroline Schiff, who shared her version of a squash and ricotta dip with me in 2019. I adapted it by roasting the squash whole (halved and seeds scooped) to save time on peeling and cutting and dubbed it a "sheet pan dip."

I engineered the dippers, chewy-crispy mini mochi flatbreads, to be made while the squash is roasting, so you can have an impressive party spread ready in just over an hour. And the name of this dip is just fun to say—you gotta have squashcotta!

1 medium butternut squash (about 3 pounds)

1 garlic head

¼ cup plus 1 tablespoon olive oil, plus more for garnish

2½ teaspoons kosher salt

1 container (15 ounces) whole milk ricotta cheese

2 tablespoons Japanese-style curry powder, such as S&B, plus more for garnish

¼ cup aggressively rough chopped fresh cilantro leaves, for garnish

1. Preheat the oven to 400°F. Line a sheet pan with parchment paper or aluminum foil and set aside.

2. Place a damp paper towel under your cutting board to hold it steady and make sure your knife is sharp before tackling the squash. Wash the squash and carefully slice off a thin piece of its roundest side so it can lay flat and secure on the cutting board. Cut the squash in half lengthwise, scoop out the seeds, and discard. Transfer to the prepared sheet pan, flesh side down. Cut about ½ inch off the top of the garlic bulb to expose the cloves.

(continued)

3. Drizzle ¼ cup of the oil evenly across both halves of the squash, inside and out. Rub the squash in your hands to distribute the oil, then sprinkle 1½ teaspoons of the salt evenly across the squash. Put the garlic bulb on a piece of foil large enough to enclose it, then drizzle the cut surface of the garlic with the remaining 1 tablespoon oil and sprinkle with ½ teaspoon of the salt. Wrap it up into a little bundle and place it on the sheet pan next to the squash. Roast for 1 hour, or until you can insert a knife into the squash with no resistance.

4. Unwrap the garlic gift and let cool. Let the squash rest until cool enough to handle, then use a large spoon to scoop out the flesh into a large bowl, leaving an inch-thick border on one of the halves. It should be so tender that you can mash it with a potato masher, but it's even easier if you use an electric hand mixer, food processor, or immersion blender. Squeeze the roasted garlic cloves out of their papery skins straight into the bowl. Mash, mix, process, or blend until smooth. Add the ricotta, curry powder, and remaining ½ teaspoon salt and transfer to the most beautiful of your squash halves.

5. Use a spoon to carve out a little *dip*vot or moat in the squash dip (see page 19), then fill with a hefty drizzle of olive oil and finish with a sprinkle of curry powder and the chopped cilantro.

MOD*IP*FICATIONS: I use Japanese curry powder, which is comparatively less spicy, slightly sweet, and includes fewer spices than Indian curry powder. But if you have a favorite curry powder, feel free to sub*dip*tute. Just add a little at a time until it tastes good to you.

CHIPPY'S TIPPY

This can moonlight as a side dish instead of a dip, eaten by the spoonful.

CAN IT BE MADE IN ADVANCE? Yes, the flavors meld as it sits.

HOW LONG WILL IT KEEP? Up to a week in the fridge in an airtight container.

DIPPER MATRIX

HOMEMADE

Double Sesame Mochi Flatbreads, 196
Wonton Lil' Scoopz, 200
Rainbow Dumpling Chips, 203
Tantalizing Tempura, 212
*Crisp*anthemum Onion Petals, 210
Shortcut Garlic Knots, 190
Garlic-Kissed Crostini, 189
Veggie Ribbons, 214

STORE-BOUGHT IS FRAN FINE

Pita chips
Tortilla chips, especially Tostitos Scoops
Crudités, such as carrots, cucumbers, celery, or sweet peppers

layered dips

To quote the great Shrek: "Dips have layers. Ogres have layers. We both have layers." Oh, is that not how it goes? Well, dips *should* have layers. There's more to love in flavors, textures, and a dynamic presentation that would knock the socks off everyone in Shrek's swamp! Historically, the only dip known for its layers is seven-layer dip, which is usually a take on tacos or Mexican flavors. I have a twist on that—as an ode to Taco Bell—but there are many more ways to layer dips together—and they don't have to have exactly seven tiers—from breakfast (Face Your Schmears Everything Bagel Dip, page 131) to *dips*sert (Fat Mint Dip, page 174). Just make sure your dippers are sturdy enough to break through all those layers!

NEW YORK'S HOTTEST CLUB SANDWICH DIP (PAGE 125)

TUNA MELT DIP (PAGE 127)

new york's hottest club sandwich dip

SERVES A BIG DIP PARTY (8 TO 10)

This dip exists in a world between a sandwich and a salad. You could eat it in a bowl with toast points or potato chips as a form of utensil, or smush a scoop between a few layers of toast and make a reconstructed deconstructed club sandwich. But there's one key *dip*ference between this dip and the sandwich that inspired it: the tomatoes are cooked. I don't like raw tomatoes because of the seedy wateriness, so these are roasted until jammy. They add another layer of texture and flavor to this layered dip, which I *do* think Stefon would proclaim New York's hottest. And for a double *SNL* feature, pair with These Bagel Pretzel Bites Have Everything (page 194).

- **8 bacon strips, preferably thick-cut**
- **2 pints cherry tomatoes, halved**
- **1 tablespoon olive oil, if not using bacon grease**
- **¼ teaspoon kosher salt**
- **10 cranks black pepper**
- **⅓ cup mayonnaise**
- **⅓ cup sour cream**
- **1 teaspoon ranch seasoning**
- **½ pound sliced deli turkey, aggressively rough chopped**
- **½ pound sliced deli cheddar cheese, aggressively rough chopped**
- **2 cups thinly sliced iceberg lettuce**
- **1 small red onion, minced**
- **6 slices of your favorite sandwich bread, toasted and cut into triangles or dipsticks, for serving**

1. Preheat the oven to 400°F. Line a sheet pan with foil for easy cleanup and set a wire rack on top.

2. **IF YOU WANT TO MAKE BACON-ROASTED TOMATOES:** Set the oven rack in the middle position, then arrange the bacon in a single layer on the prepared wire rack. Cook for 15 minutes, then check to see how crispy it's looking. If you like it more golden, continue to cook, checking every 2 minutes, until it reaches the desired doneness. Transfer the bacon to a paper towel–lined plate to drain the excess grease, remove the rack from the sheet pan (using a pot holder!), and toss the tomatoes in the bacon grease on the sheet pan. Sprinkle on the salt and pepper and toss again. Roast the tomatoes for 20 minutes, stirring halfway through cooking. The tomatoes should be soft and jammy at that point, but if they aren't, continue to cook, checking

(continued)

DIPPER MATRIX

HOMEMADE

Simple toast points (see recipe)

Garlic-Kissed Crostini, 189

Potato Skinny Dippers, 219

Everything in a Pickle, 218, or store-bought pickles

These Bagel Pretzel Bites Have Everything, 194

STORE-BOUGHT IS FRAN FINE

Potato chips

Pita chips

Bagel chips

Crudités, such as carrots, cucumbers, celery, or sweet peppers

French fries, Tater Tots, or your favorite crispy potatoes

Onion rings

Funyuns

every 2 minutes, until they are. Let cool for at least 10 minutes before handling.

3. IF YOU PREFER TO COOK THE BACON AND TOMATOES AT THE SAME TIME: Arrange the oven racks in the top and lower thirds, line a second sheet pan with foil, and toss the tomatoes with the oil. Season with the salt and pepper. Set the bacon in the top third of the oven and the tomatoes in the lower third. Roast the bacon for 15 to 20 minutes, to the desired doneness, then transfer it to a paper towel–lined plate. Roast the tomatoes for 20 to 25 minutes, stirring halfway through, until soft and jammy.

4. Let the bacon and tomatoes cool for at least 10 minutes before handling.

5. In a medium bowl, whisk the mayonnaise, sour cream, and ranch seasoning. In an 8 x 8-inch clear baking dish or a wide, shallow serving bowl, spread the ranch-accented dip, then layer on the turkey, cheese, roasted tomatoes, lettuce, and onion. Crumble the bacon and scatter it on top.

6. To serve, cut each slice of toast diagonally into 4 triangles for toast points or into 4 strips for dipsticks and get in line for New York's Hottest Club Sandwich Dip.

MO*DIP*FICATIONS: Have leftover turkey from Thanksgiving? Use it in place of the deli turkey here! And if you want to serve it for Dipsgiving, then you could also make it without the turkey layer and serve as a side dish alongside a whole roasted bird.

CHIPPY'S TIPPY

If you don't mind waiting a little longer for the dip to be ready, roast your bacon first, then toss the tomatoes in the drippings before roasting. More bacon flavor is always an improvement.

faq

CAN IT BE MADE IN ADVANCE? Yes, but chop and top just before serving so the dip confetti doesn't get brown or otherwise weird.

HOW LONG WILL IT KEEP? Up to 5 days in the fridge, covered with plastic wrap.

tuna melt dip

SERVES A LIL' GET-TOGETHER (4 TO 6)

My favorite diner sandwich is a tuna melt, which elevates a humble can of tuna into something spectacular. Homemade will never taste as good as a diner . . . so I transformed it into a dip! It has a mixture of American *and* cheddar cheese (which is normally a surcharge at the diner) and a smidge of cream cheese to make it more of a creamy dip than just tuna salad. And in spite of my hatred of pickles (I know, I'm a monster—I just really dislike cucumbers), I added them to this dip, and they bring an acidity and brightness that nothing else could. If you love pickles, try using whole spears as *dill*icous dippers!

1 can (5 ounces) tuna, preferably whole chunk in oil, drained

¼ cup mayonnaise

2 ounces cream cheese, softened at room temperature (see page 14)

¼ pound thinly sliced deli cheddar cheese, torn into pieces

¼ pound thinly sliced deli American cheese, torn into pieces

3 tablespoons minced red onion, plus more for garnish

2 tablespoons aggressively rough chopped dill pickles, plus more for garnish

¼ teaspoon kosher salt

10 cranks black pepper

2 tablespoons finely chopped fresh parsley leaves

4 slices rye bread, toasted and cut into sticks, for dipping

1. Preheat the oven to 350°F.

2. In a medium bowl, combine the tuna, mayonnaise, cream cheese, half of the cheddar and American cheeses, onion, pickles, salt, and pepper. Mix gently to combine. Spread the mixture evenly in a 1-quart baking dish and top with the remaining cheddar and American cheeses.

3. Bake for 15 to 20 minutes, until golden brown and bubbly. Top with the parsley, and more onion and pickles, if you'd like, and serve with rye toast dipsticks.

faq

CAN IT BE MADE IN ADVANCE? It can be prepped in advance, but bake it off just before serving.

HOW LONG WILL IT KEEP? Up to 4 days in the fridge, and it can be eaten cold as a schmear on a bagel or broiled atop bread for a tuna melt toast. Or mix it with some cooked elbow noodles for a version of tuna mac salad.

DIPPER MATRIX

HOMEMADE

Garlic-Kissed Crostini, 189

Roulette Charred Peppers, 216

STORE-BOUGHT IS FRAN FINE

Toast of your choice, cut into dipsticks

Pita chips

Bagel chips

Potato chips

Crudités, such as carrots, sweet peppers, cucumbers, or celery

Pickles

drive-thru taco 7-layer dip

SERVES A BIG DIP PARTY (8 TO 10)

This is the *Captain Planet* of layer dips, but instead of earth, wind, fire, air, and water, it's a bunch of my favorite items from Taco Bell. It may seem daunting to take on a seven-layer dip, but all of these are quick to assemble, and only one requires the stove—the rest can be just stirred together and/or microwaved. If you want to live más, make mini Crunchwrap-inspired Hexagon Dippers (page 199) and potato wedges. (They make excellent next-day Cheesy Fiesta Potato Nachos with leftovers. And you will have some, because this makes a lot—but can be halved.)

LAYER 1: MEXICAN PIZZA-*DIPS*PIRED GROUND BEEF

1 pound ground beef

¼ teaspoon kosher salt

1 packet (1 ounce) taco seasoning, preferably Taco Bell

1 can (19 ounces) red enchilada sauce

⅓ cup ketchup

LAYER 2: CHEESY REFRIED BEANS

1 can (16 ounces) refried beans, preferably made with lard (unless you're vegetarian)

¼ cup hot water, plus more as needed

½ cup shredded Mexican blend cheese

¼ teaspoon kosher salt

½ teaspoon ground cumin

5 dashes of your favorite hot sauce, such as Cholula, or more to taste

LAYER 3: NACHO AVERAGE CHEESE DIP

1 can (15 ounces) nacho cheese (I find the canned variety is better than the jarred for this)

1 can (10 ounces) diced tomatoes and green chiles, preferably Ro-Tel

LAYER 4: QUESADILLA-*DIPS*PIRED CREAMY JALAPEÑO DIP

1 package (8 ounces) cream cheese, softened at room temperature (see page 14)

½ cup sour cream

1 can (7 ounces) chopped jalapeños, with juice

1½ teaspoons garlic powder

1½ teaspoons onion powder

1½ teaspoons ground cumin

½ teaspoon chili powder

½ teaspoon smoked paprika

¼ teaspoon kosher salt

LAYERS 5, 6, AND 7 (MORE LIKE TOPPINGS, BUT THEY ARE LAYERED TOPPINGS!)

½ cup shredded iceberg lettuce

1 Roma tomato, seeded and diced

¼ cup shredded Mexican blend cheese

OPTIONAL BUT ENCOURAGED

Sour cream and Taco Bell sauce or hot sauce, for drizzling

LAYER 1: MEXICAN PIZZA-*DIPS*PIRED GROUND BEEF

Heat a large skillet over medium heat for at least 3 minutes, which will help the beef form a nice golden-brown crust immediately. Add the ground beef to the pan (without any oil!) and press it into an even layer with a spatula. Cook un*dips*turbed for 5 minutes, then season with the salt. Flip the ground beef in pieces and let sear on the other side for about 3 more minutes, then break up into small pieces with a wooden spoon or

DIPPER MATRIX

HOMEMADE

Hexagon Dippers, 199

Potato Skinny Dippers, 219

Roulette Charred Peppers, 216

STORE-BOUGHT IS FRAN FINE

Fritos Scoops, or another corn chip

Tortilla chips, preferably Tostitos Scoops

Potato wedges, or any type of crispy potato you love

Crudités, such as carrots, celery, or sweet peppers

spatula. Cook for 2 to 4 minutes, until golden brown all around. If there's excessive grease, remove it with a spoon or carefully soak it up with a wadded-up paper towel held with tongs, then discard it. Add the taco seasoning, enchilada sauce, and ketchup. Bring to a simmer and cook until thickened, about 5 minutes. Spread evenly across the bottom of a 9 x 13-inch baking dish and set aside.

LAYER 2: CHEESY REFRIED BEANS

In a medium bowl, stir together the refried beans, hot water, cheese, salt, cumin, and hot sauce to your liking. Microwave for 2 minutes, stir, and microwave for another minute if necessary

(continued)

to melt the cheese. Add a tablespoon of water at a time if your beans seem too thick; you want them to be dippable. Pour on top of the first layer and smooth it out, moving from the center of the dish to the outside so it spreads evenly and the layers are crisp.

LAYER 3: NACHO AVERAGE CHEESE DIP

In a medium bowl, stir together the nacho cheese and tomatoes and chiles. Microwave for 2 minutes, stir, then microwave an additional 1 to 2 minutes as needed until melted and smooth. Pour over the bean layer and smooth it out evenly.

LAYER 4: QUESADILLA-*DIP*SPIRED CREAMY JALAPEÑO DIP

In a medium bowl, stir together all the creamy jalapeño dip ingredients. Pour the mixture on top of the nacho cheese layer and smooth it out evenly.

LAYERS 5, 6, AND 7—AKA DIP CONFETTI

Top with a layer of the lettuce, then the tomatoes, then the cheese. Drizzle on sour cream and hot sauce, if desired.

MO*DIP*FICATIONS: You can try ground turkey, chicken, or plant-based meat instead of beef.

CHIPPY'S TIPPY

This dip is great warm, but it's equally *dip*lightful at room temperature, so no need to break out the slow cooker. For crisp layering tips, check out page 21!

faq

CAN IT BE MADE IN ADVANCE? Yes, but chop and top just before serving so the dip confetti doesn't get brown or otherwise weird.

HOW LONG WILL IT KEEP? Up to 5 days in the fridge, covered with plastic wrap.

face your schmears everything bagel dip

SERVES BIG DIP PARTY (8 TO 10)

After moving away from the bagel capital of the world, New York City, I haven't eaten as many bagels as a Jewish woman should. (Or any person, for that matter.) But I've found a way to enjoy half of the New York bagel experience anytime, anywhere I want, with this dip. I'm talkin' toppings, baby! This kind of fully loaded bagel would raise a lot of eyebrows in NYC, with Dill the Hand Chive Cream Cheese Dip, ribbons of smoked salmon, Plenty of Whitefish Salad Dip, and as many accoutrements as you want. It makes an excellent triple-threat schmear on bagels, whether you're using leftover dip the morning after or doing a rip 'n' dip with whole bagels at the party. Brunch is served!

DILL THE HAND CHIVE CREAM CHEESE DIP

- 1 package (8 ounces) cream cheese, softened at room temperature (see page 14)
- 1 small fistful fresh chives (about ½ ounce)
- 1 small fistful fresh dill fronds (about ½ ounce)
- 3 teaspoons caper juice, plus more as needed

PLENTY OF WHITEFISH SALAD DIP

- 2 cold hard-boiled eggs
- 1 can (3.5 ounces) smoked whitefish, tuna, or cod
- ¼ cup sour cream
- ¼ cup mayonnaise
- 1 tablespoon freshly squeezed lemon juice
- 2 tablespoons capers
- 6 cranks black pepper
- 2 tablespoons aggressively rough chopped red onion
- Kosher salt, as needed
- Caper juice, as needed
- Everything bagel seasoning (optional)

***DIP*SSEMBLY**

- 3 ounces sliced smoked salmon, cut into 1-inch pieces
- Mix-and-match dip confetti of capers, seeded and diced Roma tomatoes, thicc-cut chives, lil' fresh dill fronds, and everything bagel seasoning

CHIPPY'S TIPPY

Scallion, garlic & herb, or your favorite store-bought flavor of cream cheese works in place of making your own Do the Hand Chive Cream Cheese layer. Just thin it out with a splash of milk if need be. Say Kimcheese! Dip (page 42) also works!

DILL THE HAND CHIVE CREAM CHEESE DIP

1. Using a food processor, combine the cream cheese, chives, and dill. Scrape down the sides to make sure the ingredients are all incorporated, then add a teaspoon at a time of caper juice, processing after each addition, until you reach a dippable consistency. Although 3 teaspoons should do it, you may need a little more to make it the right *dips*cosity.

(continued)

faq

CAN IT BE MADE IN ADVANCE? Yes, but it's better to layer it the day you're serving it, as the cream cheese will become more solid than dippable after a rest in the fridge.

HOW LONG WILL IT KEEP? Up to 5 days in a covered container in the fridge, but as noted, it will become more of a spread than a dip!

PLENTY OF WHITEFISH SALAD DIP

2. To hard-boil the eggs, place them in a small saucepan and cover them with water by about 1 inch. Bring to a boil, then cover the pan and let sit for 10 minutes off the heat. Transfer the eggs to a small bowl of ice water for 5 minutes, then peel and aggressively rough chop.

3. In a large bowl, combine the eggs, whitefish, sour cream, mayonnaise, lemon juice, capers, pepper, and onion and mix well. The dip shouldn't need salt, but taste to see what you think. Add a little caper juice if it seems too thick to get a bagel chip through it. Mix in everything bagel seasoning if you'd like.

***DIPS*SEMBLY TIME**

4. In a 2-quart clear glass bowl, baking dish, or pie plate, spread the cream cheese dip across the bottom in an even layer. Add the smoked salmon in a single layer, shingled over the whole surface. You can add a sprinkle of everything bagel seasoning here if you'd like, or skip it. Next, dollop on the whitefish salad dip and spread evenly across the dish from the center to the outside edges to get clean layers. Garnish the dip with your chosen dip confetti: capers, tomatoes, chives, dill, and everything bagel seasoning.

MO*DIP*FICATIONS: Serving vegetarians? You can just serve them the base layer (chive-dill cream cheese) and *everything* else to the rest of the group.

DIPPER MATRIX

HOMEMADE

Cucumber "Bagels": Cut 1 or 2 Persian (seedless) cucumbers into ½-inch-thick rounds, hollow out the centers with a straw, and sprinkle with everything bagel seasoning

These Bagel Pretzel Bites Have Everything, 194

Potato Skinny Dippers, 219

Roulette Charred Peppers, 216

Crispy Rice Dipsticks, 207

STORE-BOUGHT IS FRAN FINE

Your favorite bagels, served whole as rip 'n' dip or cut lengthwise in half and then crosswise into half-moon-shaped bagel chips and toasted

Pita chips

Bagel chips

Crudités, such as carrots, cucumbers, celery, or sweet peppers

French fries, Tater Tots, or your favorite crispy potatoes

TRY SAY KIMCHEESE!
DIP (PAGE 42)

DIPPER MATRIX

HOMEMADE

Crispy Rice Dipsticks, 207
Tantalizing Tempura, 212
Wonton Lil' Scoopz, 200
Rainbow Dumpling Chips, 203
Double Sesame Mochi Flatbreads, 196

STORE-BOUGHT IS FRAN FINE

Tempura seaweed chips
Tortilla chips, especially Tostitos Scoops
Crudités, such as carrots, cucumbers, or sweet peppers

spicy california roll guacamole

SERVES A BIG DIP PARTY (8 TO 10)

This one is *dip*dicated to the band Phantom Planet. I invented this dip for my Instagram video series *Let's Take a Dip!*, for which I create a dip based on a musician's back catalog, an actor's IMDB page, or someone's favorite dish. It made its debut on the evening of the twentieth anniversary show for their album *The Guest*, which featured their song "California"—aka the iconic theme song of *The O.C.*

Before the show, lead singer and songwriter Alex Greenwald and I layered in*dip*vidual servings of this dip together, alternating bright green guacamole and sunset-orange spicy surimi (aka imitation crab, made of pollock and the key ingredient for my number one food, crab rangoon). I find it best to make it that way; interactive and customizable for friends! Warning: Everyone will fight over the crispy shallot topping, which is fried in—gasp—the microwave! In five minutes!

To make a full California roll bite, stack a seaweed-wrapped Crispy Rice Dipstick (page 207) on a piece of cucumber, then dip that whole thing into the krab and guacamole and rock 'n' roll. It may even inspire you to write a song . . . like how Alex and I wrote the *Big Dip Energy* theme song the night after the *BDE* shoot wrapped. Check it out on Instagram @alysewhitney, and dip 'n' dance the night away!

XXXTRA CRISPY SHALLOTS

2 shallots, sliced as thinly as possible

¼ cup neutral oil, such as vegetable or canola

Pinch of kosher salt

GUAC OUT!

3 ripe medium avocados, halved, pitted, and peeled

1 shallot, aggressively rough chopped

3 garlic cloves, aggressively rough chopped

2 scallions, white parts aggressively rough chopped and green parts thinly sliced on the bias, for garnish

½ jalapeño, seeded and minced (or the whole thing, if you like it spicier)

2 tablespoons freshly squeezed lime juice (about 1 lime)

2 teaspoons toasted sesame oil

¼ teaspoon ground white pepper

¾ teaspoon kosher salt

KRABBY SUSHI SITUATION

8 ounces imitation crab

½ cup Kewpie mayonnaise

1 tablespoon sriracha

½ teaspoon toasted sesame oil

(continued)

XXXTRA CRISPY SHALLOTS

1. In a medium microwave-safe bowl, combine the thinly sliced shallots and neutral oil. Microwave on high for 5 minutes, stir, then microwave in 30-second increments until the shallots are *very lightly* golden brown. They will continue cooking in the hot oil after you remove, so don't let them get too dark or they will burn with the carryover cooking. After removing from the microwave, drain using a slotted spoon or sieve—but don't get rid of that infused shallot oil! Transfer the shallots to a paper towel–lined plate to drain off the excess grease and sprinkle with kosher salt. About 5 minutes later, they will be nice and crispy once they cool down.

GUAC OUT!

2. In a medium bowl, mash the avocados. Mix in the rough-chopped shallot, garlic, scallion whites, jalapeño, lime juice, sesame oil, white pepper, salt, and 1 tablespoon of the reserved shallot oil. Set aside.

KRABBY SUSHI SITUATION

3. Into a separate medium bowl, shred the imitation crab by rubbing each stick between your palms like a massage—they will come apart into strands. Snip with kitchen shears or cut into smaller pieces, then add the mayonnaise, sriracha, and toasted sesame oil and mix to combine. Set aside.

4. Layer the dip however you'd like in in*dip*vidual portions (such as in coupe glasses) or in a clear bowl to see the layers. Garnish with the scallion greens and the crispy shallots.

MO*DIP*FICATIONS: A can of tuna or cooked salmon could be sub*dip*tuted in equal parts for the imitation crab. Or sushi-grade fish, if you wanna be fancy!

CHIPPY'S TIPPY

I love using vintage glassware (a coupe or martini glass) to serve layered dips like this so people have a dish with a built-in handle to walk around with, and it's easy to find space to set down, even on a crowded table.

faq

CAN IT BE MADE IN ADVANCE? Yes, but you run the chance of the guacamole turning brown after more than a day in the fridge.

HOW LONG WILL IT KEEP? It won't go bad, but it will turn brown after a day. You can safely eat it for up to 5 days, covered in plastic wrap or transferred to an airtight container and refrigerated.

dip for dinner

There is a common misconception that dip is just an appetizer. (A *dips*conception, if you will.) But dip can be more than just a snack—it can be the whole meal. Dip for dinner is a lifestyle that you should jump onto, starting with these hearty dips that are packed with protein either in the dip itself (Crab Rangoon Dip, page 140) or with the dippers (Banh Mi Dip with Universally Dippable Marinated Meat Skewers, pages 150 and 226). And all of these *dip*ner faves can and should be enjoyed while watching *Only Murders in the Building*, where Oliver Putnam (Martin Short) regularly eats dip for dinner.

crab rangoon dip

SERVES A BIG DIP PARTY (8 TO 10)

I am a crab rangoon connoisseur. A founding member of the 'goon squad. I have a custom illustration by illustrator Margalit Cutler of my best friend, Izzy, and me surrounded by crab rangoons hanging in my apartment; the same illustrations are hand-painted onto my favorite signature purse by Lorna Nixon of I Made That Bag in Brooklyn; and I have had a crab rangoon tattoo planned ever since I tried my first one at Golden Garden, my hometown Chinese restaurant in Endwell, New York, in my teens—a late rangoon bloomer, I know. I have been hooked on the crispy wontons filled with cream cheese, imitation crab, and scallions. I've tried dozens of rangoons throughout my life, in different shapes and sizes, and I am often disappointed in the filling-to-crispy-exterior ratio.

I decided to turn it into a dip in 2016 for my first-ever Dipmas (all-dips Christmas potluck), popping it into a slow cooker and serving it with homemade fried wonton chips. I've tweaked the recipe through the years, opting to bake it in the oven with the sweet chili sauce on top so it gets nice and caramelized and inventing dipper game changer Wonton Lil' Scoopz, little wonton cups to house the perfect dip-to-crisp ratio in every single bite.

1 package (8 ounces) cream cheese, softened at room temperature (see page 14)

¼ cup Kewpie mayonnaise

¼ cup sour cream

1 teaspoon garlic powder

1 teaspoon soy sauce, preferably light-colored if you can find it (not low-sodium)

1 teaspoon toasted sesame oil

1 pound imitation crab legs

1 bunch scallions, thinly sliced on the bias; reserve a handful of dark green for dip confetti

½ cup Thai sweet chili sauce, for topping

1. Preheat the oven to 375°F.

2. In a medium bowl, whisk together the cream cheese, mayonnaise, sour cream, garlic powder, soy sauce, and sesame oil. Snip or cut the crab sticks into smaller pieces using kitchen shears or a knife. Then, one piece at a time, shred the crab directly into the dip by rubbing the pieces between your palms like a massage; they will come apart into strands. Stir the scallions into the creamy dip base.

(continued)

DIPPER MATRIX

HOMEMADE

Wonton Lil' Scoopz, 200

Rainbow Dumpling Chips, 203

STORE-BOUGHT IS FRAN FINE

Tempura seaweed chips

Tortilla chips, especially Tostitos Scoops

Crudités, such as carrots, cucumbers, cauliflower, or sweet peppers

3. Spread out the dip evenly in a 9 x 13-inch glass baking dish or 9-inch glass pie plate. Bake for 15 minutes, until slightly golden brown and bubbly, then pour on the sweet chili sauce and spread it over the dip. Bake the dip for 10 more minutes, until the chili sauce starts to caramelize. Garnish with the reserved scallions.

faq

CAN IT BE MADE IN ADVANCE? Yes! Prepare the mixture and refrigerate, then bake when ready to serve.

HOW LONG WILL IT KEEP? Up to 4 days covered in the fridge.

CHIPPY'S TIPPY

Light-colored soy sauce will make the dip look less brown and a little more aesthetically pleasing. This style is light in color but slightly saltier than classic soy sauce, so if you use regular, you may need to add a splash more. Don't confuse light-colored soy sauce with low-sodium soy sauce, which is just as dark in color but less salty.

poutine on the ritz dip

SERVES A LIL' GET-TOGETHER (4 TO 6)

My first poutine experience was at a bowling alley. But because it was in Plattsburgh, New York, a mere 15 minutes from the border to Montreal, Quebec, it was actually great in a high-low way. I bowled mostly gutter balls that day, but my gut was happy. The combination of squeaky, slightly toothsome cheese curds blanketed under gravy that made parts of the fries below satisfyingly soggy changed the way I thought about sauces and dips.

To make poutine into a dip, I leaned into the low, using the dehydrated mashed potatoes I grew up with. Their flavor is punched up by cooking them in chicken stock and making a very dark gravy to drizzle on top. But what about the cheese, you ask? It's fried day, I'm in love. The cheese curds become part French fry as they're crusted in dehydrated potatoes, then tossed with a smoky-salty Montreal steak-inspired seasoning to bring it together. O, thank you, Canada!

If you don't feel like frying cheese curds as a dipper, you can dip un-fried cheese curds, too. They won't be crunchy and satisfying, but they'll be a toothsome and squeaky-chewy contrast to the soft potatoes. But if you only want to use fries as a dipper, the carb-on-carb situation will be just fine. (And remember that store-bought is Fran Fine.)

3¼ cups chicken stock

1 packet (4 ounces) instant mashed potatoes

1 tablespoon salted butter

½ cup whole milk, plus more as needed

3 tablespoons vegetable oil

3 tablespoons flour

¼ teaspoon kosher salt, plus more to taste

1 teaspoon garlic powder

1 teaspoon onion powder

1 teaspoon soy sauce

10 cranks black pepper, plus more to taste

1. In a small saucepan over medium-high heat, bring 2 cups of the chicken stock to a boil. Add the instant mashed potatoes and butter, stir to combine, cover, and turn off the heat. Let sit for 5 minutes, and then add ¼ cup of the milk; the potatoes should now be a more dippable consistency. If it still feels too stiff to dip, add a splash of milk at a time until your desired *dips*cosity is achieved.

2. In a medium skillet over medium heat, add the vegetable oil and flour. Cook, whisking constantly, until the mixture (the

(continued)

DIPPER MATRIX

HOMEMADE

Potato-Fried Cheese Curds, 222

*Crisp*anthemum Onion Petals, 210

STORE-BOUGHT IS FRAN FINE

Squeaky fresh cheese curds

French fries, whatever style tickles your fancy

Rotisserie chicken legs

Really crunchy kettle-cooked potato chips

Funyuns

roux) is dark brown and smells toasty, 4 to 6 minutes. Slowly add the remaining 1¼ cups chicken stock, whisking constantly, then add the remaining ¼ cup milk. Reduce the heat to medium-low and whisk occasionally until the gravy is thick enough to coat the back of a spoon, and then add the salt, garlic powder, onion powder, and soy sauce. Taste for seasoning and add more salt if needed, plus 10 (or more) cranks of black pepper.

3. To serve, scoop the potatoes into a medium serving bowl (preferably a shallow one), smooth it out, and make some *dip*vots or a moat using a spoon (for *dip*corating tips, see page 19). Spoon the gravy into those indentations and garnish with chives. Serve with a big ol' pile of fries and cheese curds!

MO*DIP*FICATIONS: You could use leftovers from Thanksgiving to make this dip. Just thin down homemade mashed potatoes with chicken stock and top with or mix in any other leftovers you want to eat in a dip.

faq

CAN IT BE MADE IN ADVANCE? Yes, but store the potatoes and gravy separately and then heat and plate just before serving.

HOW LONG WILL IT KEEP? A week in an airtight container in the fridge.

CHIPPY'S TIPPY

You can make your Potato-Fried Cheese Curds (page 222) and fries in advance. Either keep them warm in a low oven (250°F) or reheat at 325°F for about 15 minutes, or until golden brown and crunchy again.

DIPPER MATRIX

HOMEMADE

Tantalizing Tempura, 212
Potato Skinny Dippers, 219
Roulette Charred Peppers, 216
Garlic-Kissed Crostini, 189
Veggie Ribbons, 214

STORE-BOUGHT IS FRAN FINE

Cooked shrimp or shrimp cocktail
Korean-style shrimp chips
Potato chips
Pita chips
Bagel chips
Crudités, such as carrots, cucumbers, celery, broccoli, cauliflower, or sweet peppers
French fries, Tater Tots, or your favorite crispy potatoes
Little Gem, Bibb, romaine, or butter lettuce, cut into dippable pieces

shrimp-less scampi dip

SERVES A LIL' GET-TOGETHER (4 TO 6)

Scampi is now a verb to me, because I can scampi anything with enough garlic and lemon. I love shrimp scampi, but the idea of a hot shrimp dip made me queasy. It would overcook and become too rubbery held in a slow cooker, and I wouldn't want to have a party foul of congealed cheese dip by not keeping it warm. So I turned down the temperature and created a chilled dip inspired by the core shrimp scampi flavors. The only heat involved is sizzling a ton of garlic—the most garlic per capita in this book—in olive oil, then pouring that oil into a mayonnaise-sour cream mixture so there's the luscious richness that you associate with shrimp scampi. But vegetarians can enjoy it, too!

1 cup sour cream

1 cup mayonnaise

Zest and juice of 1 lemon

½ teaspoon kosher salt

15 cranks black pepper, plus more for garnish

2 tablespoons olive oil

8 garlic cloves, aggressively rough chopped

1 bunch chives, snipped into thicc pieces (see page 22)

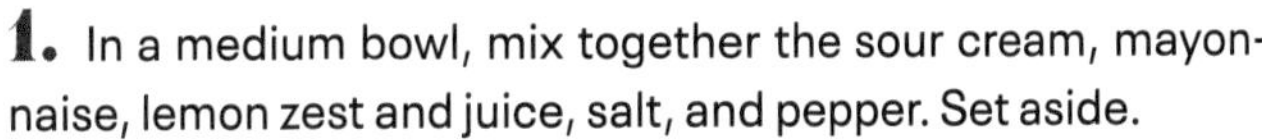

1. In a medium bowl, mix together the sour cream, mayonnaise, lemon zest and juice, salt, and pepper. Set aside.

2. In a small skillet, combine the oil and minced garlic. Set over medium-low heat and gently let the garlic infuse the oil for about 4 minutes, stirring occasionally, until it is light golden brown. Immediately remove the skillet from the heat and add the garlic *and* oil to the dip in progress.

3. Mix everything together, then add a handful of minced chives and stir again. To serve, garnish with additional chives and a few cranks of black pepper.

MOD*IP*FICATIONS: You can add more garlic, but not less.

faq

CAN IT BE MADE IN ADVANCE? Yes, and it tastes even better after a rest in the fridge.

HOW LONG WILL IT KEEP? Up to a week in an airtight container in the fridge.

CHIPPY'S TIPPY

Garlic burns fast, so when it's just starting to brown at the edges, pull it off the heat and pour it into a heat-safe bowl (like glass or ceramic) to stop the cooking. The carryover cooking will make it perfectly golden.

spanakopidip

SERVES A BIG DIP PARTY (8 TO 10)

When making spanakopita for the first time with a friend of my grammy's, I caught her sneaking bites of the filling every so often. She encouraged me to do the same, saying that sometimes she even preferred it in this slightly chilled state, before it was covered by phyllo blankets and melted butter and baked until ultra-flaky outside and tender inside. So in honor of Manoush, this dip can be enjoyed hot or cold equally, using Phyllo Lil' Scoopz (page 202) as an edible spoon or prefilled dip cups.

5 tablespoons olive oil

1 large yellow onion, aggressively rough chopped

6 garlic cloves, aggressively rough chopped

1 package (10 ounces) frozen chopped spinach, thawed and wrung out in a towel

½ teaspoon kosher salt

1 cup plain whole milk Greek yogurt

1 tablespoon freshly squeezed lemon juice

6 ounces feta in brine, crumbled

¼ teaspoon crushed red pepper

1 bunch scallions, white and green parts, trimmed and thinly sliced on the bias

3 tablespoons aggressively rough chopped fresh dill

2 tablespoons aggressively rough chopped fresh parsley leaves

2 tablespoons feta cheese brine

1. In a large saucepan or high-sided skillet over medium heat, heat 2 tablespoons of the oil. Sauté the onion, stirring occasionally, until translucent and just starting to brown, 5 to 7 minutes. Add the garlic and cook until fragrant, about 1 minute. Add another tablespoon of the oil and the spinach and cook for another 3 to 5 minutes, stirring occasionally, until warmed through. Season the mixture with the salt, but don't be tempted to add more—the feta will make things perfectly salty.

2. In a medium bowl, combine the yogurt, lemon juice, crumbled feta, crushed red pepper, almost all the scallions and herbs, feta brine, and the remaining 2 tablespoons oil. Stir thoroughly.

3. To make the hot dip version, add the creamy mixture to the spinach mixture in the saucepan, mix well, and heat on medium-low until warmed through, about 5 minutes. To make the cold dip version, add the spinach mixture to the creamy mixture, mix well, and enjoy at room temp or chill in the fridge before serving. Garnish either version with the reserved scallions and herbs.

faq

CAN IT BE MADE IN ADVANCE?

Yes (see page 15 for reheating instructions) or eat cold.

HOW LONG WILL IT KEEP?

A week in an airtight container in the fridge.

DIPPER MATRIX

HOMEMADE

Phyllo Lil' Scoopz, 202—or you can buy them!

Potato Skinny Dippers, 219

Roulette Charred Peppers, 216

Garlic-Kissed Crostini, 189

STORE-BOUGHT IS FRAN FINE

Pita chips

Bagel chips

Crudités, such as carrots, cucumbers, celery, broccoli, cauliflower, or sweet peppers

French fries, Tater Tots, or your favorite crispy potatoes

banh mi dip

SERVES A LIL' GET-TOGETHER (4 TO 6)

After trying a banh mi board at my friend Jimmy's New York City restaurant, Monsieur Vo, I had a vision of dip. It really was like doing long *dip*vision, because there were so many complex flavors and parts of the Vietnamese sandwich that I had to incorporate thoughtfully. I tried making my friend Tue's (aka @twaydabae) homemade pâté first. It was incredible, but too fussy and time-consuming for dip incorporation.

So my brilliant food stylist, Nick, suggested we take store-bought liverwurst and use it as a base instead. We blended in jalapeño, garlic, cilantro, and some pickling liquid from the pickled veggie dippers we had already made. It was a transformative experience—you'd never know the base came from behind the deli counter.

To get the full banh mi experience, go to your favorite Vietnamese sandwich shop and ask to buy their bread. (If you don't have a nearby shop, a crusty French roll will do.) Wrap a piece of tender meat (Universally Dippable Marinated Meat Skewers, page 226) inside the soft roll and dip through the pat*nay* (not pâté?) for a sublime one-bite delight.

8 ounces liverwurst, packaged or from the deli counter

½ jalapeño, seeded

2 garlic cloves

¼ cup fresh cilantro leaves, aggressively rough chopped, plus more for garnish

Pickling liquid from Everything in a Pickle (page 218)

Kewpie mayonnaise, for garnish

Sriracha, for garnish

Chopped pickled veggies, for garnish (optional)

CHIPPY'S TIPPY

Everything in a Pickle (aka quick-pickled veggies, page 218) are an essential dipper *and* are used as dip confetti in this one.

1. In a food processor (this is easiest in a small one), combine the liverwurst, jalapeño, garlic, and cilantro. Run the motor until the mixture is almost smooth, then add the quick pickle brine and run again until completely smooth and dippable.

2. Pour into a small bowl to serve, and decorate the top with a drizzle of Kewpie mayonnaise and sriracha—a spiral is the easiest and simplest. Top with chopped cilantro and a few small pieces of pickled vegetables, if desired.

3. The ultimate way to serve is to dip in a half-toasted piece of Vietnamese baguette and top with lemongrass-marinated beef or pork and extra pickled veg for the perfect mini banh mi bite.

DIPPER MATRIX

HOMEMADE

Vietnamese baguette (or crusty French bread), cut into ½-inch-thick slices, schmeared with Kewpie mayonnaise, and toasted at 400°F for 10 minutes

Everything in a Pickle, 218

Universally Dippable Marinated Meat Skewers, 226

STORE-BOUGHT IS FRAN FINE

Crudités, such as carrots, cucumbers, or sweet peppers

faq

CAN IT BE MADE IN ADVANCE? Yes, but you may need to thin it out with a bit of additional pickling liquid once it's chilled and firmed up in the fridge.

HOW LONG WILL IT KEEP? Up to a week in an airtight container in the fridge.

SPAM

deviled spam musubi dip

SERVES A LIL' GET-TOGETHER (4 TO 6)

I had my first canned deviled ham salad recently . . . and I wasn't a fan. But the pun was *right there* and I have a Spam musubi tattoo on my right arm, so it was written in the stars (or at least in ink) that I make this dip. Spam is rendered unrecognizable after it is seared. It looks like a little ham steak, and after adding a quick sauce of soy sauce, sugar, and water, it becomes glazed and shimmery. Enjoy that for a moment, because then it's all going into a food processor and will resemble cat food. I'm being honest here so you don't feel like you've been catfished. But I promise the flavor will more than make up for the questionable appearance. Beauty isn't skin deep . . . it's Spam dip.

1 tablespoon soy sauce

¼ teaspoon garlic powder

¼ teaspoon onion powder

1 teaspoon toasted sesame oil

3 tablespoons packed light brown sugar

¼ cup water

1 teaspoon neutral oil, such as vegetable or canola

1 can (12 ounces) low-sodium Spam, sliced lengthwise into 10 ¼-inch-thick pieces

½ cup Kewpie mayonnaise

2 scallions, white parts cut into big chunks, green parts thinly sliced

1 tablespoon furikake, plus more for garnish

1. In a small bowl, mix together the soy sauce, garlic powder, onion powder, sesame oil, brown sugar, and ¼ cup water. Set aside.

2. In a large skillet (preferably nonstick) over medium heat, heat the neutral oil. Add the Spam slices and cook until lightly golden brown, about 3 minutes per side. Pour on the sauce and let it bubble and thicken until the water evaporates and the sauce forms a glaze. Turn the Spam pieces for even coating and let cook 1 more minute. Remove to a plate, including any remaining glaze, and set aside to cool for at least 15 minutes.

3. Set aside 1 slice of Spam for garnish. In a food processor, pulse the fried Spam, mayonnaise, and scallion whites until evenly combined and mostly smooth (with some chunky lil'

(continued)

CHIPPY'S TIPPY

Serve this right in the Spam can!

DIPPER MATRIX

HOMEMADE

Crispy Rice Dipsticks, 207
Tantalizing Tempura, 212
Roulette Charred Peppers, 216
Everything in a Pickle, 218
Wonton Lil' Scoopz, 200
Rainbow Dumpling Chips, 203

STORE-BOUGHT IS FRAN FINE

Tempura seaweed chips
Rice crackers
Tortilla chips, especially Tostitos Scoops
Bagel chips
Crudités, such as carrots, cucumbers, celery, broccoli, cauliflower, or sweet peppers

Spam bits to keep things interesting). Transfer the mixture to a small bowl and stir in the furikake and half the scallion greens.

4. Serve in the bowl it's already in or transfer to the Spam can. Finish with the scallion greens, Spam garnish (cut into any shapes you like), and a sprinkle of furikake.

faq

CAN IT BE MADE IN ADVANCE? Yes!

HOW LONG WILL IT KEEP? Up to a week in the fridge in a covered container.

MY FRIEND ALICE HU, CAREER ASTROLOGIST, READ OUR TAROT CARDS . . .

"DIP IS YOUR FUTURE . . ."

SPAM
Lady Boba
MATCHA LATTE BUBBLE TEA

dipsserts

It would be doing you a *dips*service if I didn't take a dip into the sweet side. I don't have much of a sweet tooth, so you'll notice that all of these dips are not *too* sweet—the highest compliment in my book. One of the revelations I found when *dip*veloping this cookbook was how you can soak cake, sweet bread, or cookies in heavy cream and then whip it to make a whipped cream base for sweet dips. The result is airy and light yet packed with familiar—and often nostalgic—flavors for Strawberry Shortcake Dip (page 180), Dirt Pudding Dip (page 177), and many more. You'll find some sweet-and-savory combinations as well, like the well-rounded nuttiness and hint of salt in Black-and-White Sesame Cookie Dip (page 164), an homage to my Jewish and Korean roots with a mash-up of the famous deli cookie and a roasty-toasty duo of sesame pastes.

egg tart dip

SERVES A LIL' GET-TOGETHER (4 TO 6)

A warm egg tart with its custardy, rich center and flaky, buttery crust is my platonic ideal of dessert. Both the Chinese and Portuguese styles have special places in my heart, so this dip-and-dipper combo pays homage to both. The dip is actually a custard made with extra egg yolks and evaporated milk, a signature ingredient of egg tart fillings, and the dipper is a brûléed cracker, made by pouring a two-ingredient caramel over saltines or buttery crackers and broiling very briefly until they have a cracklingly crisp shell on top and toothsome, chewy caramel underneath.

4 egg yolks

3 tablespoons salted butter

½ cup packed light brown sugar

1 can (12 ounces) evaporated milk

1½ tablespoons cornstarch

½ teaspoon pure vanilla extract

1. In a medium bowl, whisk the yolks until they look like a sauce, about 30 seconds.

2. In a medium saucepan over medium-low heat, combine 2 tablespoons of the butter and the brown sugar. Whisking constantly, cook until the mixture starts to caramelize and brown and smells toasty, about 5 minutes. Whisk in the evaporated milk, then take off the heat.

3. Remove 1 cup of the caramelized milk mixture from the saucepan and very slowly drizzle it into the bowl of egg yolks, whisking constantly. (This is called tempering, which makes sure you don't end up with scrambled eggs.) Whisk thoroughly until combined, and then pour the mixture back into the saucepan.

4. Add the cornstarch and vanilla and whisk to combine. Bring to a boil over medium-high heat, then lower the heat to a simmer and cook the custard, whisking often, until thick enough to coat the back of a spoon, 1 to 2 minutes.

5. Turn off the heat, whisk in the remaining tablespoon of butter, and pour the mixture into a large bowl. Let cool for 30 minutes at room temperature.

CHIPPY'S TIPPY

"Tempering" is a fancy word for matching the temperatures of ingredients so they remain stable. In this case, it's using caramelized milk to take the fridge-coldness off egg yolk, so they don't curdle into scrambled eggs. Go slow and don't stress!

DIPPER MATRIX

HOMEMADE

Caramel Brûlée Crackers, 233

Phyllo Lil' Scoopz, 202

Cinnamon-Sugar Lil' Scoopz, 200

STORE-BOUGHT IS FRAN FINE

Fresh fruit, such as cut-up apples, strawberries, or bananas

Pretzels or pretzel thins

Graham crackers

Gluten-free crispy coconut rolls, such as Thai brands or Ava Organic

Buttery crackers of your choice

6. Cover the bowl in plastic wrap or transfer to an airtight container and chill for at least 4 hours, or even overnight. Let sit at room temperature for at least 20 minutes before serving.

faq

CAN IT BE MADE IN ADVANCE? Yes! It has to set for at least a few hours up to overnight in the fridge, but longer is totally fine.

HOW LONG WILL IT KEEP? Up to a week in an airtight container in the fridge.

DIPPER MATRIX

HOMEMADE

Boba and Pocky skewers (see recipe)

Cinnamon-Sugar Wonton Lil' Scoopz (page 200)

Caramel Brûlée Crackers (page 233)

STORE-BOUGHT IS FRAN FINE

Pocky, any flavor you like

Pirouette cookies, any flavor you like

Gluten-free crispy coconut rolls, such as Thai brands or Ava Organic

Fresh fruit, such as apples, strawberries, or bananas

Plain or chocolate graham crackers

Shortbread cookies

Sugar cookies

Pretzels, chocolate-covered pretzels, or pretzel thins

boba tea dips with boba skewers

SERVES A LIL' GET-TOGETHER (4 TO 6)

I'm a boba girl in a boba world. And I'm also very indecisive. So there are four *dip*ferent flavors of tea-infused dips to choose from here, all made with concentrated, aggressively strongly brewed tea to make them really taste like tea and not just sugar. The creamy base takes inspiration from the salted cheese foam available at a lot of modern boba shops, which, by the way, is actually cream cheese in both cases. And just like when you order a drink, you can adjust the sweetness to your liking. I prefer this not-too-sweet version, but if you find it a little too tea-heavy, add a teaspoon of powdered sugar at a time until it satisfies your sweet tooth.

CREAMY DREAMY BASE

1 package (8 ounces) cream cheese, softened at room temperature (see page 14)

¼ cup plus 2 tablespoons powdered sugar

½ cup heavy cream

Hefty pinch kosher salt

TEA TIME!

4 tea bags of choice, preferably black tea, such as English Breakfast or Earl Grey, but you can also try green tea, like jasmine, or oolong

¾ cup boiling water

2 teaspoons cornstarch

2 teaspoons cold water

BOBA SKEWERS

½ cup partially cooked tapioca pearls (they appear dried in the bag)

½ cup water

½ cup white sugar or packed light brown sugar

2 boxes (2.6 ounces each) Pocky, flavors of your choice, or 3- or 4-inch toothpicks or skewers

BOBA DIP FLAVOR OPTIONS

The below amounts are for a full batch of a single flavor. If *dip*viding the batch into multiple flavors, cut those amounts in the same ratio, e.g., ¼ cup brown sugar for a half batch of Brown Sugar Milk Tea Boba Dip!

CREAMY DREAMY BASE

1. In a large bowl, whip the cream cheese with an electric hand mixer on medium speed until soft and fluffy, about 2 minutes. Add the powdered sugar and mix to combine. Pour in the heavy cream and whip into the mixture on medium speed until it is extra fluffy but does not hold a peak when you turn off the mixer, and hold a beater out of the bowl, about 2 minutes more. Cover with plastic wrap and refrigerate so it sets up a bit, at least 2 hours and up to overnight.

(continued)

BROWN SUGAR MILK TEA

Before adding the cornstarch mixture to the tea, add ½ cup packed light brown sugar to the tea and stir to dissolve.

STRAWBERRY MILK TEA

Before adding the cornstarch slurry, add 3 tablespoons strawberry jelly to the tea and stir to dissolve.

THAI TEA

Use Thai tea bags (which have orange dye added). Swirl 2 teaspoons sweetened condensed milk into the finished dip.

MATCHA

Use 1 tablespoon matcha powder instead of tea bags.

TEA TIME!

2. While the creamy base is setting up, make your tea. Steep the tea in the boiling water for 4 minutes. (This works best if you boil water in a small saucepan, add the tea bags, and turn off the heat and let it sit for 4 minutes.) Remove the tea bags and discard.

3. In a small bowl, whisk together the cornstarch and cold water (cornstarch will get clumpy if added directly to hot liquid). Whisk that mixture into the tea, bring to a boil, and stir until it thickens—it should happen immediately, or within 30 seconds. Transfer the tea mixture to a small bowl to cool for at least 20 minutes at room temperature or 10 minutes in the fridge.

4. Repeat for any other tea flavors you want to make.

5. Remove the creamy base from the fridge and mix in the tea concentrate. (Again, if you *dip*vide into different flavors for one batch, make sure you use the right ratio of concentrate to creamy base.)

BOBA SKEWERS

6. Make the boba skewers by boiling the partially cooked tapioca pearls according to the package directions—usually 25 minutes with the lid off, then a 15-minute rest with the lid on. Meanwhile, make a syrup by heating ½ cup water over medium-high heat with the sugar until the sugar is completely dissolved, 1 to 2 minutes. Transfer the syrup to a medium bowl, strain the boba, and add to the syrup to soak for at least 30 minutes at room temperature, or up to 4 hours. After that, you can transfer to an airtight container and store in the fridge for up to 2 days, but the boba will get hard in the fridge. Don't fret—just microwave the boba in syrup in 20-second bursts until softened, or reheat in a small saucepan over low heat.

7. To make the skewers, you can go the extra mile and make a shallow incision with a paring knife into each boba and slide them onto a stick of Pocky or just put them onto toothpicks or small skewers. You can also just dip Pocky or other dippers in the dips if you don't want to go through the trouble of making homemade boba. Serve them in teacups, coupe glasses, or other fun vessels, ideally with boba drinks on the side for double boba!

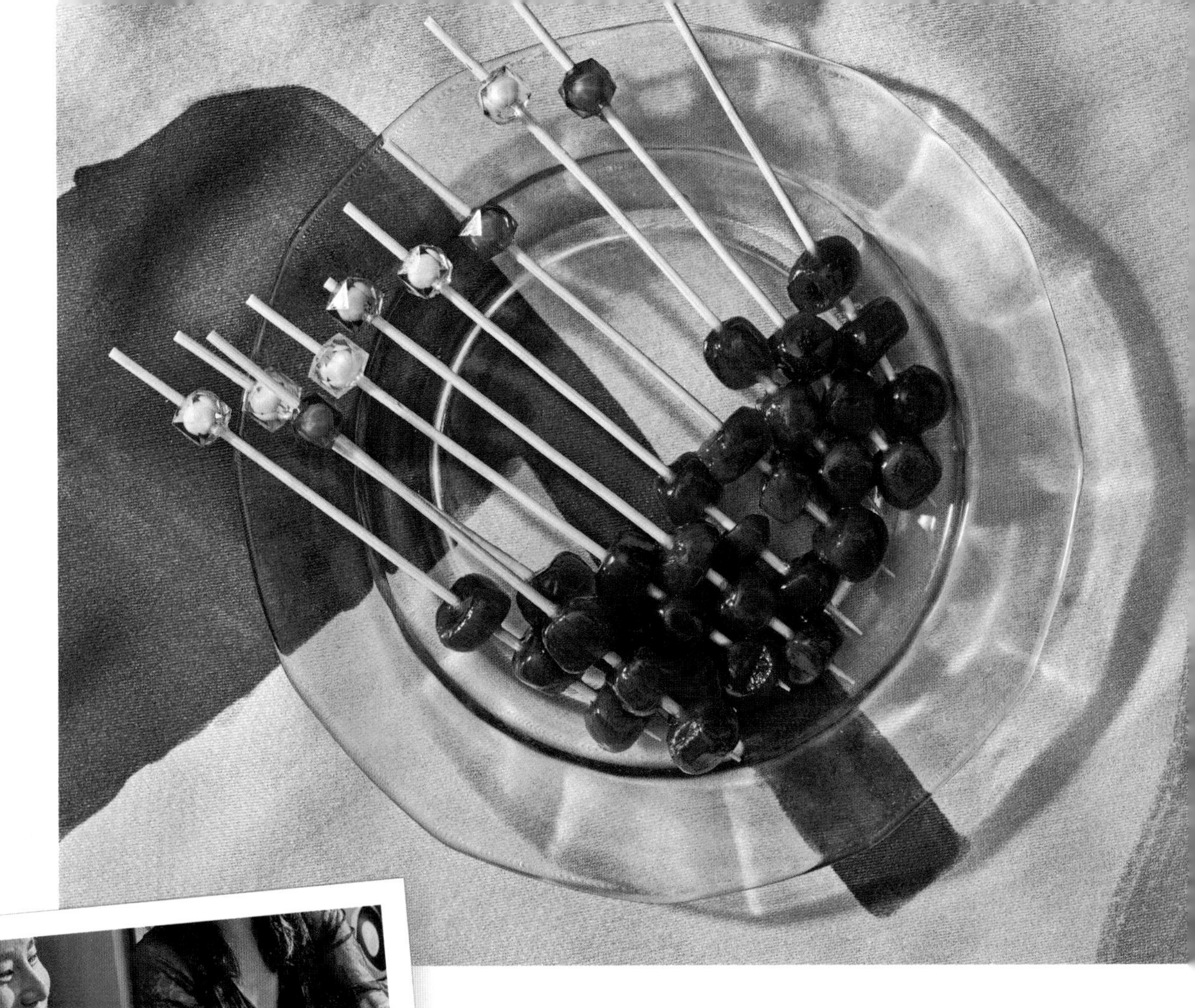

SPILLING THE TEA (DIPS) WITH SHIRLEY

MO*DIP*FICATIONS: You can alter the sweetness level or styles of tea to match your personali*tea*.

faq

CAN IT BE MADE IN ADVANCE? Yes! Let it sit at room temperature for at least 30 minutes before serving, and add a splash of milk to thin it out if it thickens too much in the fridge.

HOW LONG WILL IT KEEP? Up to 10 days in an airtight container in the fridge.

black-and-white sesame cookie dip

SERVES A BIG DIP PARTY (8 TO 10)

As a Libra, balance is an essential part of my life. As a Korean American adoptee raised by a half Jewish, half Catholic, barely religious family, I've always had my identity split into pieces. This is the dip that put them all together in a harmonious, unique, seren*dip*itous way. I was on the hunt for the best black-and-white cookies (or as upstate New Yorkers call them, half-moon cookies) in Los Angeles, which is still an ongoing journey. Then I saw black and white sesame pastes at H Mart, physically added them to my cart, and became obsessed with the idea of a black-and-white *sesame* cookie dip. So to me, *this* is the best black-and-white cookie in LA—no *dips*respect to all the amazing Jewish delis here.

It took some trial and error to figure out how to emulate the cakey texture of the black-and-white cookie in dip form. Ultimately, I came up with a new technique for this style of *dips*serts: soak store-bought cake in cream, then whip it. No straining required, and no extra sugar added on top of what's already in the cake and frosting. The cake melts into the cream but leaves a hint of the crumb on your tongue, and the sour cream is there to add the signature tang of a B&W cookie base while also balancing out the sweetness. To experience it fully, I recommend dragging a shortbread cookie across the entire dip, getting a little yin, a little yang, and a lot of bang for your buck in dip-to-dipper ratio.

1 slice (6 ounces) store-bought chocolate-frosted chocolate cake

1 slice (6 ounces) store-bought vanilla-frosted vanilla cake

2 pints heavy cream

2 tablespoons toasted white sesame paste, such as Sanfeng, Wang Zhihe, or Kadoya (found at H Mart or online)

½ cup sour cream

2 tablespoons toasted black sesame paste, such as Sanfeng, Wang Zhihe, or Kadoya (found at H Mart or online)

Toasted white and black sesame seeds, for garnish (optional)

1. Place the chocolate cake in a medium bowl and the vanilla cake in a separate medium bowl. Pour 1 pint of heavy cream over each piece of cake. Smash the cake into the cream with a potato masher, fork, or spatula until it's mostly incorporated—the rest will happen when you whip it, whip it good.

(continued)

DIPPER MATRIX

HOMEMADE

Crumble Crackers, 229

Double Sesame Mochi Flatbreads, 196

Cinnamon-Sugar Lil' Scoopz, 200

STORE-BOUGHT IS FRAN FINE

Fresh fruit, such as apples, strawberries, or bananas

Shortbread cookies

Pretzels or pretzel thins

Graham crackers, plain or chocolate

Gluten-free crispy coconut rolls, such as Thai brand or Ava Organic brand

Your favorite buttery cracker

2. Use an electric hand mixer (don't be a hero trying to whip this by hand) and whip the vanilla cake-infused cream first, starting on low speed and building up to medium until the mixture holds a loose peak when you turn off the mixer and lift a beater out of the bowl. Add the white sesame paste and ¼ cup of the sour cream, then mix again until the mixture is homogeneous, with no streaks.

3. Rinse off the beaters, dry, and repeat the whipping process with the chocolate cake-infused cream. Add the black sesame paste and the remaining ¼ cup sour cream, then again mix until well combined, with no streaks.

4. If you intend to serve in a yin-yang symbol, reserve 1 tablespoon each of the vanilla and chocolate mixtures. To serve, scoop the vanilla mixture into one side of a medium (preferably shallow) serving bowl, then carefully add the chocolate mixture into the other side. It's okay if they touch slightly, but try to keep them separate and the colors *dip*stinct. To finish, you can make a yin-yang symbol by using the reserved tablespoon of each dip as dots on the opposite flavor's side. Or just sprinkle toasted black sesame seeds over one side and toasted white sesame seeds on the other—you can go monochromatic or make opposites attract. Serve with plenty of dippers and two separate spoons if you don't want the colors to run together.

MO*DIP*FICATIONS: If another base flavor of cake speaks to you, use it! Just try to keep one darker and one lighter so you get that stark visual contrast.

CAN IT BE MADE IN ADVANCE? Yes, but the colors may bleed together, so plate it just before serving.

HOW LONG WILL IT KEEP? Up to 10 days in an airtight container in the fridge.

CHIPPY'S TIPPY

Asian-style (or Chinese-style) sesame paste is not interchangeable with Middle Eastern tahini. It's made with toasted sesame seeds for a deeper, richer flavor.

this dip is bananas!

SERVES A BIG DIP PARTY (8 TO 10)

This dip was created similarly to the way One Direction was formed. Banana bread, banana pudding, and bananas Foster are all good solo, but when parts of each are combined, they complement each other and form a supergroup. One *Dip*rection? Or maybe more like *Dip*stiny's Child? However you want to contextualize it, this is a dish that *dip*serves the spotlight. It has whipped cream infused with actual banana bread and caramelized banana-enhanced pudding layered together in an *apeel*ing aesthetic. This dip has *Styles* all its own and will *Bey* a runaway hit at your next shindig.

BREADY FOR BANANA BREAD WHIPPED CREAM

2 cups crumbled banana bread, store-bought or homemade

1 pint heavy cream

4 ounces cream cheese, softened at room temperature (see page 14), cut into small pieces

1 teaspoon pure vanilla extract

BANANAS FOSTER PUDDING (MINUS THE FLAMBÉ)

2 tablespoons salted butter

2 tablespoons packed light brown sugar

2 ripe bananas, cut into coins

2 cups whole milk

1 box (3.4 ounces) vanilla instant pudding mix

LATE NIGHT DIPPIN'

BREADY FOR BANANA BREAD WHIPPED CREAM

1. If baking the banana bread from scratch, do so at least a day in advance and let it cool completely. If using store-bought, congratulations on taking a shortcut. Either way, a few 1-inch-thick slices should do the trick to get 2 cups of banana bread crumbs.

2. In a medium bowl, combine the banana bread crumbs and heavy cream. Using an electric hand mixer—don't be a hero trying to whip cream by hand—whip it, starting on low speed and building up to medium until the mixture holds a loose peak when you turn off the mixer and lift a beater out of the bowl. Add the cream cheese and vanilla, then whip on medium-low speed until the cream cheese is fully incorporated. Set aside.

(continued)

DIPPER MATRIX

HOMEMADE

Crumble Crackers, 229

Cinnamon-Sugar Lil' Scoopz, 200

STORE-BOUGHT IS FRAN FINE

Fresh fruit, such as cut-up apples, strawberries, or bananas

Banana chips

Nilla Wafers

Pretzels, peanut butter pretzel nuggets, chocolate-covered pretzels, or pretzel thins

Graham crackers, plain or chocolate

Gluten-free crispy coconut rolls, such as Thai brand or Ava Organic

BANANAS FOSTER PUDDING (MINUS THE FLAMBÉ)

3. In a small skillet, preferably nonstick, melt the butter and brown sugar together over medium-low heat. Add the banana coins and, using a spatula, toss to coat each piece thoroughly. Spread into a single layer and cook until gently caramelized on both sides, about 2 minutes per side, then transfer to a medium bowl and mash with a fork or potato masher. Set aside to cool while you make the pudding.

4. In a medium bowl, combine the milk and vanilla instant pudding. Mix with an electric mixer on medium-low speed for 2 to 3 minutes, or until the mixture is almost doubled in volume and looks like pudding. Scrape the mashed caramelized bananas into the bowl and stir to combine.

***DIP*SSEMBLY TIME!**

5. To serve, layer the pudding and whipped cream in a coupe glass for in*dip*vidual servings, or in a 1-quart bowl for a communal portion.

MO*DIP*FICATIONS: A tablespoon or two of peanut butter mixed into the pudding or a finishing drizzle of honey or both would not suck.

faq

CAN IT BE MADE IN ADVANCE? Yes, but store the layers separately and assemble just before serving.

HOW LONG WILL IT KEEP? Up to a week in an airtight container in the fridge.

CHIPPY'S TIPPY

For a fun presentation, put the banana bread whipped cream in a zip-top bag, get as much air out as you can, push it to one bottom corner, and snip the tip. You've got a DIY piping bag to pipe swirls of infused whipped cream atop your pudding layers. You fancy.

DIPPER MATRIX

HOMEMADE

Crumble Crackers, 229

Cinnamon-Sugar Lil' Scoopz, 200

STORE-BOUGHT IS FRAN FINE

Cannoli shells

Waffle cones, broken into pieces

Pretzels or pretzel thins

Graham crackers

Pirouette cookies, any flavor you like

Gluten-free crispy coconut rolls, such as Thai brands or Ava Organic

Fresh fruit, such as apples, strawberries, or bananas

holy cannoli dip

SERVES A BIG DIP PARTY (8 TO 10)

My first experience with cannoli out of its shell (with shoes on?) was in college with a custom New Year's Eve cake I bought at Wegmans to celebrate the holiday with my best friend, Izzy. The marble cake had a thick layer of their cannoli filling between the layers, and they decorated the top with penguins drinking margaritas. Only one part of that has to do with this dip, which has evolved in the fifteen years of Izzy's and my friendship since that cake. Cannoli dip made its first appearance at Dipmas 2017, my all-dips Christmas potluck. It was the first sweet dip to go, because everyone said, "It's not *too* sweet!" which is the kind of dessert I'm always chasing.

This is not the cloyingly sweet cannoli you may have had before. This dip uses a 4:1 ratio of dairy (mascarpone and ricotta cheeses) to sugar (powdered). It's the type of dessert you can eat a lot of without feeling ill.

1 container (15 ounces) whole milk ricotta cheese

1 container (8 ounces) mascarpone cheese

1 cup powdered sugar

2 teaspoons pure vanilla extract

Zest and juice of ½ orange (about 2 tablespoons juice)

¾ cup mini chocolate chips

Hefty pinch of flaky sea salt, for garnish

1. In a medium bowl, using an electric hand mixer (or a stand mixer with the whisk attachment), whip the ricotta, mascarpone, and powdered sugar together until fluffy and slightly thickened. Add the vanilla and orange zest and juice and whip again if it looks thin. Stir in ½ cup of the chocolate chips.

2. Transfer to a medium serving bowl, then top with the remaining ¼ cup chocolate chips and a hefty pinch of flaky sea salt.

MOD*IP*FICATIONS: You can add in pistachios, extra chocolate chips, or chocolate chips *and* peanut butter chips for a peanut butter cup version.

CHIPPY'S TIPPY

The most fun way to serve this is with a waffle cone in a resealable plastic bag so people can smash their own cannoli "chips."

faq

CAN IT BE MADE IN ADVANCE? Yes! Let it sit at room temperature for at least 30 minutes before serving, and add a splash of milk to thin it out if it thickens too much in the fridge.

HOW LONG WILL IT KEEP? Up to 10 days in the fridge in an airtight container.

espressomartinimisu dip

SERVES A LIL' GET-TOGETHER (4 TO 6)

When you want to wake up and also turn up, there's nothing like an espresso martini. But if you want to level up, you'll try the *dips*sert version with Espressomartinimisu Dip, which incorporates elements of the classic Italian dessert: mascarpone cheese, ladyfinger-infused whipped cream, and a dusting of cocoa powder. It combines this with an extra kick of caffeine and booze from espresso powder and Kahlúa! Serve in a martini glass, preferably pinkies up.

8 ladyfingers (the cake kind!)

1 cup heavy cream

1 container (8 ounces) mascarpone cheese

¼ cup Kahlúa

2 teaspoons espresso powder

2 teaspoons cocoa powder, plus more for garnish

Chocolate-covered espresso beans, for garnish

1. Crumble the ladyfingers into a medium bowl or quart-size deli container and pour in the heavy cream. Refrigerate for at least 30 minutes to let the ladyfingers steep, then mash them fully into the cream with a fork.

2. Using an electric hand mixer (don't be a hero trying to whip cream by hand), whip the mixture, starting on low speed and building up to medium, until the mixture holds a soft peak when you turn off the mixer and lift a beater out of the bowl. Add the mascarpone, Kahlúa, espresso powder, and cocoa powder and beat again until thoroughly combined.

3. To serve, dish into a martini glass or a small bowl and top with a sprinkle of cocoa powder and chocolate-covered espresso beans.

MODIPFICATIONS: Replace the Kahlúa with an equal part of cream for an alcohol-free version.

CHIPPY'S TIPPY

Blue Bottle's freeze-dried espresso is my favorite version of espresso powder; find it at the coffee chain or online. Instead of adding directly, dissolve 2 teaspoons of it into 1 ounce of hot water, as it is not as finely ground as typical espresso powder and could create a weird texture in the finished dip otherwise.

faq

CAN IT BE MADE IN ADVANCE? Yes, but you may need to thin with milk as it firms up in the fridge.

HOW LONG WILL IT KEEP? Up to a week in the fridge in an airtight container.

DIPPER MATRIX

HOMEMADE

Cinnamon-Sugar Lil' Scoopz, 200

Crumble Crackers, 229

STORE-BOUGHT IS FRAN FINE

Ladyfingers

Waffle cones, broken into pieces

Pretzels, chocolate-covered pretzels, or pretzel thins

Graham crackers, regular or chocolate

Pirouette cookies, any flavor you like

Fresh fruit, such as apples, strawberries, or bananas

fat mint dip

SERVES A BIG DIP PARTY (8 TO 10)

Mint chocolate was never a flavor profile I gravitated toward, but I was encouraged to embrace it by one of my best friends, Irene. She's a mint chocolate *freak*, and this dip is a love letter to her. But it's also a reminder that "fat" doesn't have to be a negative word. It's just a descriptor, and this dip *is* fat. It's chock-full of the choco-mint flavors of Thin Mint cookies, grasshopper pie, mint chocolate chip ice cream, mint Oreos (and an ice cream called Mint Cookie Crumble that my friend Sam loves from Stewart's, a shop native to upstate New York, where we met in college), Andes mints, and even a little hint of Shamrock Shake customized with chocolate syrup. So there's more to love. It's mint to be.

1 sleeve (7.6 ounces) Mint Oreos

1 package (8 ounces) cream cheese, softened at room temperature (see page 14)

1 container (8 ounces) Cool Whip, preferably Extra Creamy

½ teaspoon peppermint extract

¼ cup mini chocolate chips, plus more for garnish

Green gel food coloring, as needed

2 Andes Crème de Menthe mints (or more!), shaved lengthwise with vegetable peeler, for garnish

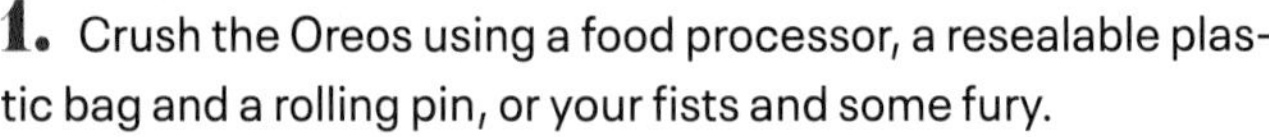

1. Crush the Oreos using a food processor, a resealable plastic bag and a rolling pin, or your fists and some fury.

2. In a large bowl, using an electric hand mixer, whip the cream cheese until it's soft and fluffy, about 2 minutes. Using a spatula, mix in the Cool Whip gently as to not deflate the mixture. *Dip*vide the mixture equally between two medium bowls. In one bowl, mix in the peppermint extract, mini chocolate chips, and a little green food coloring at a time until you reach the desired shade of minty green. Set aside. In the other bowl, gently mix in the Oreo crumbs to combine without deflating. Set aside.

3. To serve, in a clear glass pie plate or a 1-quart serving dish or bowl, layer the two dips in as many layers as you would like, spreading each layer from the center of the dish to the outside to get clean edges. (You can also scoop the dip like ice cream into an ice cream glass for a fun presentation.) When you have the number of layers you're happy with, garnish with more mini chocolate chips and the Andes mint curls.

MOD*IP*FICATIONS: If you have another mint chocolate product you love, try mixing it in!

CHIPPY'S TIPPY

Gel food coloring is the easiest concentrated food dye to find at standard grocery stores. A little goes a long way, and it won't water down the flavor of your dip or make your tongue totally green (probably).

DIPPER MATRIX

STORE-BOUGHT IS FRAN FINE

Thin Mint or Grasshopper cookies
Chocolate wafers
Chocolate biscuits, such as BelVita
Oreo Thins, regular or mint
Chocolate graham crackers
Milano cookies, regular or mint

faq

CAN IT BE MADE IN ADVANCE? Yes, but you may need to thin with milk as it firms up in the fridge.

HOW LONG WILL IT KEEP? Up to a week in the fridge in an airtight container.

DIPPER MATRIX

STORE-BOUGHT IS FRAN FINE

- Fresh fruit, such as apples, strawberries, or bananas
- Oreos or Oreo Thins
- Shortbread cookies
- Graham crackers, plain or chocolate
- Pretzels, peanut butter-filled pretzel nuggets, or pretzel thins

dirt pudding dip

SERVES A BIG DIP PARTY (8 TO 10)

The number of buckets of "worms in dirt" I was served as a treat in the nineties was remarkable. It was the hit of birthday parties and Brownie meetings, sometimes even potted in little cups or actual planters. It was *everything* . . . until it wasn't. It disappeared in the way social media trends do now, and I didn't think about it again until one night when I saw an empty bag of gummy worms on the sidewalk and was hit with a wave of nostalgia. So now, more than two decades later, my dirt pudding drought is over, reuniting me—and now you—with this delightfully weird dessert. Heal your inner child, one mouthful of dirt at a time.

1 package (14.2 ounces) Double Stuf Oreos, regular or gluten-free

4 ounces cream cheese, softened at room temperature (see page 14)

1 box (3.9 ounces) instant chocolate pudding mix

1 cup whole milk

1 container (8 ounces) Cool Whip

Gummy worms, for garnish

1. Crush the Oreos using a food processor, a resealable plastic bag and a rolling pin, or your fists and some fury.

2. In a medium bowl, whip the cream cheese, pudding mix, and milk, using an electric hand mixer (or whisk vigorously by hand; it's arm day) for 2 to 3 minutes, until completely smooth and almost doubled in volume.

3. Mix in 1 cup of the Oreo crumbs, and then gently fold in the Cool Whip with a spatula, lifting it up and over the pudding until the mixture is completely homogenous with no streaks of white.

4. Transfer the pudding into a wide serving bowl, kid-size bucket, or small planter with the bottom hole taped up—get as creative as you want!—and then evenly distribute the remaining Oreo crumbs over the top. Stick gummy worms into the "dirt" and arrange more worms all over the top.

MOD*IP*FICATIONS: You can swap in any flavor of Oreos that speaks to you, or change out the chocolate pudding for chocolate peanut butter.

faq

CAN IT BE MADE IN ADVANCE?
Yes! Let it sit at room temperature for at least 30 minutes before serving, and add a splash of milk to thin it out if it thickens too much in the fridge.

HOW LONG WILL IT KEEP?
Up to 10 days in an airtight container in the fridge.

baileys in a shoe eggnog dip

SERVES A BIG DIP PARTY (8 TO 10)

If this incredibly niche recipe name made you say, "Huh?" then please go to YouTube and search "Old Gregg." Your life will be permanently altered, you may have the desire to buy a tutu, and you'll never be able to watch *The Great British Baking Show* the same way again. Because Old Gregg? That's judge Noel Fielding, back in 2005 when he was part of The Mighty Boosh, a British comedy troupe known for their strange brand of humor.

The whole reason this recipe is in the book is not that I love eggnog. It's that I wanted to spread the gospel about Old Gregg while also making a spike-able dip.

1 box (3.4 ounces) vanilla instant pudding mix

1¼ cups eggnog

¼ cup Baileys Irish Cream

1 teaspoon pure vanilla extract

1 container (8 ounces) Cool Whip

Hefty pinch of kosher salt

Dip confetti: festive sprinkles, crushed-up gingerbread, or a sprinkle of ground cinnamon

1. In a medium bowl, mix together the pudding mix, eggnog, Baileys, and vanilla with an electric hand mixer—or vigorous whisking by hand—for 2 to 3 minutes, until completely smooth and almost doubled in volume.
2. Fold in the Cool Whip—lifting the pudding mixture up and over the whipped topping using a spatula so it is incorporated without losing its airy fluffiness—then add a pinch (or two, tasting in between) of salt to help offset the sweetness.
3. Top with festive sprinkles, crushed-up gingerbread, or a sprinkle of cinnamon.

MOD*IP*FICATIONS: Replace the booze with more eggnog or milk for an alcohol-free version.

CHIPPY'S TIPPY

This uses half the amount of liquid required for instant pudding to keep the dip thick. If your eggnog is particularly thick already, you may need to add a splash of regular milk to split the *dip*ference in texture.

faq

CAN IT BE MADE IN ADVANCE? Yes, but the boozy flavor may get stronger as it sits, so stir in the Baileys right before serving.

HOW LONG WILL IT KEEP? Up to a week in an airtight container in the fridge.

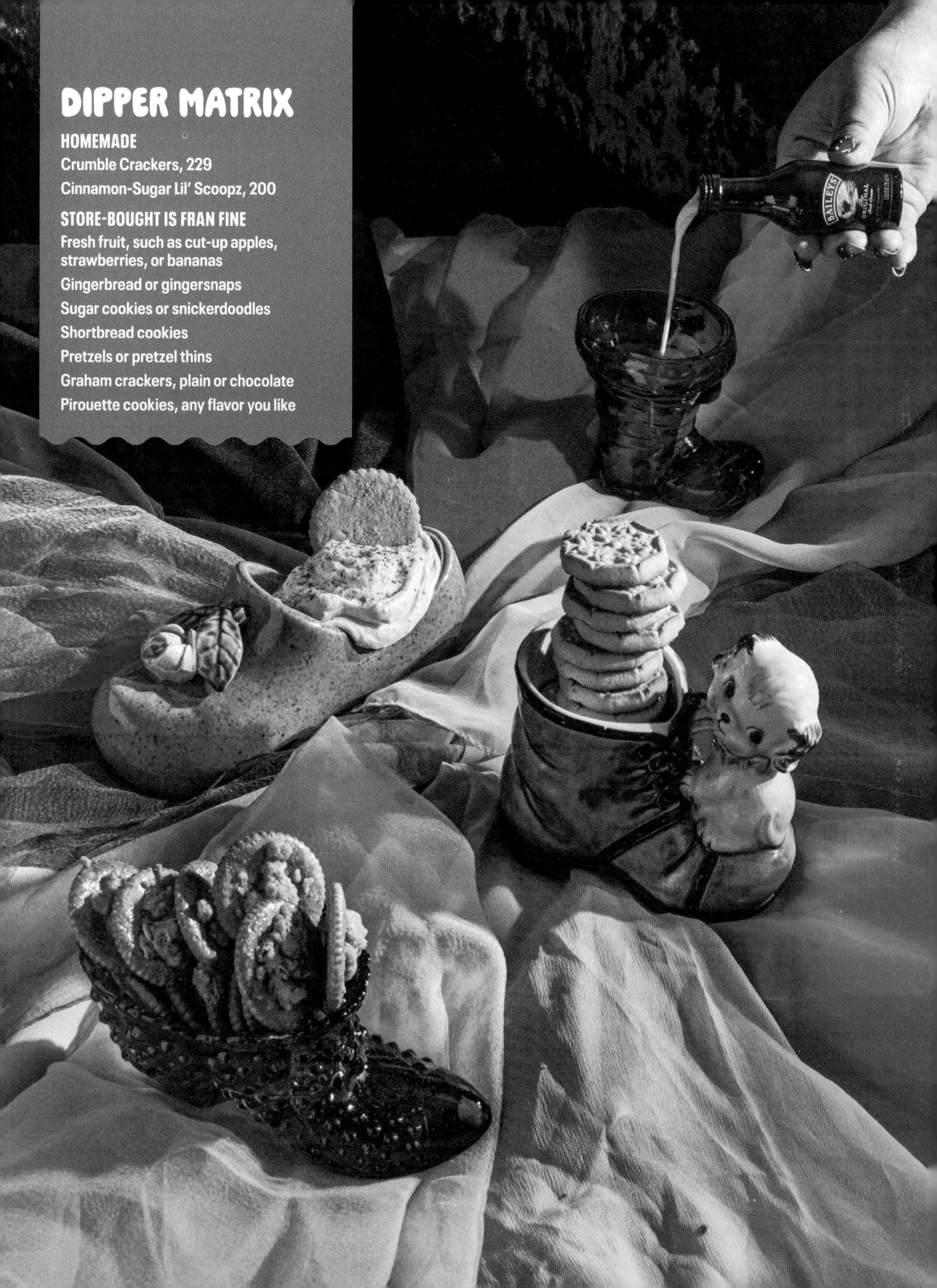

DIPPER MATRIX

HOMEMADE

Crumble Crackers, 229

Cinnamon-Sugar Lil' Scoopz, 200

STORE-BOUGHT IS FRAN FINE

Fresh fruit, such as cut-up apples, strawberries, or bananas

Gingerbread or gingersnaps

Sugar cookies or snickerdoodles

Shortbread cookies

Pretzels or pretzel thins

Graham crackers, plain or chocolate

Pirouette cookies, any flavor you like

strawberry shortcake dip

SERVES A BIG DIP PARTY (8 TO 10)

I love angelic food. I will die on the hill of loving angel hair pasta *and* angel food cake, both of which can soar far above expectations when paired with the right complementary ingredients. For angel food cake, that's always going to be strawberries. Preferably fresh, but the quick jammy strawberry situation in this recipe has been tested off-season with frozen fruit and works like a charm. This dip is made by soaking angel food cake in cream, then whipping it—no straining required—to give it a unique *dips*cosity, gentle flavor, and double the airiness, double the fun. When the strawberry situation gets swirly, it's a feast for the eyes and mouth that is downright heavenly.

1 pound fresh or frozen strawberries

⅓ cup granulated sugar

2 tablespoons freshly squeezed lemon juice

2 cups crumbled angel food cake

1 pint heavy cream

¼ cup powdered sugar

1. In a small saucepan, combine the strawberries, granulated sugar, and lemon juice. If using frozen strawberries, you'll only need 1 tablespoon water; if using fresh, add ¼ cup water. Bring to a boil over medium-high heat, then reduce the heat to a low simmer and cook for 15 to 20 minutes, until the strawberries have softened and almost melted into a jammy consistency. Transfer to a medium bowl and let cool at room temperature for at least 20 minutes, then move to the fridge until completely chilled, about 2 hours or up to overnight. This will keep the whipped cream from melting.

2. In a medium bowl or quart deli container, combine the angel food cake crumbles and heavy cream. Refrigerate for at least 30 minutes to steep, then mash the cake fully into the cream using a fork.

3. Add the powdered sugar to the cream and, using an electric hand mixer—don't be a hero trying to whip cream by hand—whip, starting on low speed and building up to medium, until the mixture holds a soft peak when you turn off the mixer and lift a beater out of the bowl.

When swirling, less is more! Start by dropping dollops of the jammy strawberries on top of the whipped cream base and drag a chopstick or butter knife through both, lifting and wiping off the utensil between swirls.

DIPPER MATRIX

HOMEMADE

Crumble Crackers, 229

Cinnamon-Sugar Lil' Scoopz, 200

STORE-BOUGHT IS FRAN FINE

Fresh fruit, such as apples, strawberries, or bananas

Chocolate-covered strawberries

Waffle cones, broken into pieces

Pretzels—even chocolate-covered!

Shortbread cookies

Graham crackers, plain or chocolate

Pirouette cookies, any flavor you like

Gluten-free crispy coconut rolls

4. Fold in the strawberry jammy situation—lifting the whipped cream up and over the strawberries using a spatula so it is incorporated without losing its airy fluffiness—and transfer to a serving bowl.

faq

CAN IT BE MADE IN ADVANCE? It can, but the whipped cream may deflate a bit, so I wouldn't recommend it.

HOW LONG WILL IT KEEP? A day or two in the fridge due to being mostly whipped cream.

whipped peanut butter cup dip

SERVES A BIG DIP PARTY (8 TO 10)

Many of the *dips*serts in this book could be eaten with a spoon like mousse. This is one of them. With a yogurt base and only ¼ cup powdered sugar in the whole thing, it could even be eaten with granola for breakfast. Peanut butter–chocolate is not a vice for me, it's a virtue. And if you're a fellow PBC fanatic, you'll go nuts for this one. It's also a chance to be artistic. Refer to the #SendDipPics section (page 19) for tips on mastering your layering, dollops, or swirls—it's a dip dealer's choice on how to style it. And grab a bag of Oreos and channel your inner Hallie and Annie!

½ cup whole milk plain yogurt

½ cup creamy peanut butter, preferably Jif or Skippy

½ teaspoon pure vanilla extract

¼ cup powdered sugar

Pinch of kosher salt

1 container (8 ounces) Cool Whip

¼ cup mini semisweet chocolate chips or chocolate shavings, plus more for garnish

1 tablespoon butter, preferably salted

1 teaspoon water

2 tablespoons roughly chopped roasted salted peanuts, for garnish

1. In a medium bowl, combine the yogurt, peanut butter, vanilla, powdered sugar, and salt with an electric hand mixer on low (or by hand with a whisk). Add the Cool Whip and mix in gently so it does not deflate, and then spoon half of the mixture into a separate medium bowl.

2. In a small bowl, combine the chocolate chips, butter, and 1 teaspoon water and melt in 30-second increments in the microwave, stirring in between, until fully melted. Let cool for 5 minutes, then fold the mixture into one bowl of the peanut butter mixture until the whole thing is smooth and uniformly chocolaty in color.

3. To serve, have fun layering the peanut butter and chocolate layers in a glass bowl; make a yin-yang situation with one peanut butter and one chocolate side; or swirl them together using a butter knife. Garnish with chocolate chips and chopped peanuts.

DIPPER MATRIX

HOMEMADE

Ritzy Crispy Treat Chips, 230

Crumble Crackers, 229

These Bagel Pretzel Bites Have Everything, 194 . . . without the everything seasoning!

STORE-BOUGHT IS FRAN FINE

Oreos or Oreo Thins, because I believe in magic in a young girl's heart!

Fresh fruit, such as apples, strawberries, or bananas

Waffle cones, broken into pieces

Pretzels, chocolate-covered pretzels, or pretzel thins

Graham crackers, plain or chocolate

Pirouette cookies, any flavor you like

Milano cookies

Shortbread cookies

MOD*IPF*ICATIONS: Swap out semisweet for dark or milk chocolate, or use crunchy peanut butter for more texture!

faq

CAN IT BE MADE IN ADVANCE? Yes, and it is the perfect consistency even after sitting in the fridge.

HOW LONG WILL IT KEEP? Up to 10 days in an airtight container in the fridge.

making dip HAPPEN!

the dippers!

Like every rose has its thorn, every dip has its dipper. You probably have noticed by now that *Big Dip Energy* has big choose-your-own-adventure energy. Every dip can be mixed and matched with the dippers in this section to find your ideal combination, whether that's dipping fried cheese into cheese (Crispy Paneer Dipsticks, page 221), *carb*ing your enthusiasm (These Bagel Pretzel Bites Have Everything, page 194), getting your scoop on (Wonton Lil' Scoopz, page 200), or somewhere in between. You won't find any recipes for tortilla chips, potato chips, or anything that is convenient and *dip*pendable to buy ready-made, because store-bought is, and will always be, Fran Fine.

garlic-kissed crostini

MAKES 16

SERVES A LIL' GET-TOGETHER (4 TO 6)

This is a kiss from a different kind of rose . . . it's more like a kiss from a clove on a piece of olive oil–toasted bread. This style of skillet crostini takes inspiration from popular tapas treat pan con tomate, in which warm toast is rubbed with a clove of raw garlic to impart just enough garlickiness.

½ a baguette, cut into ¼-inch slices on an extreme diagonal, or 4 slices of your favorite sandwich bread

Olive oil, as needed

3 garlic cloves, halved

Kosher salt, to taste

Black pepper, to taste

1. Heat a large skillet or griddle over medium heat. Generously drizzle the bread with oil on both sides and toast for 2 to 3 minutes per side, until golden brown. Set the toast aside on a plate to cool until you won't burn yourself handling it, then rub each piece with a halved garlic clove; the flavor should melt into all the nooks and carb crannies. Sprinkle with salt and some cranks of black pepper.

2. Baguette slices can be left whole for dramatically large crostini dippers that you can rip 'n' dip (see page 26 for dipping techniques) or halved lengthwise to make dipsticks. Toast can be cut into thirds or quarters *dip*ending on how big you want your crostini or dipsticks to be!

faq

CAN THEY BE MADE IN ADVANCE? Yes!

HOW LONG WILL THEY LAST? Store leftovers in a paper towel–lined airtight container at room temperature for up to 3 days. They should remain crisp, but you can also re-crisp in a skillet over medium-low heat for a minute or two per side or in a toaster oven.

shortcut garlic knots
(or garlic knot wreath!)

MAKES 16 KNOTS OR 1 WREATH

SERVES A LIL' GET-TOGETHER (4 TO 6)

"Forget me knot," says the humble garlic knot. It's time to recognize how game-changing and important garlic knots can be in the big dipper universe! Make them as individual little dippers or a full wreath for a festive *dips*play with Pizza Your Way Dip (page 79).

All-purpose flour, for kneading

1 ball (1 pound) of fresh or thawed frozen pizza dough

½ cup (1 stick) salted butter

2 garlic cloves, grated

2 tablespoons Knorr Garlic & Herb Sauce Mix (if you're not making pizza dip, page 79, and don't have it on hand, just add another clove of grated garlic)

2 tablespoons freshly grated parmesan cheese

2 tablespoons thicc-cut chives (see page 22)

1. Preheat the oven to 375°F. Line a sheet pan with parchment paper and set aside.

2. On a floured surface, knead the dough a few times so it's more pliable and elastic, then cut the ball into quarters. Cut each of those quarters into quarters so you have 16 pieces.

3. Think back to your days of playing with Play-Doh and use your palms to roll each of those pieces into a "snake" about 5 inches long, or long enough that you feel comfortable to tie it into a simple knot. (No bunny ears needed—just one loop!) Transfer the knots to the prepared pan, setting them about 2 inches apart.

4. (If making a garlic knot wreath, trace a pie plate on a sheet of parchment paper—or draw a 9-inch circumference circle by hand—and place the parchment paper in the sheet pan. Arrange the knots on and around that line, snuggled close like the grandparents in *Willy Wonka & the Chocolate Factory*, and after baking, they will perfectly rest as a wreath around the edge of a pie plate full of pizza dip.)

5. Melt the butter in a small saucepan over medium-low heat or in a medium bowl in the microwave. Stir in the garlic, Knorr mix, and parmesan. Using a pastry brush or a small spoon, brush or drizzle about half the garlic butter mixture over the knots.

6. Bake the knots for 8 to 10 minutes, until golden brown; a wreath may take up to 12 minutes to fully bake. While it's hot, drizzle or brush the remaining garlic butter all over the wreath so it sparkles festively. Let it cool for at least 10 minutes on the tray, if you can bear it, before serving so no one burns themselves! Top with the chives.

faq

CAN THEY BE MADE IN ADVANCE? Yes, but it's *knot* recommended for the garlic knot wreath, as it is fragile and you risk breaking it. Reheat regular knots in a toaster oven or conventional oven at 300°F for about 5 minutes, or until warmed through and with a slightly crisp exterior.

HOW LONG WILL THEY KEEP? Store leftovers in an airtight container in the fridge for up to 4 days.

mini ham and cheese croissants

MAKES 20

SERVES A LIL' GET-TOGETHER (4 TO 6)

What if you could eat pigs in a blanket for breakfast? That's really what ham and cheese croissants are to me. They're my favorite French pastry, and this is a cheater's version using store-bought crescent dough. They are apples to oranges, meaning they're different but both great, and I'm not here to ask you to laminate your own dough at home in a dip cookbook.

1 tube (8 ounces) crescent dough sheet or rolls

4 slices of deli ham, each cut into 5 strips

4 slices deli sharp cheddar or Swiss cheese (or a combination), each cut into 5 strips

1. Preheat the oven to 375°F. Line a sheet pan with parchment paper and set aside.

2. Unroll the tube of crescent dough onto a cutting board. If it's a sheet, cut it in half crosswise then in 10 strips lengthwise. If it's the precut rolls, pinch and press the seams together with your index fingers until the perforations are sealed, then cut as above. You should have 20 small strips of dough.

3. Place 1 piece of ham and 1 piece of cheese inside each strip of dough (ripping, folding, and stacking as needed to fit) and roll it all together into a baby croissant. Arrange on the prepared pan, about 1 inch apart. Bake for 8 to 10 minutes, until evenly golden brown. Let cool for about 5 minutes before serving.

CHIPPY'S TIPPY

If you have a choice, buy the crescent dough sheet. It's so much easier to work with!

faq

CAN THEY BE MADE IN ADVANCE? Yes! They can be served fridge-cold or reheated at 300°F for about 5 minutes, or until warmed through with melty cheese.

HOW LONG WILL THEY KEEP? Store leftovers in an airtight container in the fridge for up to 4 days.

these bagel pretzel bites have everything

MAKES 40

SERVES A BIG DIP PARTY (8 TO 10)

These fluffy bites are cooked like pretzels but seasoned like bagels. Both get a boil-then-bake method anyway, so it just made sense to combine them into a super carb. The first dip you should make them with is New York's Hottest Club Sandwich Dip (page 125), because Stefon would want you to have *everything*.

1 ball (1 pound) of fresh or thawed frozen pizza dough

½ cup baking soda

1 egg

1½ tablespoons water

Everything bagel seasoning, sesame seeds, chopped dried onion, chopped dried garlic, flaky salt, ground black pepper, or other seasonings of choice

1. Preheat the oven to 425°F. Line a sheet pan with parchment paper and set aside.

2. Cut the pizza dough into 4 pieces and roll each piece into about a foot-long log. Cut each log into 10 pieces.

3. In a large pot, bring 3 quarts of water to a boil. Lower the heat to medium-low and add the baking soda; it will violently bubble up! Stir to dissolve the baking soda, then return the heat to high to bring to a boil. Add the dough nuggets in batches of about a dozen at a time—making sure to stir gently so they don't stick together in the process—and boil until they float, 30 to 45 seconds. Using a strainer or spider, transfer to a tea towel or paper towels to dry, then arrange on the prepared pan about ½ inch apart. Repeat with remaining dough; you can bake two pans at a time, arranging the racks in the top third and lower third of the oven. If you're only baking one pan at a time, arrange the rack in the middle of the oven.

4. Whisk together the egg and 1½ tablespoons water in a small bowl. Dunk or brush each nugget with the egg wash, then sprinkle with crunchy seeds and spices of your choice. Bake for 10 to 12 minutes, until golden brown.

CHIPPY'S TIPPY

Ask your favorite pizza place if you can buy a ball of their dough and then invite friends over and make an assembly line to have pretzel day happen faster.

faq

CAN THEY BE MADE IN ADVANCE?
Yes!

HOW LONG WILL THEY KEEP?
Store leftovers in an airtight container at room temperature for up to 4 days. Add a slice of bread to the container to soak up extra moisture so it gets stale instead of the pretzels.

double sesame mochi flatbreads

MAKES 16

SERVES A LIL' GET-TOGETHER (4 TO 6)

This gluten-free bread is made with glutinous rice flour (a confusing term, I know), aka mochi flour, that makes the inside chewy and tender. Rolled in sesame seeds and griddled, these pillowy-yet-toothsome pockets are flavorful but also neutral enough to be used for savory or sweet applications.

2 cups glutinous rice flour (mochiko), such as Koda Farms

1 teaspoon kosher salt

2 tablespoons toasted sesame oil

1 cup plus 2 tablespoons warm-to-the-touch water

½ cup toasted white sesame seeds

½ cup toasted black sesame seeds

¼ cup neutral oil, such as vegetable or canola, for shallow-frying

1. Line a sheet pan with parchment paper and set aside.

2. In a large bowl, combine the rice flour, salt, sesame oil, and 1 cup of the water using your hands. It will be sticky and messy at first, but as you work, it will come together into a smooth ball. Knead until it's smooth and pliable, about 5 minutes. Cut the dough into 16 pieces—it's easiest to cut the dough into 8 pieces, then cut each of those into 2 pieces. Roll each piece into a ball, press it into a flattened disc that is 2½ to 3 inches wide, and set it on the prepared pan. Repeat the process with the remaining pieces, about ½-inch apart so they don't stick together.

3. Set up a station with the remaining 2 tablespoons of the water in one small bowl and both sesame seeds mixed together in a separate small bowl. Working one at a time, dip a disk into the water, shake off the excess, and press into the sesame seeds to coat fully. Return to the prepared sheet pan while you finish coating the rest.

4. Heat a large skillet (preferably nonstick) over medium heat for 3 minutes. Pour in 2 tablespoons of the neutral oil and place as many flatbreads as you can fit without crowding the pan. Cook for about 5 minutes, until one side is golden brown, then flip and cook for 2 to 3 minutes on the other side, until also golden. Repeat until all the flatbreads are cooked, and be sure to eat at least one while it's warm for the best experience.

CHIPPY'S TIPPY

This is ideal for a rip 'n' dip—see page 26 for more on this dipping technique.

faq

CAN THEY BE MADE IN ADVANCE? Yes. Reheat in a toaster oven for crunch, or wrap in a damp paper towel and microwave for 30 seconds for more of a pillowy-soft experience.

HOW LONG WILL THEY KEEP? Store in an airtight container at room temperature for up to 4 days. Add a slice of bread to the container to soak up extra moisture so it gets stale instead of the flatbreads.

hexagon dippers

MAKES 20

SERVES A BIG DIP PARTY (8 TO 10)

Honey, I shrunk the Crunchwrap Supreme. And this hexagonal homage to Taco Bell's signature item is not supreme at all—it's actually empty inside. But in this case, it's what's on the outside that counts, because these little dippers are almost too cute to eat yet they are sturdy enough to get through all the layers of Drive-Thru Taco 7-Layer Dip (page 128)! This is made to be a fun accent dipper, served alongside tortilla chips or another store-bought dipper to offset the time it takes to fold each little hexagon.

5 large flour tortillas, ideally 12-inch for the most bang for your buck

1 tablespoon neutral oil, such as vegetable or canola

Kosher salt

1. On a cutting board or large plate, using a 3-inch cookie cutter or a cup with approximately that diameter, punch out mini tortillas from the flour tortillas. (You should get about 4 per 12-inch tortilla.) You can do all the tortillas at once, or take a break halfway through to start folding and cooking.

2. To fold your hexagons, put some water in a small bowl and use your finger to dab it into the center of a mini tortilla. Fold from the outside into the center six times so it forms a hexagon, applying firm pressure after each fold so it sticks to the middle. Put a little water inside the final fold, press to seal, and then turn the hexagon over to rest seam side down on a plate or sheet pan while you work on the rest so it's less likely to pop open. Repeat with the remaining tortillas.

3. In a large skillet or griddle over medium heat, heat the neutral oil. Add the little hexagons seam side down and cook for 2 minutes per side, until golden brown on both sides. Sprinkle with salt.

CHIPPY'S TIPPY

Use leftover bits of tortillas to make chilaquiles or irregular-shaped dippers!

faq

CAN THEY BE MADE IN ADVANCE? No.

HOW LONG WILL THEY KEEP? Leftovers risk falling apart or getting stale, but you could punch out your mini tortillas in advance and keep them in the fridge until you're ready to fold and cook.

wonton lil' scoopz

MAKES 48 (OR MORE)

SERVES A BIG DIP PARTY (8 TO 10)

The "scoop"-style chip has always been my platonic ideal of a dipper, but no one in the packaged food game has made them out of wonton wrappers . . . yet. This started as a dipper custom-made for Crab Rangoon Dip (page 140), but evolved into a versatile chip for many dips—with and without Asian flavor profiles, and savory *and* sweet, especially with cinnamon-sugar dusted on top.

Nonstick cooking spray

1 package round wonton or dumpling wrappers

Kosher salt

1. Preheat the oven to 375°F. Grease the cups of two mini muffin tin trays (24-cup capacity each) with nonstick cooking spray. Remove your wonton wrappers from the packaging and place on a small plate underneath a damp paper towel to keep them from drying out as you work. (FYI: There are typically about 60 wrappers per package, so it's up to you whether you want to make the full 60 with another partial batch or stop at 48!)

2. Gently press a wonton wrapper into each mini muffin cup, being careful not to break them. As the wrappers are bigger than the cups, they will look slightly squished and crinkled together in spots, but that's okay. It will add texture once they bake! Spritz the tops with more cooking spray and sprinkle with salt.

3. Bake for 10 to 15 minutes, until lightly golden brown all around. They will continue to cook from residual heat after coming out of the oven, so pull them before they get too crispy.

4. Sprinkle with a little more salt when they first come out of the oven, and then you can either dip them or fill them with dip for easy-to-serve appetizers.

VARIATION: Cinnamon-Sugar Lil' Scoopz: Mix together 1 tablespoon of cinnamon with ¼ cup sugar (white or packed light brown) in a small bowl. Sprinkle thoroughly over Lil' Scoopz just after they come out of the oven.

CHIPPY'S TIPPY

If you let wonton wrappers sit at room temperature for at least five minutes before using, they are less likely to split or crack.

faq

CAN THEY BE MADE IN ADVANCE? Yes!

HOW LONG WILL THEY KEEP? Store leftovers in a paper towel–lined airtight container at room temperature for up to a week. They will stay crunchy this way for snacking, and the paper towel will soak up any moisture and grease.

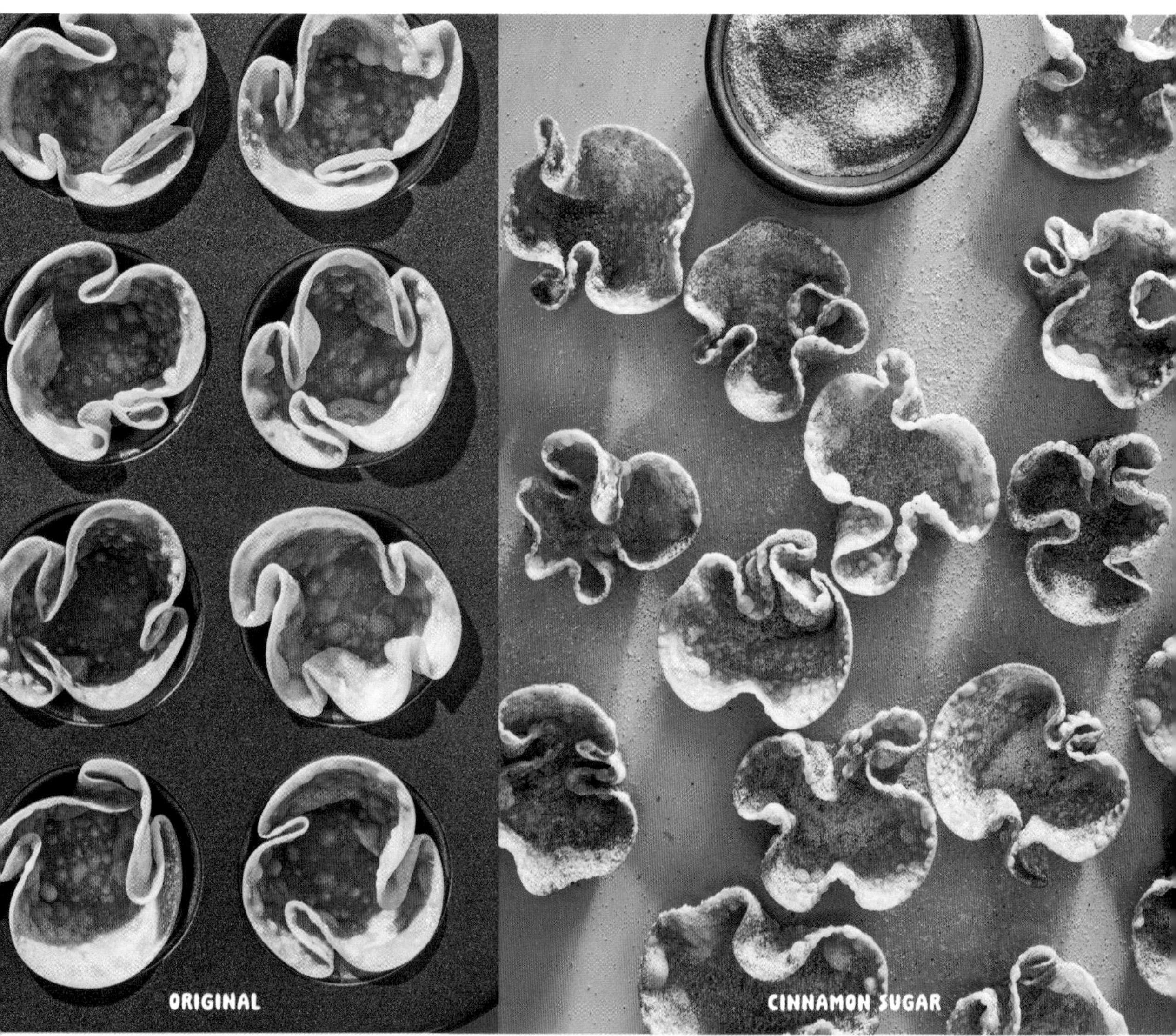

phyllo lil' scoopz

MAKES 15

SERVES A LIL' GET-TOGETHER (4 TO 6)

Phyllo cups exist in the frozen section, but when working on this recipe, I found they were often sold out, they were expensive per cup, and there was no room for customization. The homemade versions are almost soothing to make as you paint butter over thin sheets of dough, stack them, and smush them into mini muffin tins to make edible cups.

6 sheets frozen phyllo pastry, thawed

¼ cup (½ stick) salted butter, melted

Kosher salt

1. Preheat the oven to 375°F.
2. On a clean countertop or cutting board, lay down a sheet of the phyllo dough. Brush butter from edge to edge, really saturating the sheet with butter (this will help them be lighter and crispier after baking, similar to making a croissant but without having to make the dough). Lay another sheet of dough on top and repeat, for six total layers. Brush the top layer with a little extra butter and sprinkle a pinch of kosher salt.
3. Cut the dough lengthwise (the hot dog way) into thirds, then cut those strips into 5 pieces each. (You'll have slightly smaller than 3 x 3-inch squares.) Press each stack of dough into a mini muffin well, filling 15 of the wells.
4. Bake for 10 minutes, until lightly golden brown. Remove from the oven and let them cool in the muffin tin for a few minutes before removing carefully to a plate to either dip in or fill with dip!

CHIPPY'S TIPPY

Customize these by sprinkling sesame seeds, everything seasoning, cinnamon sugar, or your favorite spice blend as desired between the dough and butter layers.

faq

CAN THEY BE MADE IN ADVANCE? No.

HOW LONG WILL THEY KEEP? It's not ideal, but they can last a day if you store leftovers in a paper towel–lined airtight container at room temperature. Phyllo is fragile and gets soggy quickly, but you can pop them in a 300°F oven for about 5 minutes to re-crisp.

rainbow dumpling chips

MAKES 30 (OR MORE)

SERVES A BIG DIP PARTY (8 TO 10)

I affectionately call my friend Jen Kwong "Rainbow Dumpling Brite" because we met due to her colorful handmade dumplings. During the pandemic, she started her business, Kwong Shop, selling beautiful and delicious vegetarian dumplings out of her home. A few years after we met, she finally showed me how she does it, with a technique to make even store-bought dumpling wrappers colorful. We used them to make these dumpling chips and Rainbow Crab Rangoon for my *Cosmopolitan* column, "Doing the Least with Alyse." This is a new version of tie-dyeing or dyeing Easter eggs with friends, a fun arts-and-crafts project to tackle at a dinner party.

We opted to make half-moon dumpling shapes instead of more commonly seen triangular wonton chips, but they can also be served as giant circular chips that guests can dip 'n' snap (see page 26 for that technique). These chips are shallow-fried, but you can also air-fry or even use them to make Wonton Lil' Scoopz (page 200).

30 round dumpling or wonton wrappers (about half a 12-ounce package)

3 different colors of gel food coloring

2 cups neutral oil, such as vegetable or canola, if shallow-frying, or nonstick cooking spray, if air-frying

Kosher salt

Ground spices, such as garlic powder, onion powder, seasoned salt, ranch seasoning, or chili powder (optional; play around to complement the dip you're pairing with!)

EQUIPMENT

Small food-safe paintbrushes of varying thicknesses

1. To start, you have to choose whether you want these to aesthetically look like dumplings. If you do, on a cutting board, cut the wonton wrappers in half at a curve across the middle so that half the stack looks like half-moon dumplings. The other half will be more of an oval-ish blob, but that's okay—equally delicious. If not, just leave 'em whole, and either way, remember to cover them with a damp paper towel as you work so they don't dry out on you.

2. Now it's time to make it rain(bow)! Set up your painting station with either a large plate or platter or a sheet pan to paint on. Arrange as many dumpling wrappers as will comfortably fit on your surface of choice without touching so the colors don't run together.

(continued)

3. In a few small bowls, add a few squirts of gel food coloring (which is very concentrated) and a drizzle of water to thin into paintable consistency. Have a small bowl of water ready nearby, to clean your brush when you switch colors. A little food coloring goes a *long* way—the color can be as intense or light as you'd like by reducing or adding water to the food coloring. Wet your brush in the water bowl, then paint just one side of the wrappers in any style you'd like, with as many colors as you'd like. It's best to do more color-blocking than attempting to marble your first time, but as you gain comfort you can try different techniques, like splattering on with brushes or swirling two colors together on the wrapper. Just remember to dip your brush in water to switch colors, or use multiple brushes.

4. You can either paint them all at once on multiple plates, or paint, then fry, then paint again until you've made the amount of chips you need. This recipe calls for using half a package of wrappers, which is about 30 full-size circular chips or 60 half-moon chips, but you can keep going for as many chips as you need. (Psst . . . it's a good idea to invite friends over to make this a collaborative, fun, "Paint and Dip Night" so you aren't *Dip*casso-ing all by yourself.)

5. Once your dumpling chips are painted, it's time to fry, fry away. Set a wire rack over a sheet pan covered with paper towels off to the side of the stove, and have a tiny bowl of salt ready to season once they get out of the skillet.

6. To fry on the stove, heat the oil in a wide, high-sided skillet or wok over medium heat for at least 5 minutes. To test if the oil is ready to fry, put a wooden chopstick or the handle of a wooden spoon into the oil; if it bubbles immediately and rapidly, you're ready to fry. You can also put a small piece of plain dumpling wrapper in the oil and see if it bubbles up and fries right away.

7. Carefully lower a few chips in, one at a time, releasing them away from you into the oil. Fry until they turn golden brown on the edges; it will take just about 1 minute. Using a strainer or spider, remove the chips from the oil to the prepared sheet pan to drain. Sprinkle immediately with kosher salt and/or your favorite spices, if using. Repeat to cook batches of 5 to 7 chips at a time, depending on the size of the pan.

CHIPPY'S TIPPY

Gel food coloring—even the cheap stuff from the grocery store—is a nonnegotiable. It's concentrated and so the wrappers will retain vibrant color even after being chip-i-fied.

8. If you'd rather air-fry, spray the air fryer basket with nonstick cooking spray and arrange an even layer of dyed dumpling wrappers in the basket, making sure they don't touch. Spray thoroughly with more cooking spray and air-fry at 350°F for 2 minutes. Shake the basket and continue cooking for 1 to 2 minutes, until the chips are golden brown.

9. Sprinkle with salt or your favorite spices when they come out. Repeat to air-fry the rest of the chips.

faq

CAN THEY BE MADE IN ADVANCE? Yes!

HOW LONG WILL THEY KEEP? Store leftovers in a paper towel–lined airtight container at room temperature for up to a week. They will stay crunchy this way for snacking, and the paper towel will soak up any moisture and grease.

crispy rice dipsticks

MAKES 18

SERVES A BIG DIP PARTY (8 TO 10)

Crispy rice is normally only associated with spicy tuna, but you don't need to be at a sushi restaurant to enjoy this delightful delicacy. These are normally served as bricks of deep-fried goodness, but this version is a thinner stick that is still sturdy enough for dipping, and shallow-fried so it's overall golden brown but not as oily or messy to make. They do require at least 4 hours of chilling time to set up in the fridge, so plan in advance if you want to make them.

2 cups short-grain rice or sushi rice

2 cups water

1 teaspoon kosher salt

2 teaspoons sugar

2 tablespoons unseasoned rice vinegar

2 tablespoons furikake

2 cups neutral oil, such as vegetable or canola, for shallow-frying

Seaweed snacks or nori, for wrapping (optional)

1. Line a 13 x 9-inch sheet pan or a similar-size baking dish with parchment paper overhanging on the two short sides of the pan to form handles for later. Set aside.

2. Wash the rice by swishing around in a bowl of water and straining it in a colander up to three times, until the water runs clear. Combine the rinsed rice with 2 cups water, salt, and sugar in a medium saucepan and bring to a boil over high heat. Cover, reduce to a simmer, and cook for 20 minutes, until all the water is evaporated and the rice is tender when you sneak a bite. Fluff the rice, then cover and let sit for 10 minutes to steam.

3. Spread the rice across the prepared sheet pan, and then evenly drizzle on the rice vinegar and sprinkle on the furikake. Mix with a spatula to combine, then press the rice into the pan, pushing it to fill the pan evenly to the edges. Lay another piece of parchment paper on top and set another quarter sheet pan or a similarly sized, flat-bottomed pan on top to press it as flat as possible.

4. Transfer this setup to the fridge, set a couple unopened cans or other heavy items on the top sheet pan to weigh it down, and chill for at least 4 hours and up to overnight.

(continued)

These can be cooked at 400°F in an air fryer after being coated with oil or cooking spray, but they'll never get quite as crispy as shallow-frying, even after 30 minutes.

5. Remove the rice from the pan using the parchment paper Remove the rice from the pan using the parchment paper handles you made before and transfer the whole thing to a cutting board. Cut the rice into 1-inch-wide strips crosswise (across the longer side), then cut the strips crosswise in half, to make 18 total pieces.

6. In a wide, high-sided skillet or wok, heat the oil over medium heat for at least 5 minutes. To test if the oil is ready to fry, put a wooden chopstick or the handle of a wooden spoon into the oil; if it bubbles immediately and rapidly, it's ready. Add the dipsticks and shallow-fry them until golden brown and crispy, 4 to 6 minutes per side, working in batches so the rice is able to fry, not steam.

7. Wrap the dipsticks in pieces of seaweed snacks or nori for more of a sushi roll (Spicy California Roll Guacamole, page 135) or musubi vibe (Deviled Spam Musubi Dip, page 153).

faq

CAN THEY BE MADE IN ADVANCE? Yes, but they are better fried just before serving if possible, and don't wrap in nori if you will be storing in the fridge or they will get soggy.

HOW LONG WILL THEY KEEP? Store leftovers in a paper towel-lined airtight container in the fridge for up to 3 days. They will stay crispy even when fridge-cold, and the paper towel will soak up any moisture and grease.

CALIFORNIA ROLL GUACAMOLE, HERE WE COMEEEE! PAGE 135

pasta la vista chips

MAKES ½ POUND

SERVES A BIG DIP PARTY (8 TO 10)

I've had fried pasta at Olive Garden, but I didn't bring it into my dip setup until recently. My favorite shape to use is Cascatelli, invented by Dan Pashman of *The Sporkful* podcast. It has copious ridges and swoops that get ultra crispy and can be filled with dip to the max. But for a wider dipper option, I also like paccheri, which are wide-yet-stout tubes (aren't we all?), or rigatoni. They may not stay totally tubular after frying (squish happens) but some can be *filled with dip* if they do stay open for business.

Kosher salt

½ pound pasta of your choice, preferably a shape with lots of ridges

2 tablespoons olive oil

1. Preheat your oven or air fryer to 400°F.

2. Bring a large pot of water to a boil, add 1 tablespoon kosher salt, and cook the pasta according to the package directions until al dente (a little toothsome bite). Drain and rinse the pasta, then dry it thoroughly with a tea towel. Transfer to a large bowl and toss with the oil.

3. Arrange in the basket of an air fryer or on a parchment-lined sheet pan in one even layer (try to make sure there are no clumps stuck together; you may need to do batches) and cook at 400°F for 5 minutes in the air fryer or 15 minutes in the oven. Toss, then cook for 2 minutes more if not crispy and golden enough, but be mindful that they do get crispier as they sit and you don't want to break a tooth! The idea is for them to be crispy yet toothsome, not brittle.

CHIPPY'S TIPPY

These dippers are kept neutral-flavored on purpose, but you can sprinkle on your favorite spices or grated cheese just after cooking, if you'd like to punch 'em up.

faq

CAN THEY BE MADE IN ADVANCE? Yes!

HOW LONG WILL THEY KEEP? Store leftovers in a paper towel–lined airtight container at room temperature for up to 4 days. They will stay crunchy this way for snacking, and the paper towel will soak up any moisture and grease.

crispanthemum onion petals

MAKES ABOUT 32 PETALS

SERVES A BIG DIP PARTY (8 TO 10)

I love Outback Steakhouse's iconic Bloomin' Onion, which I nicknamed a "*Crisp*anthemum" because it looks like a big stinky flower. But making a whole fried onion is almost as scary as deep-frying a turkey, so Honey, I Shrunk the Bloomin' Onion! These onion petal dippers (the new petal pushers?) are quick to fry, crispy all around, and already a scoop shape to dip into Bloom Bloom Room Onion Dip (page 45) *and* they have the same seasonings as the dip so you get an extra boom of flavor. (Or should I say *bloom* of flavor?) This is the only acceptable form of double dipping!

1 large sweet onion

1 cup tempura batter mix, or 1 cup all-purpose flour, ½ cup cornstarch, and ½ teaspoon baking powder

Kosher salt

1 teaspoon paprika

1 teaspoon garlic powder

1 teaspoon onion powder

½ teaspoon dried oregano

16 cranks black pepper

¼ teaspoon cayenne pepper

1 cup ice-cold club soda or sparkling water

2 cups neutral oil, such as vegetable or canola, for deep-frying

½ cup all-purpose flour, for dusting the onion petals before battering

1. Line a sheet pan with paper towels, and set a wire cooling rack over the paper towels. Set aside.

2. To make the petals, first cut off the root end of the onion. Slice the onion in half lengthwise, then set it cut side down and cut the halved onion into quarters. Separate the onion layers to make "petals" and repeat with the other onion half. Set petals aside while you make the batter.

3. In a medium bowl, whisk together the tempura mix, 1 teaspoon salt, and the paprika, garlic powder, onion powder, oregano, black pepper, and cayenne.

4. Pour the club soda into an ice-filled 2-cup measuring cup. Let it sit to chill for a minute, then remove the ice or strain the water into another measuring cup to get ¾ cup cold bubbly water. Gently whisk the cold water into the dry mix for about 30 seconds, taking care not to overmix—some small clumps

CHIPPY'S TIPPY

You can cut your onion petals smaller—each half into sixths instead of quarters—if you'd like to have more petals, or if your onion is a BFO (Big Friendly Onion).

I WANT YOU IN MY BLOOM BLOOM ROOM ONION DIP (PAGE 45)

are okay and will make the end result better. Set aside to rest and re-whisk gently just before dipping the petals.

5. In a large saucepan, high-sided skillet, or wok, heat the oil over medium-high heat for about 5 minutes. Dip a wooden chopstick or the handle of a wooden spoon into the oil to test the temperature—if it bubbles rapidly, you're ready to fry!

6. In a second medium bowl, add the flour. About a handful at a time, toss the onion petals in the flour to lightly dredge, shaking off any excess. Add the dredged petals to a slotted spoon or spider and dip into the batter bowl, which will allow them to get coated and the excess to drip off. This may seem tedious, but add each piece one at a time gently into the oil so it can start to bubble and not stick to the other pieces, which would happen if you tried to add that whole spoonful at a time! You can fry about 8 pieces per batch, cooking for 3 to 5 minutes, turning occasionally with chopsticks or metal tongs, until the batter is golden brown on all sides.

7. Using a slotted spoon, spider, or tongs, remove the *crisp*-anthemum onion petals from the oil and let drain on the paper towel–lined sheet pan. Repeat with the remaining batches of petals. Immediately sprinkle with salt so it adheres to the petals, then get ready to take a dip! These are best eaten hot, but okay to sit out at a party for an hour or so before they start getting limp.

8. Now make Bloom Bloom Room Onion Dip (page 45) and you're ready for a garden of eatin'.

faq

CAN THEY BE MADE IN ADVANCE? No, not ideally.

HOW LONG WILL THEY KEEP? If frying the day of, you can keep them warm in a 200°F oven on a wire rack over a sheet pan, or let sit at room temperature and refry, or air-fry at 350°F for 3 to 5 minutes, to get crispy again.

tantalizing tempura

MAKES ABOUT 25 PIECES

SERVES A LIL' GET-TOGETHER (4 TO 6)

Other than becoming dip royalty and hosting the most fabulous dip-centric parties, I hope your biggest takeaway from *Big Dip Energy* is to get over your fear of frying! Buy a splatter screen if you're worried about hot oil spitting at you, and use a deep saucepan or skillet and long tongs to keep your appendages safe from burns. I hope this tantalizing tempura will tempt you to tackle the terrifying thought of hot oil and tickle your fancy. (A lot of alliteration went into that plea, so please listen.) This lighter-than-air batter can be shortcut with tempura batter mix from the store, or you can make your own with three common ingredients (flour, cornstarch, and baking powder). Both use either club soda or sparkling water to keep things light 'n' crispy for fried food that won't weigh you down—especially after it's been dipped into something delectable.

1 cup tempura batter mix, or 1 cup all-purpose flour, ½ cup cornstarch, and ½ teaspoon baking powder

Kosher salt

1 cup ice-cold club soda or sparkling water

3 cups neutral oil, such as vegetable or canola, for frying

½ cup all-purpose flour

VEGETABLE OPTIONS

One batch of batter will coat about 2 pounds of cut vegetables. Mix and match from these!

1 bunch (about 1½ pounds) broccoli, stem removed and crown separated into 1-inch-wide florets, or 1 bag (12 ounces) precut broccoli florets

1 head (about 1½ pounds) cauliflower, stem and core trimmed and crown separated into 1-inch-wide florets, or 1 bag (12 ounces) precut cauliflower florets

¼ pound green beans, trimmed

¼ pound mixed mushrooms, such as shiitake caps and oyster

1. Line a sheet pan with paper towels, and set a wire cooling rack over the towels. Set aside.

2. In a medium bowl, whisk together the tempura batter mix and 1 teaspoon salt. Pour the club soda into an ice-filled 2-cup measuring cup. Let it sit to chill for a minute, then remove the ice or strain the water into another measuring cup to get ¾ cup cold bubbly water. Gently whisk the cold water into the dry mix for about 30 seconds, taking care not to overmix—some small clumps are okay and will make the end result better. Set aside to rest and re-whisk gently just before dipping your vegetables.

3. In a large saucepan, high-sided skillet, or wok, heat the oil over medium-high heat for about 5 minutes. Dip a wooden chopstick or the handle of a wooden spoon into the oil to test the temperature—if it bubbles rapidly, you're ready to fry!

4. In a second medium bowl, add the flour. Working with one type of veggie at a time for even cooking, toss a handful of veggies in the flour to lightly dredge, shaking off any excess. Add the dredged veg to a slotted spoon or spider and dip into the batter bowl, which will allow the vegetables to get coated and the excess to drip off. This may seem tedious, but add each piece one at a time gently into the oil so it can start to bubble and not stick to the other pieces, which would happen if you tried to add that whole spoonful at a time! You will have about 8 pieces per batch, and cook for about 5 minutes, turning occasionally with chopsticks or metal tongs, until the batter is golden brown on all sides.

5. Using a slotted spoon, spider, or tongs, remove the crispy veggies from the oil and let drain on the paper towel–lined sheet pan. Repeat with the remaining veg. Immediately sprinkle with salt so it adheres, then get ready to take a dip! These are best eaten hot, but are okay to sit out at a party for an hour or so before they start getting limp.

faq

CAN THEY BE MADE IN ADVANCE? No, not ideally.

HOW LONG WILL THEY KEEP? Fry them day of, and keep them warm in a 200°F oven on a wire rack over a sheet pan (no paper towels this time!), or let sit at room temperature uncovered (for up to a few hours, whilst partying) and refry or air-fry at 350°F for 5 to 7 minutes to get crispy again.

CHIPPY'S TIPPY

You can tempura fry many other veggies! If using a starchy or root veg—like potatoes, squash, or carrots—cut into ¼-inch-thick slices so they can cook inside as fast as they get crispy on the outside. Though it's possible, avoid watery produce like eggplant or zucchini—I find it's *dip*ficult to get them the right texture inside and out without extra prep of salting and drying them, which I found not worth it for what can be an otherwise quick dipper!

veggie ribbons

MAKES ½ POUND

SERVES A LIL' GET-TOGETHER (4 TO 6)

Baby carrots are not actually baby carrots. They're just the discarded "ugly" carrots that are peeled down to little nubs, and then used as an easy-to-pack healthy lunchbox snack. I don't love baby carrots as a dipper, but they've always been one of the most convenient options for veggie dippers . . . until now. In mere minutes, you can have a pile of carrot ribbons ready for dippin', and they are much more dippable due to their slight curved shape from curling up in a quick ice water bath.

These shaved crudités (fancy name) were introduced to me by my friend Eric Ehler, chef-owner of Outta Sight Pizza in San Francisco. He serves 'em with wings and house-made Maggi Seasoning–spiked ranch that made me see stars.

The ribbons are made by shaving or peeling vegetables into ⅛-inch-thick ribbons (using a mandoline or Y-peeler), which are thin yet flexible—they fold instead of breaking—and surprisingly sturdy. They have a better dip-to-dipper ratio due to the thinness; baby carrots are a big chunk of carrot for a little dip. They are a stunning centerpiece to a dip platter, and only require some careful cutting and plunging your hands into ice water—making them refreshing in more ways than one!

1 POUND OF ASSORTED DIPPIN' VEGETABLES, SUCH AS

Carrots in any color of the rainbow, ends trimmed and peeled

Persian (seedless) cucumbers, ends trimmed

Celery stalks, "center cut," aka tops and bottoms removed for even-width pieces

Radishes, tops trimmed

Asparagus, woody ends trimmed (snap to see where the woodiness ends)

EQUIPMENT

Mandoline set to ⅛-inch blade or Y-peeler

Cut-proof gloves, if using a mandoline

1. Set up an extra-large bowl of ice water next to a cutting board. Carefully shave each vegetable lengthwise on a mandoline, aiming for long, smooth strokes away from you with your palm pressed against the vegetable (ideally while using protection of cut-proof gloves) for even, steady pressure—and safety.

2. If you don't have a mandoline, you can also use a Y-peeler, which is easier to make ribbons with thanks to blades on both sides and an ergonomic grip, unlike a standard swivel peeler. When shaving vegetables with a Y-peeler, cut off a slice of the

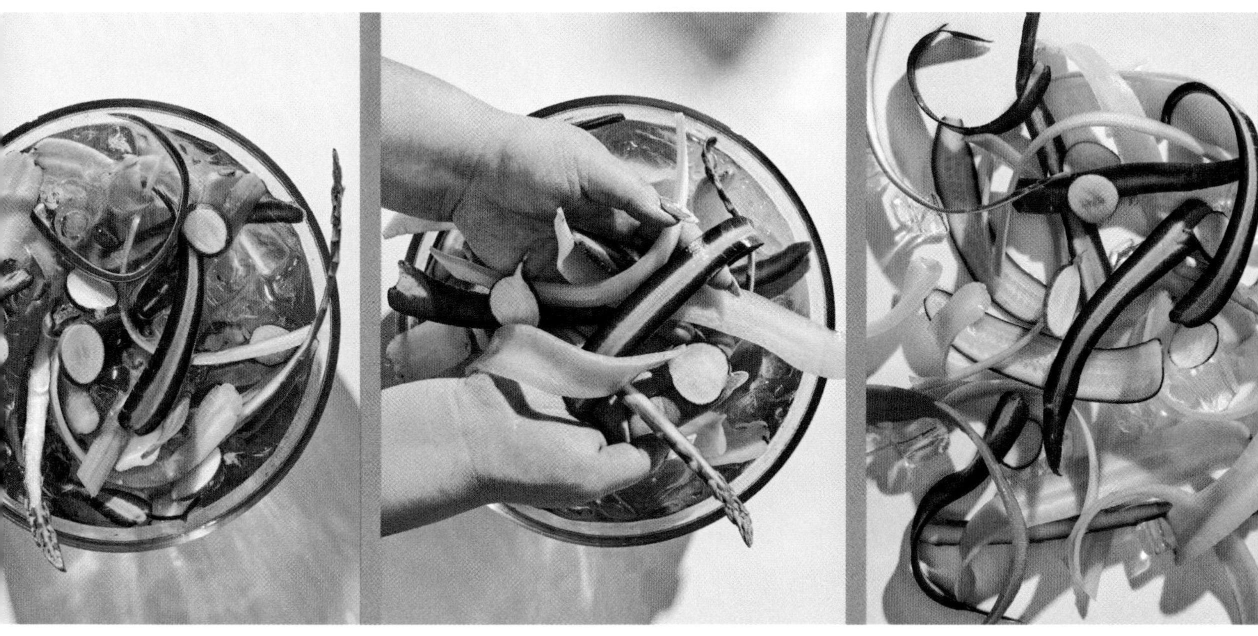

vegetable on one side so it can lay flat on the cutting board and not roll around. Hold down the vegetable with one hand, and use the peeler to shave across the veg, away from your hand. It should be one smooth pull, if possible, but it may take a few times to get the hang of it.

3. Repeat this process until you have as many Veggie Ribbons as you'd like, and then transfer them to the bowl of ice water. Let them sit for 30 seconds, then lift them out of the water using a colander or your hands (*brrr*) and dry them on a tea towel or paper towels.

4. For every pound of vegetables, you'll get about ¾ pound of ribbons, or about 40 pieces. This recipe scales up easily, so you can shave more vegetables or shave down your guest list.

CHIPPY'S TIPPY

Wear cut-proof gloves and quit while you're ahead when using a mandoline. It's not worth trying to get the last little ribbon out of a carrot when it could mean sacrificing a fingertip!

faq

CAN THEY BE MADE IN ADVANCE? Yes!

HOW LONG DO THEY KEEP? Stored in a resealable container in the fridge, they will last for up to 5 days.

roulette charred peppers

MAKES 1 POUND

SERVES A LIL' GET-TOGETHER (4 TO 6)

As a sadly spice-averse person (because I sweat and cry when things are too spicy), the idea of taking a gamble on whether something will delight me or ruin my night is a constant threat. And yet here I am, turning dippers into a sick game, with a mix of peppers all charred and served together for a game of Russian roulette mixed with I Spy or *Where's Waldo?* to identify which pepper is a shishito, which is a Fresno, and which is a nice little sweet baby bell pepper. It's a risky activity, but a fun conversation starter when you put down a platter of colorful peppers that could make you cry if you grab at random. This should come with a *dips*claimer!

1 pound mixed peppers, including baby bell, shishito, and small Fresnos or jalapeños if you really want to take a gamble

2 tablespoons olive oil

1 teaspoon kosher salt

Heat a large skillet over medium-high heat until when you tap a pepper against its surface it sizzles immediately. Spread all the peppers in the skillet in an even layer and cook for 1 to 2 minutes, until blistered on the bottom, then shake the pan and keep cooking (and sh-sh-shakin' occasionally, ideally while listening to "I'm Shakin'" by Rooney) for a few minutes more, until evenly charred. They will be tender-crisp inside and excellent for dipping. Remove the shishitos first as they are smaller and may cook faster, and any peppers that look like they've had too much time in the sun. Let cool slightly before serving so no one burns their mouth . . . at least from physical heat, anyway. You can also cut them in half lengthwise for easier-to-dip dippers and remove the seeds to calm the spice level down across the board.

CAN THEY BE MADE IN ADVANCE? Yes, served cold or at room temperature.

HOW LONG WILL THEY KEEP? Up to 5 days in an airtight container in the fridge, but they will soften over time to be less crunchy.

everything in a pickle

MAKES ABOUT 3 CUPS

SERVES A BIG DIP PARTY (8 TO 10)

I may not be a pickle fan (because of a hatred of cucumbers), but I like things that are pickled. And this easy base both puts your vegetables in a pickle and gets you out of a pickle (not having pickles in the fridge) at the same time. Memorize this formula and customize it to your taste if you like more garlic, sweeter pickles, or a little spice. (Perplexed by the cinnamon stick? It's an old-school Alton Brown hack via my friend and food stylist, Nick, to add warmth and balance.) This recipe scales up easily if you want to make multiple jars at a time. But keep in mind these need to pickle for at least 24 hours in the fridge, so patience is the last ingredient.

BRINE

¾ cup unseasoned rice vinegar

2 tablespoons kosher salt

1 tablespoon sugar

4 garlic cloves

1 teaspoon whole black peppercorns

1 cinnamon stick

¾ cup water

PICKLED VEGGIE OPTIONS (ABOUT 3 CUPS TOTAL)

Baby carrots

Baby cucumbers, halved lengthwise

Cauliflower, cut into small florets

Baby sweet peppers, stemmed, halved lengthwise, and seeded

1. Combine all the brine ingredients and ¾ cup water in a microwave-safe measuring cup or small bowl (or a small saucepan). Microwave for 3 minutes (or simmer over low heat on the stove) until the sugar dissolves.

2. Arrange your assortment of cut veggies in a 24-ounce glass jar (such as a mason jar) or other glass container, then pour in the pickling liquid. Let it sit at room temp until cooled, about 1 hour, then cover with a lid, move to the fridge, and wait at least 24 hours before enjoying, so the pickling action can happen. Since this is sealed but not canned, you *can* enjoy for up to 2 weeks.

CHIPPY'S TIPPY

Pre-shaved baby carrots are a sleeper hit because they soak up the pickling liquid quickly and strongly.

faq

CAN THEY BE MADE IN ADVANCE? Yes—at least 24 hours *minimum* for pickling!

HOW LONG WILL THEY KEEP? Up to 2 weeks sealed in the fridge.

potato skinny dippers

MAKES 20 TO 30

SERVES A BIG DIP PARTY (8 TO 10)

Potato skins were meant to be stuffed with dip. They have finally reached their peak form here. You can use any small potatoes you like, but the buttery baby dutch yellow potatoes are my favorite. Plus, you can make mashed potatoes with the scooped-out parts . . . or perhaps even for Poutine on the Ritz Dip (page 143)?

P.S. *Skinny* Dippers is just a play on words with potato skins. This is not a calorie-counting, carb-discarding book. I only scoop my potatoes to make 'em better dippers, and I will *never* scoop my bagels!

1½ pounds baby dutch yellow potatoes, such as Melissa's, washed and dried thoroughly

2 tablespoons olive oil

1 teaspoon seasoned salt, such as Lawry's

faq

CAN THEY BE MADE IN ADVANCE?
Yes! Reheat at 350°F in an air fryer, toaster, or conventional oven for 5 to 7 minutes, or until re-crisped.

HOW LONG WILL THEY KEEP?
Store leftovers in an airtight container in the fridge for up to 4 days.

1. Preheat the oven to 425°F. Line a sheet pan with foil for easy cleanup.

2. Place the potatoes on the prepared sheet pan. Drizzle with 1 tablespoon of the oil, toss to coat, then sprinkle on the seasoned salt and toss to coat again. Arrange in a single layer with a smidge of space (about ¼ inch) between each tater and roast for 20 minutes. Check for doneness by inserting a paring knife; if it meets with resistance, roast for 5 more minutes.

3. Transfer the potatoes to a plate to cool at room temperature for at least 20 minutes. Slice each potato in half lengthwise using a serrated or very sharp paring knife. Using the smallest spoon you have, carefully scoop out the insides of the potatoes, leaving a thin layer (about ⅛ inch) of potato around the skin to protect it from ripping. Reserve the scooped-out parts for making home fries or mashed potatoes.

4. If the foil doesn't look too gnarly, return the potatoes to the same sheet pan, scooped side down. If not, replace the foil. Drizzle with the remaining 1 tablespoon oil (no need to toss; just drizzle evenly) and bake for 10 minutes. Flip and cook for 10 minutes more, until sizzling and golden brown. Now they're sturdy enough for dippin'! They can be enjoyed warm or at room temperature.

CHIPPY'S TIPPY

If you have a serrated grapefruit or melon spoon, use it to scoop out the potato insides.

crispy paneer dipsticks

MAKES 16

SERVES A LIL' GET-TOGETHER (4 TO 6)

Crispy cheese. Not a mozzarella stick, but a paneer stick, a firm Indian cheese that can be griddled or grilled or otherwise cooked without melting. It's tamer in flavor than halloumi, another grill-able cheese, with a less prominent saltiness so it is easier to pair with all sorts of flavorful dips! Not to play favorites, but it was meant for Saag Paneer Artichoke Dip (page 60)—it's the paneer namesake.

1 block (12 ounces) paneer cheese

1 tablespoon ghee, for shallow-frying

1. Halve the block of paneer lengthwise into two squares. Slice each square into 4 thin pieces crosswise, and then stack them all together again on your cutting board. This way you can cut those 4 thin pieces in half all at once, giving you 8 dipsticks. Repeat with the other half of the paneer so you have 16 dipsticks total.

2. Heat the ghee in a large skillet (preferably nonstick) over medium-low heat for 2 minutes. Place the paneer fries in an even layer without crowding, cooking in batches if necessary, and cook for 1 minute per side—on two sides is fine, but you get extra cre*dip* if you sear on all four sides for beautiful sturdiness—until golden brown and crisp all over. Drain on a paper towel–lined plate.

MO*DIP*FICATIONS: If you can't find paneer, halloumi *can* work as a sub*dip*tute, but it's much saltier, so proceed with caution and cut the cheese into smaller pieces.

CHIPPY'S TIPPY

You can cut paneer into any shape you'd like, using cookie cutters or your imagination, just make sure to keep an eye on smaller pieces so they don't burn.

faq

CAN THEY BE MADE IN ADVANCE? You can cut in advance and store in the fridge in an airtight container, but cook them just before serving.

HOW LONG WILL THEY KEEP? If you have leftovers, you can store in an airtight container in the fridge for up to 3 days and reheat in a low skillet, but they won't taste the same as if they were fresh. I highly recommend against it!

potato-fried cheese curds

MAKES ABOUT 25

SERVES A LIL' GET-TOGETHER (4 TO 6)

When creating Poutine on the Ritz Dip (page 143), I wanted to find a unique way to incorporate cheese curds. Fried cheese curds are more of a Midwestern thing, but somehow they reached me as a kid in upstate New York via A&W. Not my initials, but the root beer company and fast-food restaurant. Their fried cheese curds were always a little exploded with gooey, melty cheese, which was both stressful and delightful (burning your mouth was inevitable). My version of fried cheese curds uses instant potatoes, another childhood staple, as part of the batter, so it's kind of like the French fry and cheese curd lived happily ever after . . . inside mashed potatoes and gravy dip.

1 cup all-purpose flour

¼ cup instant mashed potatoes, preferably a buttery one

1 teaspoon Homemade Montreal Steak Seasoning

1½ teaspoons baking powder

2 teaspoons Montreal steak seasoning, store-bought or see the following ingredients

2 cups ice-cold club soda or sparkling water

1 cup neutral oil, such as vegetable or canola

1 bag (5 ounces) cheese curds

HOMEMADE MONTREAL STEAK SEASONING

3 tablespoons ground black pepper

1 tablespoon ground coriander

1 tablespoon paprika

1 tablespoon garlic powder

1 tablespoon onion powder

1 teaspoon dried dill

1 teaspoon ground mustard

1 teaspoon celery seeds

1 teaspoon crushed red pepper

1 teaspoon kosher salt

1. Line a sheet pan with paper towels, and place a wire cooling rack on top. Set aside.

2. In a medium bowl, combine ¾ cup of the flour, the instant mashed potatoes, baking powder, and 1 teaspoon of the Montreal steak seasoning. Pour the club soda into an ice-filled 4-cup measuring cup. Let it sit to chill for a minute, then remove the ice or strain the water into another measuring cup to get 1½ cups cold bubbly water. Gently whisk the cold water into the dry mix for about 30 seconds, taking care not to overmix—some small clumps are okay and will make the end result better. Set aside to rest and re-whisk gently just before dipping your curds.

3. In a large saucepan, high-sided skillet, or wok, heat the oil over medium-high heat for about 5 minutes. Dip a wooden chopstick or the handle of a wooden spoon into the oil to test the temperature—if it bubbles rapidly, you're ready to fry!

4. Add the remaining ¼ cup of flour to a medium bowl and toss the cheese curds in the flour all at once to lightly dredge, shaking off any excess. Add the dredged curds to a slotted spoon or spider and dip into the batter bowl, which will allow them to get coated and the excess to drip off. This may seem tedious, but gently add each piece one at a time to the oil so it can start to bubble and not stick to the other pieces, which would happen if you tried to add that whole spoonful at a time! You will cook about 10 curds per batch, and fry for 2 to 3 minutes, turning occasionally with chopsticks or metal tongs, until the batter is lightly golden brown on all sides.

5. Using a slotted spoon, spider, or tongs, remove the crispy curds from the oil and let drain on the paper towel-lined sheet pan. Repeat with remaining batches. You can keep them warm in a 200°F oven on a paper towel-less wire rack over a sheet pan, or let sit at room temperature and refry or air-fry at 350°F for 3 to 5 minutes to get crispy again. These are best eaten hot, but they surprisingly stay crisp at room temperature and the curds get squeakier as they cool. (Music to my ears . . .)

CHIPPY'S TIPPY

Pull the curds out before they are deep golden brown, as they are small and will continue to cook after removing from the oil. If you wait too long, they can burn or explode a bit of cheese out of the side.

faq

CAN THEY BE MADE IN ADVANCE? No.

HOW LONG WILL THEY KEEP? If you have leftovers, store in a paper towel-lined airtight container in the fridge for up to 4 days and reheat in a 350°F oven or air fryer for 3 to 5 minutes, or until re-crisped. Or eat them cold! But they won't be as good as they were originally.

rice cake and sausage skewers

MAKES 32 SKEWERS

SERVES A BIG DIP PARTY (8 TO 10)

I am Korean American, but I've never been to Korea. Physically. Mentally, I've made enough street food (like these skewers of crispy-chewy rice cakes and juicy Korean pork Vienna sausages), experimented with many ingredients, and sung enough karaoke that I feel like I'm there. As an adoptee, sometimes it's hard to figure out how to merge my identities, but dippin' these skewers into In Queso Emergency Dip (page 41) was a *dip*fining moment for me.

16 frozen garae-tteok (Korean cylindrical rice cakes)

Toasted sesame oil

1 package (12 ounces) Korean Vienna sausages, such as Beksul

2 tablespoons vegetable oil

EQUIPMENT

Thirty-two 3- or 4-inch wooden or bamboo skewers

1. In a medium bowl, combine the rice cakes with water just to cover. Microwave for 5 minutes if from the fridge and 7 minutes if from frozen. They should be squishy to the touch, and if you bite into one—and you should—it should be delightfully chewy with no hard parts. Drain, rinse in cool water, toss them in a large bowl with a hefty drizzle of sesame oil to keep them from sticking together, and set aside.

2. Using 2 parallel skewers, thread on a sausage, a rice cake, another sausage, and another rice cake. They should be gently touching but not squished like the middle seater on an airplane! Repeat until all the rice cakes and sausages are skewered.

3. In a large skillet (preferably nonstick) over medium heat, heat the vegetable oil for at least 3 minutes. Add the skewers, taking care not to crowd them—you can work in batches!—and cook for about 4 minutes per side, until evenly golden brown.

4. Let cool on a cutting board for a few minutes, then slice the rice cakes and sausage down the middle between the two skewers, giving you two smaller, easier-to-bite-daintily skewers to dip with gusto—without making a total mess.

CHIPPY'S TIPPY

Try to remember to thaw the rice cakes the night before, but if not, you'll just have to add some more time to the microwaving.

faq

CAN THEY BE MADE IN ADVANCE? Yes!

HOW LONG WILL THEY KEEP? Store leftovers in an airtight container in the fridge for up to 4 days. Microwave for 30 seconds each, or put in a dry skillet over medium-low heat for 2 minutes per side, to reheat.

universally dippable marinated meat skewers

MAKES ½ CUP MARINADE AND ABOUT 24 SKEWERS

SERVES A BIG DIP PARTY (8 TO 10)

Meat on a stick is universally beloved, so why not make it a universal dipper? This master marinade and oven-cooking method for a whole batch of skewers will have you *dip*ertaining without breaking a sweat. It does require a 4-hour marinade, but it's worth it. This is a stickup!

6 garlic cloves

½ yellow onion, cut into a few chunks

2 tablespoons soy sauce

2 tablespoons fish sauce

2 tablespoons packed light brown sugar

¼ teaspoon ground white pepper

2 tablespoons neutral oil, such as vegetable or canola

1½ pounds meat of your choice, such as flank steak, pork belly, or chicken thighs, cut into ½-inch cubes or ¼-inch-thick slices

Nonstick cooking spray

EQUIPMENT

Twenty-four 3- or 4-inch wooden or bamboo skewers

1. In a food processor, combine the garlic, onion, soy sauce, fish sauce, brown sugar, white pepper, and oil and blitz until it is as smooth as you can get it. If you don't have a food processor, you can grate the garlic and onion and mix everything together in a medium bowl.

2. Place one resealable plastic storage bag inside another. Combine the meat and marinade in the inner bag, and smush to combine. Get as much air out of the bags as possible before sealing and refrigerate for at least 4 hours and up to overnight but not longer.

3. Preheat the oven to 350°F. Line a sheet pan with foil, set a wire rack on top, and spray with nonstick spray. Set aside.

4. Skewer the meat by threading 3 cubes or 1 slice per skewer. Cook until the meat reaches your desired doneness or temperature—about 15 minutes for medium-cooked steak

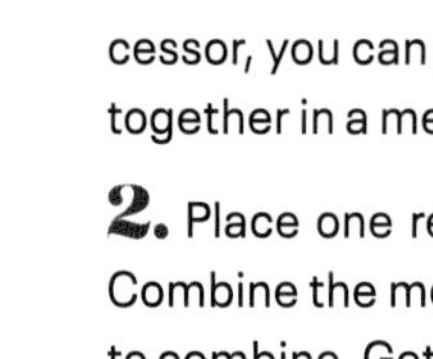

CHIPPY'S TIPPY

This marinade can be doubled easily. Use ½ cup marinade for every 1½ pounds meat as a quick calculation.

(140°F internal temperature), 20 minutes for pork (145°F), and 25 minutes for chicken (165°F)—then broil for 2 to 4 minutes until charred and resembling grilled skewers—but in the oven. Magic!

faq

CAN THEY BE MADE IN ADVANCE? Yes!

HOW LONG WILL THEY KEEP? Store leftovers in an airtight container in the fridge for up to 4 days. They can be enjoyed cold, or you can warm them in the microwave for 30 seconds or in a 325°F oven for 5 to 10 minutes, until warmed through.

MEAT CUTE WITH BANH MI DIP (PAGE 150)

piggies in snuggies

MAKES 20

SERVES A LIL' GET-TOGETHER (4 TO 6)

Piggies in Snuggies, they're coming down the stairs . . . okay, that doesn't have as much of a ring as *Bananas in Pajamas*, but the rhyme and overall coziness of both the food and idea of a pig wrapped in a Snuggie are pretty fantastic. Usually pigs in a blanket are made to only have a thin strip of dough in the middle of a small sausage, and that ratio makes me sad. So these Piggies in Snuggies only have a tiny bit of each tip exposed, much like being wrapped up in a Snuggie and allowing for dough and sausage in every bite. Plus, for Halloween, you can add little strips of dough to make them Mummies in Snuggies (check them out on page 244).

1 tube (8 ounces) crescent dough sheet or rolls

20 Lit'l Smokies (about half a 14-ounce package)

1. Preheat the oven to 375°F. Line a sheet pan with parchment paper and set aside.

2. Unroll the tube of crescent dough onto a cutting board. If it's a sheet, cut it in half crosswise (hamburger style) and in 10 strips lengthwise (hot dog style). If it's the standard precut rolls, pinch and press the seams together with your index fingers until the perforations are sealed, then cut the same way. You'll have 20 small strips of dough; wrap each Lit'l Smokie almost completely, only leaving the two tips exposed, by stretching and pulling the dough up and around like you're swaddling it.

3. Arrange the pigs in Snuggies on the prepared sheet pan, about an inch apart. Bake for 10 to 12 minutes, until evenly golden brown.

CHIPPY'S TIPPY

Prefer chicken over pork? Want an all-beef hot dog instead or a heartier sausage? Vegetarian? Vegan? You can swap in anything you want inside these Snuggies—just cut them to approximately the size of a Lit'l Smokie. You could even add some cheese if you want . . .

faq

CAN THEY BE MADE IN ADVANCE? Yes. Reheat in a toaster oven or conventional oven at 325°F for 5 to 7 minutes until warmed through and slightly crisp again on the outside.

HOW LONG WILL THEY KEEP? Store in an airtight container in the fridge for up to 5 days.

crumble crackers

MAKE 32

SERVES A BIG DIP PARTY (8 TO 10)

This is a crumble-topped pie with a buttery crust, but in cracker form. The pie "filling" is the dips that you choose to dip these into. Somehow these also taste a little like the best, warm-spiced granola I've had, thanks to the oats inside. So maybe try crumbling them over some yogurt for breakfast?

1 sleeve buttery crackers, such as Ritz (about 32 crackers)

½ cup (1 stick) salted butter, cold, cut into cubes

½ cup packed light brown sugar

½ cup all-purpose flour

½ cup old-fashioned rolled oats

1 teaspoon ground cinnamon

½ teaspoon ground ginger

½ teaspoon ground nutmeg

1 teaspoon pure vanilla extract

¼ teaspoon kosher salt

1. Preheat the oven to 350°F. Line a sheet pan with parchment paper. Arrange the crackers in an even single layer—so they are touching but not piled on top of each other—on the prepared sheet pan.

2. In a medium bowl, combine the butter, brown sugar, flour, oats, cinnamon, ginger, nutmeg, vanilla, and salt. Mash with a fork until the butter is in pea-size pieces.

3. Pinch a bit of the mixture to compact it slightly into a little crumble blob and dollop or sprinkle it on each cracker; it doesn't have to be perfect or even on every single one. Bake for 12 to 14 minutes, until golden brown. It's nice to eat them when they're still warm, but they are equally wonderful at room temperature.

CHIPPY'S TIPPY

Use your pinchers (thumb and pointer finger) to make sure you get a good amount of compacted crumble topping on each cracker.

faq

CAN THEY BE MADE IN ADVANCE? Yes.

HOW LONG WILL THEY KEEP? Store leftovers in an airtight container at room temperature for up to 5 days, with pieces of parchment or wax paper separating each layer of crackers to protect them from . . . crumbling.

ritzy crispy treat chips

MAKE 20

SERVES A BIG DIP PARTY (8 TO 10)

I love Rice Krispies Treats, but as someone who enjoys desserts (and *dips*serts) not too sweet, I needed to tweak them to make them perfect for my palate—and hopefully your dippin' pleasure. I added crushed-up Ritz Crackers to the Rice Krispies cereal and used salted butter for sweet-and-savory balance, but after a few tests, they weren't chewy enough. Then I added half a jar of Marshmallow Fluff and it changed everything. They were crispy on the outside and chewy on the inside, and sturdy enough to dip into an assortment of *dips*-serts without breaking or making a mess. To make them even more delightfully toothsome, I added mini rainbow mochi (found at many Asian grocery stores or online), inspired by my friend Tiffany Kim, who makes Mochi Krunchies in fun flavors like Ube Oreo and Pandan Coconut under her company Loaf Language in Los Angeles. They're optional but encouraged to add a fun extra-chewy texture and a burst of color.

½ cup (1 stick) salted butter

1 bag (10 ounces) mini marshmallows

1 cup marshmallow crème, such as Marshmallow Fluff

2 sleeves of Ritz Crackers (about 64 crackers), crushed into small, irregular pieces in a resealable plastic bag with a rolling pin, bottle of wine, or your fists and some fury

5½ cups Rice Krispies cereal

½ cup mini mochi (any flavor and color), such as Hwagwabang or Royal Family (optional)

1. In a large nonstick skillet over medium-low heat, melt the butter. Cook, stirring frequently, for about 5 minutes until it foams, then the foam dissipates and brown flecks start to form on the edges of the butter, 3 to 5 minutes more. Add the marshmallows and marshmallow crème and stir with a spatula until they melt and form one homogeneous mixture. Add the crushed Ritz Crackers and Rice Krispies and stir until well combined. Take off the heat and mix in the mini mochi, if using.

2. Press the mixture into the bottom of the pan that you cooked the brown butter marshmallow mixture in and let set at room temperature for at least an hour. Use a spatula to loosen the big ol' circle of Ritzy Crispy Treats around the perimeter of the pan and move to a plastic cutting board (easier to clean) or a parchment paper–lined wooden cutting board. Cut into 10 even-as-you-can wedges, and then cut each wedge crosswise into two thinner chips.

CHIPPY'S TIPPY

Use a nonstick pan when making this, or you'll regret it.

faq

CAN THEY BE MADE IN ADVANCE? Yes.

HOW LONG WILL THEY KEEP? Store leftovers in an airtight container at room temperature for up to 5 days, with pieces of parchment or wax paper separating each layer of "chips" so they don't stick together.

caramel brûlée crackers

MAKES 24

SERVES A BIG DIP PARTY (8 TO 10)

These crackers are better than any version of "bark" I've had in my life. Peppermint bark, peanut brittle . . . none of them do it for me. But none of them are composed of a quick salted caramel poured over saltines and broiled until brûléed with a crackling, crispy top. Sturdy as a dipper, but remarkable as a small handheld dessert.

½ cup (1 stick) salted butter

½ cup sugar or packed light brown sugar

24 saltines or buttery crackers, such as Ritz

Flaky salt, for finishing

1. In a small saucepan over medium heat, melt together the butter and sugar. Bring to a boil and let bubble without stirring or disturbing for 2 minutes. You don't want it to cook any longer or it can become a hard caramel, so immediately take off the heat to cool slightly.

2. Set the oven to broil (on low, if you can), with the rack three positions from the top so your saltines won't be in the direct line of fire. This will ensure the caramel evenly browns and turns into a crackly crust on top rather than burning. Line a sheet pan with parchment paper.

3. Arrange the saltines on the prepared sheet pan, snug as a bug in a rug so you don't waste any of that precious caramel. Pour the hot caramel evenly over the saltines. Broil for a mere 1 minute, until the tops are crackly and brûléed but still soft in some places. Remove from the oven, and sprinkle with flaky salt. Let cool for a few minutes, and break into dippable crackers.

Making a double batch of these is super easy, as 48 saltines fit perfectly onto a sheet pan.

faq

CAN THEY BE MADE IN ADVANCE? Yes.

HOW LONG WILL THEY KEEP? Store leftovers in an airtight container at room temperature for up to 5 days, with pieces of parchment or wax paper separating each layer of crackers so they don't stick together.

I Love You
SPAM

dip-ertaining

3 STEPS TO DIP PARTY SUCCESS

Just like a chip gliding through a bowl of dip, you want the dip plate-making process to be smooth. To set up the right flow for people to help themselves—without too much babysitting and explaining—just follow these simple steps to build out your dip buffet, no matter the size of your entertaining space. I've done this in a 300-square-foot New York City studio apartment (and hosted thirty-six people) and in a big private room at Gagopa Karaoke two years in a row for Dipmas (more on that and photographic proof on page 237), so size doesn't make a *dip*ference. The method remains the same; you just might have to get more creative with surfaces that can safely hold all the dips and dippers. And if you want to illustrate how to build the perfect dippy plate, reference Graze Anatomy on page 29.

PIANO DIP > PIANO ROCK?

SURFACE-LEVEL OBSERVATIONS: Don't limit yourself just to the kitchen to make dip happen! Any flat surface can be cleared to make a dip buffet. I always keep hot dips in the kitchen, whether in mini slow cookers, warmers, or covered pots on the stove over a low flame, with serving spoons on a spoon rest or plate nearby (to prevent messy cheesy spills). Keeping them in the kitchen ensures there are outlets nearby and less chance of someone burning themselves on the hot exterior of a slow cooker. Cold dips and dips that are okay at room temp for the duration of a party (like Miso Eggplant Dip, page 113) can be housed anywhere throughout your space, on coffee tables or side tables. For cold dips, see page 29 for a *dips*plainer on dippers; they can either be paired with their dips on a dual platter, or put in bowls and organized on a separate buffet in the communal space (so people can fill their plate with dips and lessen the threat of double dipping).

LOW-LABOR LABELING: For a more casual dip party, buy a few thick plastic tablecloths and dry-erase markers. You can label each dip and dipper—if it's more complex than just chips or crudités—directly on the tablecloth. (I say "thick" because I found out the hard way that the super-thin dollar ones will rip when the pressure of a marker drags against them . . .) Colorful masking tape, sticky notes, or stick-on labels also work. If you are feelin' fancy, source some fun name tags—there are so many unique vintage ones on Etsy—or make your own using wrapping paper, cardstock, or whatever speaks to you creatively.

***DIP*VIDED PLATES UNITE US:** Never have plastic kids' plates been more popular than at a dip party. The sectioned—or as I call them, *dip*vided—plates are built for separating dips and dippers into organized chaos. I have tips for finding them on the cheap on page 18, but they're readily available in both *dips*posable form (if you don't have a dishwasher and are okay hurting the environment just a teeny bit in the name of dips) or reusable. Vintage trays are my favorite large format to serve a *lot* of *dip*ferent types of dips or even to plate dips and dippers for a smaller party. Hit thrift stores, antique malls, and sites like Etsy, eBay, Mercari, and Poshmark to find a wide array of styles, colors, and even patterns to fit your Big Dip Energy aura.

introducing dipmas: dip the halls with bowls of hot cheese

get to know the holiday version of friends-giving: an all-dips potluck!

A DIPMAS STORY

I became the Dip Queen on December 1, 2017, when I hosted my first Dipmas. On the night of the inaugural all-dips potluck, December became *Dip*cember, and I go back to *Dip*cember all the time. The idea came about because my friends and I wanted to have a holiday potluck that captured the spirit of Friendsgiving but was less formal and more snacky. I started singing "Dip the halls with bowls of hot cheese," and thought that was the name: Dip the Halls. But Dipmas rolled off the tongue better, and "Dip the Halls" just became the slogan and theme song for the new holi*dip*.

The original menu featured the greatest hits from *Now! That's What I Call Dips*, including Buffalo chicken dip, artichoke dip (sans spinach, a recipe that my then-colleague Alex shared with me), a now-iconic sausage dip (page 62), pizza dip (page 79), guacamole, 7-layer taco dip (page 128), s'mores dip, cookie dough dip, and a few wild cards that friends bought. (There was notably a corned beef cheese ball, which I *dip*bated putting in this book, but it was more of a spread than a dip when it came to *dips*cosity.) Altogether we had thirteen dips, plus Dirty Shirleys as the signature cocktail, and the menu was scribbled on the chalkboard front of my cupboard. And for those who didn't feel confident in their dip-making abilities, I asked them to bring chips or other dippers, and underestimated the ratio of people who would opt for that. With twenty-three people in attendance, there was a pile of chips and pretzels a few feet high leftover post-Dipmas; it took months to eat through.

DIPFINITELY SINGING "NOBODY WANTS TO BE LONELY"

IZZY AND AJ DIPPIN' IT LOW!

Every year since 2017—except *Dip*cember 2020, during peak pandemic—I've hosted Dipmas in four different locations, and I even did a mini Dipmas Eve for my family one year. Every party was memorable for its own reasons, whether because my friend Joel accidentally dropped a potholder in molten dip in the oven (which dripped everywhere and set off the smoke alarms) or an ugly sweater contest entry that made multiple people cry laughing (which physically jingled all the way with bells on—literally sewn on—and had some scary looking toys embroidered all over). The next year got more extravagant, with a custom bejeweled Dipmas banner (which sadly somehow got wet when I moved to LA and had to be thrown away) and glittery backdrops for a photobooth, and eventually I moved the whole shebang to Gagopa Karaoke, my second home in New York City.

A GUIDE TO HOSTING DIPMAS, THE FRIENDSGIVING OF THE HOLIDAY SEASON

I hope you are sufficiently *dip*sired by my Dipmas story to think about hosting your own, or at least suggest that your more organized friend with the biggest home hosts. (Bookmarking this page if you gift it to a dip-loving friend is a nice hint.) The first rule of Dipmas is that you do talk about Dipmas to anyone who will listen. And the second is that there are no rules—just some guidelines to help make it run smoothly:

- *Dip*vide and conquer by making a sign-up sheet at least a month in advance. You probably won't get anyone actually committing to what dip or dipper they're bringing until a week before, but this ensures you won't double up on dips and get a good balance of sweet and savory. Make fields for name, dip, dipper options, and whether the dip needs to be heated up on site, so you can plan for oven or stovetop space. You can also include sections for people who'd rather bring drinks or dippers.

- The host should make at least one hot dip, so it will be hot and ready when guests arrive. Having a selection of dippers ready isn't a bad idea, either. Dipmas can be a drop-in event, but encourage your most reliable friends to make dips and arrive toward the start so the dip buffet isn't sparse and sad. People who arrive late will just re-up the dip supply and keep the party going, so if you are someone who likes people out of your house by nine p.m., either start the party in the afternoon or offer to-go containers around eight p.m. to encourage exits.

I'd been a regular at Gagopa for nearly a decade, hosting ten- to thirty-person ragers at least once a quarter and smaller "happy hour" karaoke drop-ins with friends on random weeknights. There were three photos of me on the wall as of the time of this photoshoot. Gagopa has always been BYOB and BYO-food, but I asked special permission to bring in mini slow cookers just to keep dip warm for Dipmas 2021. They were Pioneer Woman–branded colorful floral dip warmers that I had shipped directly to my hotel, and I made the first iteration of Corn Cheesy Like Sunday Morning Dip (page 37) using plastic cutlery in my

KAREN AND JESS KICKING DIPMAS INTO HIGH GEAR

Ask people to BYO containers to take dips to go if you don't have a big supply. If you'd rather provide for your guests, plastic deli containers from restaurant supply stories (online or in person) are inexpensive and come in bulk, and you don't have to chase anyone down to get them back later.

Use the tips from the dip buffet how-to (page 235) to set up a festive spread, where a mix of hot and cold dips, savory dips and *dip*sserts, and dippers abound. If you're serving potent drinks (I usually do a big-batch punch, like Dirty Shirleys), make sure to also leave room for people to set their plates down or have a garbage can or bag close by so you aren't scrubbing queso off the floor for hours later. I speak from *dip*sperience.

Dipmas can be renamed to a pun more suitable to the holiday you celebrate (even if you don't celebrate any holidays). So far I've only plotted Dipmukkah 2023 with my Jewish grammy, using latkes as a dipper for the Face Your Schmears Everything Bagel Dip (page 131), but everyone loves dips, so I encourage you to make it as inclusive and inviting as possible. Dips are a shareable, joyful food meant to be enjoyed with others, and whether you're with family, chosen family, friends, or only your pets, just have fun dippin' in.

A FULL DIPMAS-OKE SPREAD!

hotel room instead of borrowing someone's kitchen, because I like a challenge. There was a spike in COVID-19 cases that month, so a small group of us—Izzy, AJ, Karen, Jess, Joel (who flew in from Portland just for Dipmas), and Carson—got PCR'ed and gathered in the giant room I reserved with a ri*dip*ulous amount of dip for seven of us. The following year, in 2022, we had our most epic Dipmas yet, which my friend Laura Murray photographed beautifully, so you can see us singing "All I Want for Dipmas Is You" and feel like you were dipping the halls with us.

NOW! THAT'S WHAT I CALL DIPMAS MENU

I made this menu using the dips that have appeared the most on Dipmas menus since its *dip*ception as well as ones that can look the most festive, but this is just a dipping-off point. The below menu of four dips is a combination of what the host could make and what you could ask others to bring, and includes a mix of hot, cold, sweet, and savory. These all feel celebratory, serve a crowd, and aren't ultra garlicky, in case mistletoe is involved. This is the base other potluck contributors can build around, and the host doesn't have to make all four, either. Make a*dip*tations based on what dips from this book speak to you, or make nostalgic family recipes to add to the Dipmas dip mix and let the chips fall as they may.

THE COLD *DIPPETIZER*: Shrimp-less Scampi Dip (page 147), great for vegetarians, pescatarians, and carnivores alike. And is it even a holiday party without shrimp cocktail? If you are crafty, you could even take a piece of Styrofoam shaped like a tree and use toothpicks to make a crudités Christmas tree and hang a few pieces of shrimp from it. (But use the ice double bowl method, page 16, to keep the rest of the non-decorative shrimp cold and prevent food poisoning . . .) Would also go great with Potato Skinny Dippers (page 219) underneath the mistletoe.

THE HOT *DIPPETIZER*: Pizza Your Way Dip (page 79) in a Garlic Knot Wreath (page 190), with pepperoni and mini mozzarella balls as ornaments and basil leaves and pimientos mimicking holly on the dip and/or wreath. To really make it festive, you could brush the garlic knot wreath with pesto to make it even more green.

DIP FOR DINNER MAIN COURSE: Crab Rangoon Dip with red- and green-dyed Rainbow Dumpling Chips (pages 140, 203), because all I want for Christmas is rangoooon! If you have too many vegetarian friends to serve, a runner-up is Tteokbokki Sausage Dip (page 62), served with rice cake-only skewers (page 224), a Dipmas classic that has a slightly red hue from the gochujang in the spicy-but-not-too-spicy base.

***DIPSSERT*:** Baileys in a Shoe Eggnog Dip (page 178), topped with festive sprinkles and served with gingerbread and sugar cookies. And maybe Crumble Crackers (page 229) with sprinkles, too?

other holidips, dipcasions, and theme party menus

Looking to celebrate more good times with dips? Here are my four-course dip menus for some of the heavy hitters, but I encourage you to not let a theme *dip*-ter you from making whatever you damn well please, whenever you want. That's what Big Dip Energy is about, after all—the confidence of knowing how to create the best party atmosphere.

HOLIDIPS

DIP CLARK'S ROCKIN' NEW YEAR'S EVE (OR AWARDS SEASON VIEWING PARTIES)

COLD *DIPPETIZER*: **Devils on Horseback Dip** (page 93) with **Potato Skinny Dippers** (page 219) and caviar, if you're feelin' extra fancy.

HOT *DIPPETIZER*: **Broccoli Cheddar Soup Fon*dip*** (page 76) with **Tantalizing Tempura Broccoli** (page 212), served in a vintage fondue pot.

DIP FOR DINNER MAIN COURSE: **Poutine on the Ritz Dip** (page 143) with **Potato-Fried Cheese Curds** (page 222). Carbs on carbs: the ideal way to close out one year and ring in another.

DIPSSERT: **Espressomartinimisu Dip** (page 172), served in martini glasses, with some **Crumble Crackers** (page 229) arranged artfully inside.

FRIENDS WHO DIP TOGETHER, STAY TOGETHER

SUPER BOWLS OF DIP

COLD *DIPPETIZER*: **Buffalo Cranch** (page 54) as a meatless Buffalo Chicken Dip alternative for vegetarians, but also served with wings, nuggets, or tenders and **Potato Skinny Dippers** (page 219) made to look like mini footballs on the sidelines! Think of this as the "Star-Spangled Banner" before *dip*-off.

HOT *DIPPETIZER*: **Classique Spinnie Artie Dip** (page 58) with store-bought Tostitos Scoops, because this pairing is as iconic as the 2001 halftime show. (Walk this way toward Google if you don't know the reference, person who found this now-vintage cookbook at an estate sale in the year 3000 . . .)

DIP FOR DINNER MAIN COURSE: **Cincinnati Chili Dip** (page 65), with the option to dip in or eat the chili by itself on top of hot dogs, with **Piggies in Snuggies** (page 228) and **Pasta la Vista Chips** (page 209).

DIPSSERT: **Whipped Peanut Butter Cup Dip** (page 182) with **These Bagel Pretzel Bites Have Everything** (page 194) . . . but without the everything seasoning! Unless you wanna get weird. Please report back, if so.

PIZZA YOUR WAY DIP (PAGE 79) IN A GARLIC KNOT WREATH (PAGE 190)

HOLY CANNOLI DIP (PAGE 171)

CHILI CRISP CRANCH (PAGE 54)

CURRY SQUASHCOTTA SHEET PAN DIP (PAGE 119)

LUNAR NEW YEAR

COLD *DIPPETIZER:* **Toum Raider Dip** (page 100) or **Miso Eggplant Dip** (page 113) with **Universally Dippable Marinated Meat Skewers** (page 226).

HOT *DIPPETIZER:* **Corn Cheesy Like Sunday Morning Dip** (page 37) with **Double Sesame Mochi Flatbreads** (page 196) or scallion pancakes. Roti would also be fantastic.

DIP FOR DINNER MAIN COURSE: **Banh Mi Dip** (page 150) with **Everything in a Pickle** (page 218) and some more of those skewers!

*DIP*SSERT: **Boba Tea Dips with Boba Skewers** (page 161) in an abundance of flavors.

DIPSGIVING ME LIFE!

COLD *DIPPETIZER:* Technically room temp, but **Herbalicious Oil Is Bready for Dippin'** (page 98) can be an appetizer or served as part of the main meal with crusty bread or your favorite Thanksgiving carb.

HOT *DIPPETIZER:* **Poutine on the Ritz Dip** (page 143) with fried onions or Funyuns as a dipper if you don't want to fry **Potato-Fried Cheese Curds** (page 222) on such a chaotic cooking day!

DIP FOR DINNER MAIN COURSE: **New York's Hottest Club Sandwich Dip** (page 125), with roasted turkey instead of deli turkey. You could also make the dip without meat and then serve alongside a full roasted turkey. Big Turkey Day flex.

*DIP*SSERT: **Cranberries and Cream Protein Dip** (page 103, swapping in whole-berry cranberry sauce for the peach mixture) with buttery crackers and graham crackers.

VALENTINE'S (OR GALENTINE'S) DAY

COLD *DIPPETIZER:* **Roasted Red Pepp in Your Step Whipped Feta Dip** (page 110), served with heart-shaped puff pastry bites. Or broken hearts. Depends on how your day is going.

HOT *DIPPETIZER:* **Cheesesteak Me Out Fon*dip*** (page 74) with little bites of actual steak for date night *or* Galentine's (but that should also be served with fries so you can say, "Whatever, I'm getting cheese fries" to your gal or pal).

DIP FOR DINNER MAIN COURSE: **Deviled Spam Musubi Dip** (page 153) with **Crispy Rice Dipsticks** (page 207).

*DIP*SSERT: **Strawberry Shortcake Dip** (page 180), served with **Cinnamon-Sugar Lil' Scoopz** (page 200) with little chocolate-dipped strawberries nestled inside!

HALLOWEEN

COLD *DIPPETIZER:* **Shrimp-for-Brains Dip,** made by simply mixing a 16 ounces of softened cream cheese with a 12-ounce bottle of cocktail sauce and ½ pound of thawed frozen salad shrimp (aka tiny shrimp). This is a vintage recipe my friend MaryAnn's mom made, and it sounds weird but it's surprisingly great with buttery crackers dipped in. Serve it in a brain-shaped mold for extra spookiness.

HOT *DIPPETIZER:* **In Queso Emergency Dip** (page 41) served in a bubbling cauldron (or maybe a black slow cooker that resembles one?) with Fritos Scoops marked in a bowl that says "Witches' Fingernails."

DIP FOR DINNER MAIN COURSE: **Beanie Weenie Hummus** (page 108) with **Piggies in Snuggies** (page 228) that are actually MUMMIES! Save a bit of dough to roll into little wrappings for your Mummies in Snuggies. You could also make the mummies with **Toum Raider Dip** (page 100).

*DIP*SSERT: **Peaches 'n' Cream Protein Dip** (page 103) with splatters of red food coloring to make it Peaches 'n' *Scream* Dip, served with puff pastry or **Ritzy Crispy Treat Chips** (page 230) cut to look like knives. **Dirt Pudding Dip** (page 177) with tombstone-shaped Ritzy Crispy Treat Chips would also be a graveyard smash!

EASTER BRUNCH

COLD *DIPPETIZER*: **Guava Cheesecake Dip** (page 49) with **Mini Ham and Cheese Croissants** (page 193). The cheesecake can double as *dips*sert if you also serve fruit and cookies with it!

HOT *DIPPETIZER*: **Garlic Bread Baked Brie in an Edibowl** (page 85), but try to find a bread that is more oval so it looks like an Easter egg.

DIP FOR BRINNER MAIN COURSE: **New York's Hottest Club Sandwich Dip** (page 125) with These Bagel Pretzel Bites Have Everything (page 194).

DIPSSERT: **Fat Mint Dip** (page 174) served in a halved hollow giant chocolate bunny to dip 'n' snap as an edibowl.

YOM KIPPUR (BREAK FAST BREAKFAST)

COLD *DIPPETIZER*: **Say Kimcheese! Dip** (page 42), my Korean-Jewish dip medley, with **Double Sesame Mochi Flatbreads** (page 196).

HOT *DIPPETIZER*: **Tuna Melt Dip** (page 127) with the double dipper that won't be double dipped: those sesame flatbreads! Or rye toast dipsticks.

DIP FOR BREAKFAST MAIN COURSE: **Face Your Schmears Everything Bagel Dip** (page 131) with, you guessed it . . . sesame flatbread! Or bagel chips. Or actual bagels! Carb it up.

DIPSSERT: **Egg Tart Dip** (page 158) with **Caramel Brûlée Crackers** (page 233) with caramel that's extra salty.

DIPCASIONS AND THEME PARTIES

MURDER *DIPSTERY* DIPNER

COLD *DIPPETIZER:* **Death Breath Dip** (page 69) with **Hexagon Dippers** (page 199), a mysterious dipper!

HOT *DIPPETIZER:* **Curry Squashcotta Sheet Pan Dip** (for when the *sheet* hits the pan; page 119) with whodunit **Wonton Lil' Scoopz** (page 200).

DIP FOR DINNER MAIN COURSE: **Spicy California Roll Guacamole** (page 135) with **Crispy Rice Dipsticks** (page 207), because revenge is a dish best served cold.

DIPSSERT: **This Dip Is Bananas!** (page 167) with a bit of strawberry jam dolloped on top for a bloody good time.

BAT *DIPZVAH* AND/OR SLEEPOVER-THEMED BIRTHDAY PARTY

COLD *DIPPETIZER:* **Bloom Bloom Room Onion Dip** (page 45) with ***Crisp*anthemum Onion Petals** (page 210) and shrimp on the barbie. Not to be confused with Greta Gerwig's *Barbie*. That would be shrimp on the beach. I don't have the rights to any of that Big Shrimp Energy!

HOT *DIPPETIZER:* **Classique Spinnie Artie Dip** (page 58) with those onion petals and your favorite tortilla chips. I've been loyal to Tostitos Scoops since I was a teen.

DIP FOR DINNER MAIN COURSE: **Drive-Thru Taco 7-Layer Dip** (page 128) with **Hexagon Dippers** (page 199) shaped like paper fortune tellers. And you know what? Doritos! Specifically Cool Ranch Doritos as dippers. That's a *dip*ception that's *dip*ceptively *dip*licious. If you've made it this far into *Big Dip Energy*, you know that's like "xoxo," an unbeatable combination, according to Seth Cohen. That was a lot of references in one, hope you're keeping up *dip* with the times!

DIPSSERT: **Dirt Pudding Dip** (page 177) in a plastic bucket with gummy worms running amok, lots of ripe strawberries, and a sense of glee all around. Peace be dip you.

'TIL DIP DO US PART BACHELORETTE/BACHELOR PARTIES

COLD *DIPPETIZER:* **Miso Eggplant Dip** (page 113) with *crude*ités, shaped like, well . . . use your imagination. ;)

HOT *DIPPETIZER:* **Elote to Love Dip** (page 38) layered with **Toum Raider Dip** (page 100), because there's ssamjang, and you found *ssam*body to love!

DIP FOR DINNER MAIN COURSE: **Spanakopidip** (page 148) with **Phyllo Lil' Scoopz** (page 202), which you *could* call *Spank*akopidip to be cheeky.

DIPSSERT: **Holy Cannoli Dip** (page 171), or Holy Cannoli*trimony* Dip, with the same Phyllo Lil' Scoopz who found true love with *dip*ner *and dip*ssert, ooh la la!

SUMMER *DIPNIC*

COLD *DIPPETIZER* 1: **Caesar Salad Dip** (page 97) with a bunch of beautiful dippin' lettuces (page 25) or **Veggie Ribbons** (page 214) and **Garlic-Kissed Crostini** (page 189).

COLD *DIPPETIZER* 2: (Because hot food at a picnic is sad): **Green Goddess Hummus** (page 104) with the same dippers as Caesar doing double duty but remember: *no double dipping*.

*DIP*NIC MAIN COURSE: **Shrimp-less Scampi Dip** (page 147) with cocktail shrimp. I love the tray from Costco. This is not sponsored, but I am fiercely loyal to those plump shrimp.

DIPSSERT: **Simply the Zest *Dip*ssert Trio: Lemon Bar, Key Lime Pie, and Creamsicle** (page 50) with **Crumble Crackers** (page 229) and singing Tina Turner too loudly in public.

diploma

Big Dip

UNIVERSITY

This certifies that

NAME

has dippendably completed the necessary requirements of study as prescribed by Dr. Meredith Graze and is hereby presented with

'big diploma energy'

and is entitled to all the dipper and dippee privileges pertaining to dipertaining on

DATE

CLASS OF 2023

Andrew Bui
#DipPics Specialist
(Photographer)

Nick Torres
Dip Detailer
(Food Stylist)

Casha Doemland
Big Dip Vibes Officer
(Prop Stylist)

Irene Choi
Emotional Support Human
(Set Producer)

Malina Syvoravong
Commander-in-Crudités
(Food Styling Assistant)

Francesca Gabrielle
Executive Bejeweler
(Prop Styling Assistant)

dipknowledgments

thanks for making dip happen!

BEFORE WE DIP IN, LET ME FIRST THANK YOU, dear reader, for making it this far. I hope you've found your spirit dip, embraced your own BIG DIP ENERGY, and are ready to host the Dipmas (or Dipmukkah or other non*dip*nominational, international dip party) of your dreams. Now, please imagine me in *nacho* average ballgown made of bejeweled chips and a vibrant orange-yellow queso-inspired train as I make this speech, and the only song that can play me off is Latto's "Big Energy."

I wouldn't have an ounce of my BDE without my **Grammy**. I will forever be trying to pull off a velvet tracksuit as well as you, and thank you (and our Lil' Dipper of a pup, **Marshall**) for providing endless support and love throughout this whole cookbook process—and my life.

Mom and Dad, thank you for making my dreams possible. I am so lucky that you are my parents and I was adopted by such a loving, giving, kind, and dip-loving family. Sarang hae yo! I love you forever, I like you for always.

And to my brother, **Alex**, thank you for testing my recipes from afar—especially with mo*dip*fications—and letting food be our love language as siblings. It means the world to me.

Now for my dream team—WHAT TEAM?! Say it back, Wildcats!—I'm not going in any particular order, because you are all equally important to me.

Nick Torres, food stylist extraordinaire, you've been a Day 1 Dipper, and I couldn't have *dip*veloped this concept to its fullest without you. Your brilliant ideas, patience in my chaos, ability to make dip breathtakingly beautiful, and truly becoming an extension of both my brain and body are all unreal. You can anticipate my needs before I even know I'm missing something, and I can't imagine doing this life—let alone this cookbook!—without you, and I'm glad I never have to. I'm thrilled that you brought on **Malina Syvoravong** as your assistant. Malina, thank you for your fine-tuned attention to dip deets, providing necessary caffeine and snack breaks, and almost always being my first hug when I walked into the studio.

Andrew Bui, the greatest #dippics photographer in the game, I can picture—pun intended, obviously—the moment every photo in this book was taken, because you created an environment where I could take a breath and enjoy each shot. Even on the most hectic days, your calming presence, kindness, and ability to pivot like nobody's business helped accommodate my increasingly wilder ideas and make a cookbook that accurately *dip*icts the inside of my brain.

Casha Doemland, the title "prop stylist"

is not enough to encompass everything you did. You created objects and scenes that only existed in my imagination—and made them even better. I'm in awe of your talent, big heart, creativity, and willingness to go all-in and dive into the *dip* end every single time. And thank you for bringing on the wonderful **Francesca Gabrielle** as your assistant. Francesca, thank you for being a master of bejeweling, sourcing spectacularly, and being an endless source of light and happiness. The way you two worked together lock-step—even holding meat clouds!—will change the way everyone will look at dip forever. And thank you Casha, **Jack Strutz**, *and* Dollar for letting us use South of Seventh Studio as our Haus of Dip!

Irene Choi, my unofficial unnie, thank you for being my rock. Our rock, really, throughout this whole shoot. Thank you for keeping us on schedule and well-fed, giving hand massages disguised as nail art prep, calming me down and hyping me up, and making me the best version of myself. A party isn't a party without you!

Caitlin Krenz, hair and makeup maven, just *wow*. I've never looked better than when you're making me into living art. But not only in the skills of your combination of bright, glittery eyeshadow, and big hair—also as a hype woman, fan girl (literally keeping me cool), wardrobe malfunction preventer, and *dip*sco dancing queen.

Marina Tahari, your impeccable nail art and press-on perfection made every dip shot more dynamic. You are such a gifted artist who really gets me, and I am thrilled to be able to share your artwork on my fingertips. And fellow nail artist **Tanya Barlow**, thank you for sliding in my DMs and nailing my highly specific ideas—like all my favorite emo album covers and Miso in a teacup—all the way from *New Zealand*!

Lisa Rose, I am so lucky to have you as a stylist. Thank you for helping me see myself in a new light and curating my closet with me to *dip*scover all-new lewks for these big dip parties!

Cassie Jones, my brilliant editor, there are not enough words in the English language to *dip*scribe how much you complete me. You're the chip to my dip, and you dipped in deep from day one to not only embrace my big dip energy, but somehow make it . . . even bigger? And punnier? Our creative collaborative process—alongside your Assistant to the Regional Dipper, **Jill Zimmerman**, an absolute legend and *dip*pendable soul—made every single part of this book better, and I can't wait to see what magic we all create together next. Thanks also to the William Morrow production and design team, including Amanda Hong, Ploy Siripant, Brian Moore, Alison Bloomer, Renata De Oliveira, Anna Brower, Justine Gardner, and Kelsey Heiss-O'Brien, for their *dip*votion to the cause!

I *CAA*nnot believe that I have an entire CAA team to thank. Still pinching myself that the **Ben Levine** is my talent agent and, to quote the great Mia Thermopolis, "You saw me when I was invisible." Not quite invisible, but not the BDE self I know I am now, thanks to you seeing something in me and helping me tell my story through the lens of dip. Bringing on **Anthony Mattero** and **Cindy Uh** as my literary agents was the best *dip*cision I could ever have made. Thank you for letting me be my authentic self every step of the way and taking the time to get to know me well enough that we operate as one big dip entity. I don't know what I would have done without your support and guidance. And **Sophie Kavanagh** and **Jordan Solomon**, my partnerships agents, I know there's so much still to come so I'm thanking you in advance for leading the #partnerdips ship on its journey ahead.

Izzy Magliari, my Izzy Baby. We have been best friends for fifteen years now and this is our first official collaboration—but *dip*finitely not our last. Thank you for making Chippy into a real girl and designing such brilliant work, making and eating so much dip with me over the years, and being my person.

Zach Vitale, thank you for using your retouching genius to make the cover the biggest, dippiest version possible, as well as the magic you worked to make some of the photos even more multi-*dip*mensional than before.

Joel Russo, thank you for documenting my dip journey with your fantastic filmmaking, running post-production on many "Let's Take a Dip" episodes on Instagram, and providing fun (mostly food-centric) memories and puns throughout our near-decade of friend*chip*.

Jenn Kwong, thanks for sharing and helping create the painting technique for my Rainbow Dumpling Chips—and always being the first to volunteer as dip tribute for taste tests.

Sean Roach, huge thanks for letting us use your fun home and expansive, unique art to create six *dip*stinct party scenes throughout *Big Dip Energy*.

Laura Murray, thank you for capturing Dipmas karaoke (page 237) with an epic set of photos—and screaming "Hands Down" with us at Gagopa!

Taylor Penton, I am still in awe of the design you made for my cookbook proposal. You helped me shape what *Big Dip Energy* could be, and I'm so grateful the internet brought us together!

Thank you to the brands who helped make dip happen! **Material Kitchen** (specifically co-founder Eunice Byun) for providing all the cookware, bowls, cutting boards, and knives we could ever need; **Fazeek Home** for loaning us some magical glassware; **East Fork Pottery** for supplementing my collection of colorful ceramics; **Breville** for supplying a countertop oven that allowed us to make all of the recipes in this book without a proper kitchen in-studio; **Ooni** for a pizza oven that can be used for much more; **ELOQUII** for select wardrobe; and **Smallhold** for mushroom *dip*livery so we could have an epic disco 'shroom moment.

To my *Big Dip Energy* partygoers, thank you for being in the shoot and making it feel like a real rager every time. In*dip*vidual thanks for each scene: **Panic! at the Dipsco** featuring Ashley Fee, Lizzie Spellman, Josh Weaver, and Caitlin Krenz; **Tiki Time** featuring Jean Bentley, Irene Choi, Kathy Liang, and Miso; **The Bébé Dippers' Club** featuring Lauren Lorentz, Lara Prawat, Irene Choi, and Kaleigh Gaynor; **Boba High Tea** featuring Kady Moore, Alice Hu, and Shirley Chung; **Campfire Singalong** featuring Alex Greenwald, Darren Robinson, Chris Lorentz, Andrew Parker, and Joel Russo; and **Dipmas Karaoke** featuring AJ Mitchell, Jess Kane, Karen Ho, MaryAnn Bodansky, Carolyn Menyes, Kevin Rutheford, Kelsey Ragsdale, and Dan Glaser. (And to Frances Kim, Carson Blackwelder, Elizabeth Lilly, and Regan Burns, who were all there in spirit.)

I could fill up an entire chapter's length of thank yous to every friend who helped me talk through ideas, taste dips, make dips, or remind me to breathe or eat while I was on a mad dash to deadlines. In fear of leaving someone out, I'm not going to list everyone here, but please know my heart is so full of gratitude (and probably dip?) for every single one of you.

mad props: a custom prop index

I WISH I COULD TELL YOU every single prop that was used in this cookbook, but most of it was sourced over the course of a few years through antiquing, estate sales, thrift stores, yard sales, and other secondhand shopping online (Mercari, eBay, Poshmark, Facebook Marketplace, Craigslist, and Etsy). However, I *can* share all the custom creations made for *Big Dip Energy*! These small businesses and makers helped make my dreams come true, including a little strawberry figurine of me and one of my pups, *dips*co bowls, and a "pool" spoon rest with chips floating in it! You may even *dips*cover that some of them are being sold by the time you dip into this index . . .

CRAB RANGOON EARRINGS, featured in Crab Rangoon Dip (page 140), made by Gimme Swords (instagram.com/gimmeswords)

CRAB RANGOON WALL RUGS, featured in Crab Rangoon Dip (page 140), made by JESSC.X (instagram.com/jesscx_)

DIPMAS ORNAMENT, featured in Pizza Your Way Dip in a Garlic Knot Wreath (page 79), has adapted original illustration by Kelly Jackson/Kitschy Delish (instagram.com/kitschydelish)

DIPPED CHIP EARRINGS, featured in the In Queso Emergency Dip (page 41) portraits, made by Mackenzie Becker/MackBecks (instagram.com/mackbecks)

DIPPED STRAWBERRY EARRINGS, featured in Strawberry Shortcake Dip (page 180) and Boba Tea Dips (161) party scene, made by Mackenzie Becker/MackBecks (instagram.com/mackbecks)

DIPSCO BOWLS, featured in Trippin' Dip (page 115) and *dips*co party scene, made by Mackenzie Becker/MackBecks (instagram.com/mackbecks)

DUMPLING DIP BOWL, featured in The Dips! (page 32), made by Bao Bao Pottery (instagram.com/baobaopottery)

FRUIT FRIENDS HAVING A PICNIC and Alyse and Miso as strawberries with Strawberry Shortcake Dip (page 181), featured in the Simply the Zest *Dips*sert Trio (page 51), made by Wobbly Pottery (instagram.com/wobbly_pottery)

GLITTERY CHIP EARRINGS, featured in Spicy California Roll Guacamole (page 135) party photos, made by Debbie Tuch/Glitterlimes (instagram.com/glitterlimes)

GLITTERY CHIP NECKLACE, featured in Garlic Bread Baked Brie in an Edibowl (page 85) and '90s party scenes, made by Debbie Tuch/Glitterlimes (instagram.com/glitterlimes)

GLITTERY STRAWBERRY RING, featured in Strawberry Shortcake Dip (page 180), made by Debbie Tuch/Glitterlimes (instagram.com/glitterlimes)

GLITTERY CHIP RING, featured in Elote to Love Dip (page 38), made by Debbie Tuch/Glitterlimes (instagram.com/glitterlimes)

MUSHROOM AND DIP WOODEN CUTTING BOARDS, featured in Green Goddess Hummus (page 105), made by Brandy Wayne (Instagram.com/handydandy_brandy)

POOL SPOON REST, featured in Chopped Cheese(burger) Queso (page 87), made by Shistine Peterson (instagram.com/_shistine)

the big dip energy compundium

MY PUNS ARE ALWAYS INTENDED. It's almost involuntary, like a reflex to make a pun—or make it all about the wordplay, like Mr. A–Z. (Semi-niche reference.) To no one's surprise, there are a ton o' puns in *Big Dip Energy*. I don't know if I'm now eligible to be a Guinness World Records holder for most puns in a cookbook, but I have the next best thing: a com*pun*dium of the puns the copyediting team created as part of the book's style guide. *Dip* is always italicized in the pun, too! I originally wanted to have an official pun counter, but that was a daunting task, and also up for *dip*liberation when it comes to what's a pun or wordplay or just nonsense. However, if someone counts the number of puns and DMs me on Instagram @alysewhitney, I will love you forever. I will not fact-check this before *dip*claring my devotion, so please be honest and diligent in your pun counting. May the puns be ever in your favor!

ad*dip*tion
ad*dip*tive
a*dip*tation
cre*dip*
*dip*bate
*Dip*cember
*dip*ception
*dip*cibel
*dip*cide
*dip*clare
*dip*corate
*dip*dicate
*dip*ending
*dip*ertain
*dip*ference
*dip*ferent
*dip*ferentiate
*dip*ficionado
*dip*ficult
*dip*fine
*dip*finity
*dip*fy
*dip*gress
*dip*idends
*dip*liberate
*dip*liberation
*dip*licious
*dip*lightful
*dip*liver
*Dip*mas
*Dip*mukkah
*dip*ner
*dip*pendable
*dip*petizer
#*Dip*Pic
*dips*appoint
*dips*claimer
*dips*co
*dips*conception
*dips*cosity
*dips*count
*dips*cover
*dips*covery
*dip*serve
*Dips*giving
*dips*graceful
*dips*ire
*dips*pense
*dips*perience
*dips*perse
*dips*piration
*dips*pire
*dips*placement
*dips*plainer
*dips*play
*dips*posable
*dips*proportionate
*dips*respect
*dips*sembly
*dips*sential
*dips*sert
*dips*service
*dips*tinct
*dips*tinctly
*dip*ter
*dip*termine
*dip*th
*dip*tionary
*dip*velop
*dip*velopment
*dip*vide
*dip*vision
*dip*visive
*dip*vot
edibowl
fon*dip*
fruitités
*grate*ness
holi*dip*
in*dip*ative
in*dip*vidual
plattery
pre*dip*termined
pre*dip*tion
ri*dip*ulous
ri*dip*ulously
snackternoon
sub*dip*tute
sub*dip*tution
un*dip*feated
un*dips*turbed

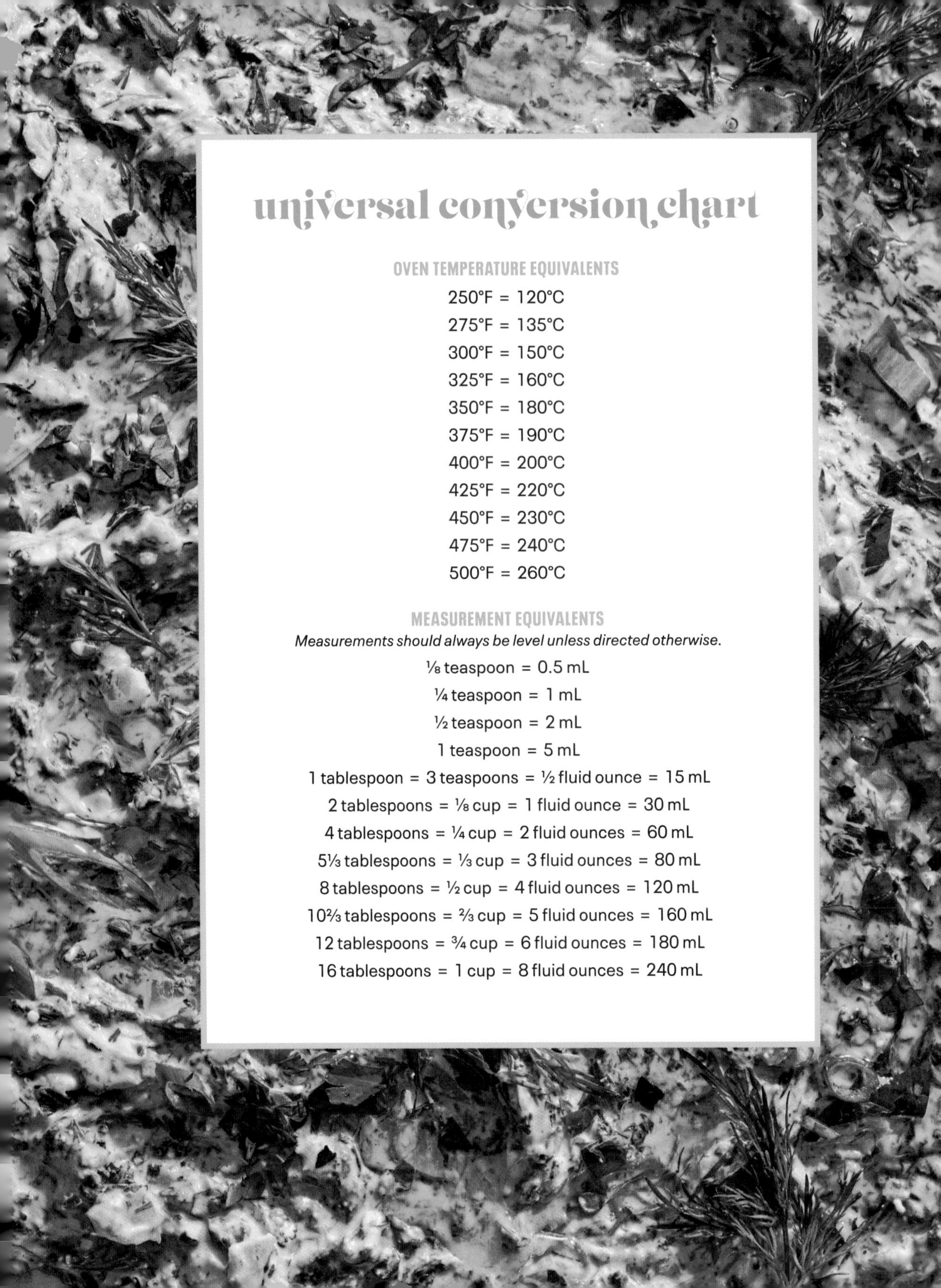

universal conversion chart

OVEN TEMPERATURE EQUIVALENTS

250°F = 120°C

275°F = 135°C

300°F = 150°C

325°F = 160°C

350°F = 180°C

375°F = 190°C

400°F = 200°C

425°F = 220°C

450°F = 230°C

475°F = 240°C

500°F = 260°C

MEASUREMENT EQUIVALENTS

Measurements should always be level unless directed otherwise.

⅛ teaspoon = 0.5 mL

¼ teaspoon = 1 mL

½ teaspoon = 2 mL

1 teaspoon = 5 mL

1 tablespoon = 3 teaspoons = ½ fluid ounce = 15 mL

2 tablespoons = ⅛ cup = 1 fluid ounce = 30 mL

4 tablespoons = ¼ cup = 2 fluid ounces = 60 mL

5⅓ tablespoons = ⅓ cup = 3 fluid ounces = 80 mL

8 tablespoons = ½ cup = 4 fluid ounces = 120 mL

10⅔ tablespoons = ⅔ cup = 5 fluid ounces = 160 mL

12 tablespoons = ¾ cup = 6 fluid ounces = 180 mL

16 tablespoons = 1 cup = 8 fluid ounces = 240 mL

NOTE: Page references in *italics* indicate photographs.

D

I

K

L

M

S

T

FIRST EDITION

Designed by Alison Bloomer

Photographs by Andrew Bui with the exception of the following: pages 4 (left), 43, 237, 238, 239, and 240 by Laura Murray
Chippy illustration by Izzy Magliari

Library of Congress Cataloging-in-Publication Data has been applied for.

ISBN 978-0-06-332049-9

24 25 26 27 28 LBC 5 4 3 2 1